TRUTH IS THE FIRST CASUALTY

The Gulf of Tonkin Affair—Illusion and Reality

Also by JOSEPH C. GOULDEN

The Curtis Caper (1965)
Monopoly (1968)

TRUTH IS THE FIRST CASUALTY

The Gulf of Tonkin Affair —Illusion and Reality

BY JOSEPH C. GOULDEN

A JAMES B. ADLER, INC., BOOK

Published in association with

RAND McNALLY & COMPANY

Chicago   •   New York   •   San Francisco

For Troy and Jim,
with hopes your generation doesn't have a Vietnam.

AUTHOR'S NOTE

Historians who walk through what the late President Kennedy called the "minefield" of contemporary events must tread carefully lest their own reputations, or those of persons about whom they write, be blown skyward by misstatement or misinterpretation. *Truth Is the First Casualty* is a reconstruction of an event that will remain politically volatile for years; unsurprisingly, therefore, the Johnson Administration and its officials are anxious that as little as possible be said about it. "Official" cooperation in this compilation was minimal, although many persons within and without the Administration offered background material and impressions. The lack of attribution in certain portions of the book, though deplorable, is unavoidable for obvious reasons; as the old Washington journalistic adage puts it, "He who names a source loses a source." Portions dealing with electronic espionage, the inner workings of the White House during the Tonkin crisis, and certain Central Intelligence Agency activities came from persons with a justifiable claim to anonymity, which has been granted. Other sources are identified in chapter notes or in the text.

Revisionism on the entire Vietnam situation is now rampant, as former Kennedy and Johnson officials busily attempt to restate or minimize their roles in a ghastly national venture. For my purposes, actions taken and recommendations tendered in 1964 weigh more heavily on the scales of history than self-exculpatory memoirs written four years after the fact.

Joseph C. Goulden

Arlington, Virginia
April 16, 1969

CONTENTS

EPILOGUE   239

TRUTH IS THE FIRST CASUALTY

The Gulf of Tonkin Affair—Illusion and Reality

"I am sure the great American people, if only they know the true facts and the background to the developments in South Vietnam, will agree with me that further bloodshed is unnecessary. And also that the political and diplomatic method of discussions and negotiations alone can create conditions which will enable the United States to withdraw gracefully from that part of the world. As you know, in times of war and of hostilities the first casualty is truth."

—U Thant, Secretary-General, United Nations

From *Remnants of Power: The Tragic Last Years of Adlai Stevenson*, Richard J. Walton (Coward-McCann, 1968).

PROLOGUE

Near midnight, Tuesday, August 4, 1964. The world of Patrick N. Park, United States Navy, consists of a round, greenish-hued radar screen, occasionally crossed by wavering, pencil-thin scratches of light or dotted by shapeless blurs that appear and vanish as rapidly as a speck of dust floats past the eye. Park stands in the main gun director of the destroyer USS Maddox, *the posture of the experienced sailor holding him steady as the vessel lurches at full speed, 34 knots, through the eight-foot swells of the Gulf of Tonkin.*

Outside, total darkness: the kind of night when a man listens for voices to know which shipmate stands beside him; when rain squalls and wave slaps against the hull are background for the deeper-pitched engine sounds. Somewhere off in the night the USS C. Turner Joy, *the Maddox's companion destroyer, is also speeding south on an erratic, evasive course—both warships, with lights out, weaving through the water like a pair of drunken porpoises.*

During three hours, only seconds of fleeting light: the sudden orange flash of the Turner Joy's *five-inch guns; twice, maybe three times, but no more, flickers of lightning creating a lingering, silverish glow under the low, heavy cloud cover; a fast-burning flare plunging from the sky, dying before it provides enough illumination to do more than attract one's attention.*

Into Park's earphones come the confusing sounds of an apparent sea battle. At 9:12 P.M. the combat information center (CIC) below deck announces its radar has detected fast-closing targets, to all appearances the repetition of a bold daylight attack two days earlier when the Maddox *had driven off three North Vietnamese torpedo boats, leaving one dead in the water. More than 20 times, the sonarman calls out "Torpedoes in the water," sending the* Maddox *and* Turner Joy *into zigzag turns. The* Turner Joy *time and again reports the ranges of "targets" upon which it is firing. But the* Maddox's *own radar room, near to anguish, says it has found nothing since the first contacts; that it is having trouble locating even the* Turner Joy.

Accompanying the darkness and the speed and the confusion are anticipation and excitement: the dread of unseen enemy boats with primed torpedoes trailing the slower United States destroyers, maneuvering for firing positions, then racing back to the safety of the North Vietnam mainland, 60 miles westward.

For Patrick Park, however, there are three hours of staring at the meaningless green quivers of the gun director's radarscope, blank even when he seeks the "targets" at which the Turner Joy *is firing so enthusiastically. His radar controls the* Maddox's *six five-inch guns and, at short ranges, is more sensitive than the ship's main radar. But for Park, no targets —only the occasional roll of a wave as it breaks into a whitecap.*

Then, a few minutes before midnight, the bridge gives Park a range reading from CIC. "The firmest target we've had all night," the voice tells him. Park hastily directs the gun-control radar toward the area of the contact.

"It was a damned big one, right on us. No doubt about this one," he says. "About 1,500 yards off the side, a nice fat blip." Park asks for the "firing key"—that is, for control of the triggering device on the five-inch gun mounts—and for permission to fire. "Open fire!" is the response. Park tells what happened:

"Just before I pushed the trigger I suddenly realized, That's the Turner Joy. *This came right with the order to open fire. I shouted back, 'Where is the* Turner Joy?' *There was a lot of yelling of 'Goddamn' back and forth, with the bridge telling me to 'fire before we lose the contact,' and me yelling right back at them. (I really wasn't thinking about what I was saying.)*

"I finally told them, 'I'm not opening fire until I know where the Turner Joy *is.' The bridge got on the phone and said, 'Turn on your lights,* Turner Joy.'

"Sure enough, there she was, right in the cross hairs. I had six five-inch guns right at the Turner Joy, *1,500 yards away. If I had fired, it would have blown it clean out of the water. In fact, I could have been shot for not squeezing the trigger."*

The averting of near-disaster was the peak of the night's tension; Park says a "great sense of deflation" followed. "People started asking, 'What are we shooting at? What is going on?' We all began calming down. The whole thing seemed to end then."[1]

Only the "whole thing" did not end with Park's refusal to be swept along with the heady excitement of sea battle. The Tonkin Gulf incidents—the attack by North Vietnamese boats on the *Maddox* on August 2, 1964, and the supposed engagement between the *Maddox,* the *Turner Joy,* and North Vietnamese vessels the night of August 4, 1964—mark a major turning point in the military and political conduct of the Vietnam War. On August 5, 12 hours after the second episode, United States war planes swept over North Vietnam for the first time, bombing four patrol-boat bases and a large oil-storage depot, retaliating for what Secretary of Defense Robert S. McNamara called "unprovoked and deliberate attacks in international waters on our naval vessels."[2] On August 7, 1964, at President Lyndon B. Johnson's bidding, Congress passed with but two dissenting voices a resolution approving and supporting "the determination of the President . . . to take all necessary measures to repel any armed attack against the armed forces of the United States and to prevent further aggression." It also affirmed the United States' readiness "as the President determines, to take all necessary steps, including the use of armed force," to assist any member or protocol state of the Southeast Asia Treaty Organization "in defense of its freedom."

Thereafter Johnson used the Tonkin Gulf Resolution as his basic congressional authority for conduct of the war. Never again did he go to Congress and directly pose the question: "Do we want to fight a conventional war in Vietnam with American boys?" At the time of Tonkin, the United States had only slightly more than 16,000 men in Vietnam and Johnson was opening a campaign for election in which his theme was to be, "We are not going to send American boys nine or ten thousand miles away from home to do what Asian boys ought to be doing for themselves" (as stated October 21, 1964). But within a year of Tonkin the buildup of men that was to pass the half-million mark was under way, and war dissenters seized upon the Tonkin Gulf Resolution as a symbol of Administration duplicity.

The Administration firmly denied any abuse of its powers. Undersecretary of State Nicholas deB. Katzenbach told the Senate Foreign Relations Committee on August 17, 1967, that the resolution, taken in company with the SEATO treaty, is the "functional equivalent of the constitutional obligation expressed in the provision of the Constitution with respect to declaring war"—the functional equivalent of a declaration of war by Congress. Katzenbach asked, "What could a declaration of war have done that would have given the President more authority and a clearer voice of the Congress than that did?"[3]

Yet the Tonkin Gulf Resolution contains the fatal taint of deception. The incidents from which it stemmed were not events of black-and-white simplicity, as Congress and the American people were led to believe in

August 1964. In this context the experience of young Patrick N. Park is, with one exception, a microcosm of the entire Tonkin affair, illustrating the confusion between illusion and reality and the inclination of man to act upon facts as he anticipates they *should be,* rather than what rational examination shows them *to be.* The exception is that Park refused to squeeze the firing key, while Washington acted on the basis of assumption, not fact—hastily, precipitously, perhaps even unnecessarily—firing at an unseen enemy lurking behind the blackness of misinformation. Park demanded that the *Turner Joy* show its lights and thereby averted naval disaster. But his superiors in Washington were content to remain in the dark. At the very moment American bombs began falling on North Vietnam, cables to the Pacific were pleading frantically for verification that enemy patrol boats had actually attacked the United States destroyers— and answering cables raised substantial doubts that they had in fact done so.

The conduct of the high naval commanders in the Pacific throughout this period can charitably be described as astounding. In one instance, the commanders forced the *Maddox* to maintain a patrol course which its ranking officer, an experienced combat veteran, wished to abandon as overly risky, and despite his warnings that the North Vietnamese considered the *Maddox* a belligerent. After the North Vietnamese attacked the *Maddox* on August 2, as the officer had predicted they would, the Pacific command ordered him to resume the patrol, and on a course even more provocative than before. Further, the Pacific commanders withheld from Washington the reports of South Vietnamese commando activities in the patrol area on August 3—information that should have had a crucial bearing on the Johnson Administration's decision making on August 4, following the second controversial episode.

None of this, of course, was made known to the Congress when it passed the "functional equivalent" of a declaration of war. Senator Wayne Morse of Oregon declared in 1968: "The controversy over the Tonkin Bay* incident will continue for decades to come in American history as one of the most controversial subjects connected with our 'undeclared war' in Southeast Asia. In my judgment, it will take a historic position alongside the sinking of the *Maine* in the war against Spain."[4]

Tonkin contains another microcosm—that of the institutional shortcomings of the national security organization, and of many of the issues which affect, for better or for worse, the conduct of American foreign policy. The workings of national security are not nearly so efficient and foolproof as its operators appear to believe. Thomas L. Hughes, director throughout the Johnson Administration of the State Department's Bureau of Intelli-

* *Gulf* of Tonkin is the correct term, although senators and other persons involved in the issue frequently used *Bay* of Tonkin. For accuracy and consistency, *gulf* will be used hereafter, except in quoted material.

gence and Research, once jested about what he called *"ex post facto intelligence,"* which he defined as the need to produce intelligence to justify actions already taken.

The Johnson Administration's obsession with secrecy (even in the internal sense, with high officials and executive departments kept unaware of operations going on around them) greatly increased the possibility of left hand-right hand blunders. Late in his tenure, Secretary McNamara estimated that he had "perhaps 25" different security clearances—some broad and overlapping, but all based on the "question of need to know." William D. Moyers, a longtime aide to Johnson, has said, "A President must sometimes reach conclusions before all the evidence is in. The choice may be between acting on the basis of information at hand—inconclusive though it may be—or not to act at all." Moyers cites specifically the dispatch of United States Marines to the Dominican Republic in 1965 to protect Americans gathered in the Embajador Hotel because the United States Ambassador "was telling the President that those lives were endangered." Moyers comments: "Later the press and others, with the benediction of hindsight, would argue that they [the Marines] were not required. The President, at the moment of decision, was not conducting a postmortem. He was acting on the basis of immediate but inconclusive reports from the field; his decision was to commit. Only later would he be able more dispassionately to analyze more complete information."[5]

That the Tonkin incidents occurred in the Johnson Administration is really of secondary import, for the problems illustrated by them have existed in one degree or another under every president since Franklin D. Roosevelt, and they will be with us again, regardless of who is in the White House.

Prominent among these problems are the electronic-espionage ships which the United States deploys throughout the world. Our national leaders assure us, periodically and most solemnly, of the usefulness of the information these vessels gather. Yet what is useful is not always wise. One of the prime pieces of electronic intelligence gathered by the *Maddox,* as we shall discover, was the warning she was about to be attacked. The *USS Liberty* incident, in which Israeli planes and ships shot a United States spy vessel to pieces, killing 34 officers and enlisted men, brought us closer to nuclear Armageddon than Washington cared to admit for months. The *USS Pueblo* seizure by North Korea—its bizarre denouement notwithstanding—was something less than a national triumph. On March 12, 1969, summarizing testimony taken in secret session, a Navy court of inquiry quoted the *Pueblo's* skipper, Commander Lloyd M. Bucher, and intelligence chief Lieutenant Stephen R. Harris, as saying "the ship's mission was unproductive up to the point of seizure." Harris had complained of "certain low job-proficiency levels among the research personnel which lessened their intelligence collection ability"—that is, the inability of anyone on board to interpret the Korean broadcasts heard by the ship.

One also notes disturbing parallels between the Tonkin and *Pueblo* incidents: Both the *Maddox* and the *Pueblo* had intelligence personnel aboard who worked independently of the regular ship's officers. Both the *Maddox* and the *Pueblo* were sent into dangerous waters at a time of quickening international crisis. Commanders of both the *Maddox* and the *Pueblo* questioned their ability to defend their ships against enemy attack— one because of the course ordered by higher commands, the other because of the unseaworthiness of his vessel and its lack of armament.

The dangers of electronic-espionage vessels have been stated succinctly:

> The itinerary of any naval vessels close along a foreign coast or through strategic waters may be tantamount to creating tension and precipitating crises, even among otherwise friendly states. Visibility may come into play to further complicate the situation. Ships only three miles offshore may easily be seen, adding to the emotional factor in the case of naval craft rights. *The most peaceful coastal patrol may loom as a war scare if alarm is generated to an uninformed and gullible citizenry.*

NOTE: Unless otherwise stated, emphasis in quoted material throughout the book has been added by the author.

An attack by Senator J. William Fulbright (Arkansas) or Senator Eugene J. McCarthy (Minnesota) on the United States' use of spy ships? No; the quotation comes from a 1965 publication*[6] of the State Department's Bureau of Intelligence and Research, the office which represents State when the intelligence community is planning such missions as those of the *Maddox* and *Pueblo*.

Another issue raised by the Tonkin affair is the constitutional division of powers between the legislative and executive branches in the conduct of foreign affairs. Is this division outmoded? What latitude should be given the president in deciding whether prior treaty commitments can justify dispatch of American troops into foreign battle? None of the 42 treaties signed since World War II *require* the United States to go to war, although all *permit* it. Congress is now attempting to regain, through the so-called "National Commitments Resolution," the powers that it surrendered to the Executive through "uncritical and sometimes unconscious acquiescence."[7] But more is required than simply a resolution, or simply the prolonged *mea culpa* by Fulbright for his floor managership of the Tonkin Gulf Resolution through a trusting and obliging Congress.

* Materials quoted from the Congressional Record, press releases, and all other official communications have been reproduced in this book exactly as they appear in their original form, regardless of inconsistencies.

The Senate claims, on the one hand, that there is no monopoly on foreign policy expertise, and derides those in the executive branch who claim to possess it: "Like the newly rich who go beyond the bounds of good judgment in material display, the newly powerful may go beyond the bounds of good judgment in their intellectual display."[8] Yet foreign affairs *competence* (as distinct from foreign affairs *expertise*) is available in Washington for the asking, and until recently the Senate, collectively and individually, displayed little interest in acquiring any of it. A prime example: Senator Albert Gore of Tennessee, since early 1965 a loud critic of Johnson war policies, was a member of the Foreign Relations Committee in 1964 during its hearings on the Tonkin Gulf Resolution—yet he didn't interrupt campaigning in Tennessee to attend them. Further, when interviewed in 1968, Gore had not the faintest recollection of what he and other senators were told earlier in 1964, when the Administration made decisions which started the United States sliding inexorably down the slope (past Tonkin) toward a major land war in Asia. "I regard this as one of the most tragic mistakes in American history," Gore cried of the Tonkin episode in August 1967—exactly three years too late.

Senator Morse attempted to warn his colleagues of what was happening; indeed, he put the basic outline of the Administration's deception into the *Congressional Record* for all to read. But Morse's Senate colleagues didn't join him in probing further; they hushed him so that the President could obtain his resolution and hurry to Atlantic City to accept the Democratic presidential nomination. Assuming that Gore's equivalents will always be with us, one must be skeptical that the Senate's current [June 1969] burning interest in foreign affairs will endure. Continuing hard work and study, not *ex post facto* complaining and whining, are the stuff of which foreign policy is made; the Senate thus far shows a penchant for the latter, but not the energy to undertake the former.

The Foreign Relations Committee, in its report on the 1967 national commitments hearings, stated: "The concentration in the hands of the president of virtually unlimited authority over matters of war and peace has all but removed the limits to executive power in the most important area of our national life."[9] In matters of national security, an administration is also peculiarly capable of orchestrating both public and internal response to events.

First, and most significantly, the government controls access to the event itself and to the information arising from it. If a Soviet aircraft flies over United States territory, taking photographs of Denver or Cleveland, the White House can choose either to remain silent and keep the incident a state secret, or to make a public protest over the violation of its borders and create an international crisis. If the Soviets install offensive missiles in

Cuba, the White House can elect to say nothing until it is prepared to put announcement and response into one dramatic package and unwrap it in a manner sure to produce maximum impact. When a crisis is precipitated on the high seas in a remote corner of the world (as in the Tonkin encounter), the government reveals at the time only what it chooses to make known. A questioning congressman or editor cannot make an on-the-spot independent inquiry. If government cables or radio facilities are the only means of communication with persons on the scene, and if those persons happen to be military, subject to security regulations and other strictures, all that is heard of their voices are the sentences which the government wishes to be heard. In time, much of what happens in secret in official Washington becomes general knowledge (although, some White House veterans avow, not nearly so much as the press and populace would like to believe). But in a crisis, when a president decides to act swiftly and secretly, Congress learns the full facts upon which his decision was based only long after the event.

The temper of public reaction, save in rare instances such as Pearl Harbor, can be manipulated by the manner in which the government chooses to present its own reaction. An unruffled president calls reporters into his Oval Room office in the White House and matter-of-factly reads a statement; the secretary of state leaves town for a previously scheduled ceremonial appearance; State Department and Pentagon briefing officers suggest to their respective "regulars" in the press corps that Washington isn't particularly excited about whatever incident is at issue. Result: national calm and indifference, even when sheer uniqueness propels the event onto the front page and the seven o'clock news.

At the other extreme is a sudden appearance by the president on the three television networks at an unexpected hour, solemnly informing the nation of grave danger and of the stern action he has been forced to take. A president sitting behind his seal of office, flanked by flags, and intoning the words, "Good evening, my fellow Americans..." is a sight calculated to bring the most lethargic of citizens to the edge of his living room chair or barstool. Result: a quickening of the collective national pulse; a joining of ranks to follow wherever the president chooses to lead; stirrings of chauvinism or blood lust—in sum, the mid-20th-century equivalent of booming drum and flashing saber, and all within the comfort of one's own home.

The Congress and the public, entirely reliant upon the Executive for information in a crisis, must put their total trust in him. Similarly, he must put his trust in the military, diplomatic, and intelligence agencies which furnish the raw data upon which decisions are based. Executive deception of the Congress is one evil; when the Executive himself acts on the basis of incomplete or inaccurate or misleading information, the potentiality for disaster increases geometrically. And here we return to the immediate

instance of the Tonkin incidents. The Johnson Administration anticipated—
perhaps even subconsciously desired—one set of facts on August 4, 1964,
when a flash report from the *Maddox* said she was under attack. The
Administration seized upon this report, clung to it despite subsequent
cables from the *Maddox* saying the whole episode could have been a
mistake, and proceeded to bomb a foreign country without congressional
authorization. Then the Administration gave Congress an "account" of
what happened that can only be termed mendacious and misleading—and
deliberately so, considering the information available to Johnson, Mc-
Namara, and others. Johnson's short-term gain was a broad congressional
mandate to run the war as he saw fit (something that he had wanted, in
his own words, since at least the previous May). Johnson's long-term loss
was the confidence of the American people and of the Congress—more so
than any war president in United States history. In this respect, Johnson
is the overall loser at Tonkin; considered more broadly, we all are the
losers, for Tonkin came to be a synonym for national disunity and distrust.

More than three years later, when the Senate obtained the raw data
essential to intelligent inquiry into the incidents—specifically, naval communications and logs of the *Maddox* and *Turner Joy*—the Johnson Administration's conduct was equally unfortunate. McNamara's insistence that
he had given the Senate a complete and accurate account of the incidents
immediately after they occurred in 1964 is not borne out by the record,
and his repeated resorting to semantical nuances confused senators all the
more and worsened a situation which was wretched from the outset. The
omissions and distortions of fact during the 1964 hearings were so frequent,
so skillful, that one must suspect something more sinister than honest
misunderstanding or accidental verbal vagueness.

But to suspect is not to convict: The weight of the evidence presented
in these pages is that the Administration acted hastily, upon incomplete
and misleading information, and then refused to admit error. McNamara
has called it "monstrous" for anyone to insinuate that the August 4 incident was a manufactured lie, product of a plot of the White House and
the military; I agree, and also note that the Senate Foreign Relations Committee made no such charge. However, we may ask why high naval commanders in the Pacific insisted on putting United States war vessels into
positions off the North Vietnam coast where an attack upon them was
inevitable, and kept them there when warned of danger? Deception is
deception, be it deliberate or unwitting, and the facts warrant conviction
of the Johnson Administration on this count—both for its recitation of
the "facts" of the August 4 incident to Congress in 1964, and for its use
thereafter of the Tonkin Gulf Resolution.

Why would Johnson resort to deception to obtain such a document as
the Tonkin Gulf Resolution? Here some brief background is in order.

South Vietnam's President Ngo Dinh Diem was overthrown three weeks before Johnson took office, and in succeeding months the war situation deteriorated rapidly. By early June 1964, Washington faced political collapse in Saigon, international pressures for a negotiated end to the war, and physical imbalance on the battlefield. From the testimony of his subordinates, it is clear that the President did not wish to "escalate" the United States role in the war until after the November election, although contingency plans put before him early in 1964 said that massive intervention eventually would be necessary to stem the Viet Cong.

Thus Tonkin was useful to Johnson for several reasons. It gave the United States a pretext to draw blood from North Vietnam and to demonstrate Washington's resolve. It boosted the morale of the South Vietnamese, who had complained that the enemy homeland was immune from the carnage of war. And it united—temporarily, at least—Congress and the public behind the President. A high Johnson Administration official once told me privately, "Regardless of all the griping three years later, Tonkin saved the war for us. It was a life raft that kept us afloat from the summer of '64 through the election, when Mr. Johnson felt the political freedom to make the decisions that had to be made. This might sound cynical, but the fact that Tonkin prevented a national disaster outweighs any of the questions that have been raised about the incidents, and the resolution, and people should be mature enough to accept it on that basis."

Of what relevance is Tonkin to us today? Johnson and the men who handled the Tonkin affair are out of office. The Senate, in all likelihood, is baying after another suspect hare. But the legacy of mistrust Johnson bequeathed will be in the minds of Congress and of the discerning public for years to come. The Senate is now keenly aware of its constitutional role in the war-making process. As Senator Clifford Case of New Jersey has said, "For the President to come to the Congress with a resolution which turns over the whole matter to him for an indefinite time seems to me was taking advantage of a situation in which Congress had no choice, and had to go along with the form of words which later is thrown back in its teeth as a complete abdication of constitutional authority on the part of Congress." Or, in the words of Senator Sam Ervin of North Carolina, "In all generations, some presidents have sent American troops abroad, usually on a small scale, without any authorization of the Congress, and a lot of people use that as an argument to justify the theory that he has that power. But my reply to that is that that is like murder and larceny. People have been committing murder and larceny in all generations, but that has never made murder meritorious or larceny legal."

Truth Is the First Casualty consists of three broad sections. The first, entitled "The Illusion," reports the Tonkin incidents exactly as related to the Congress and the public in August 1964. The next, "The Reality," tells what actually happened, beginning with an exploration of the shadow worlds of electronic espionage and covert military and sabotage operations in North Vietnam and Laos, culminating in a detailed account of the *Maddox's* ill-fated mission, and of the hectic 15 hours during which the Johnson Administration decided to bomb a country with which the United States was not formally at war. The concluding section, "The Revelation," recounts the manner in which the Senate Foreign Relations Committee, through equal parts of luck and energy, exposed the Johnson Administration's duplicity and used Tonkin as a starting point for the first serious study ever undertaken of the division of war-making powers between the president and the Congress.

Part One

THE ILLUSION

An account of the Gulf of Tonkin incidents as related to the United States Congress and the American people by the Johnson Administration between August 2 and August 9, 1964.

Chapter One

MR. JOHNSON'S CRISIS

The first public announcement of trouble in the Gulf of Tonkin came at 10:15 A.M. on Sunday, August 2, in a simultaneous press statement from the Pentagon and from the Hawaii office of Admiral Ulysses Grant Sharp, Jr., commander in chief of United States forces in the Pacific (CINCPAC):

> While on routine patrol in international waters at 020808 GCT (1608 local time) the US destroyer *Maddox* underwent an unprovoked attack by three PT type boats in latitude 19-40 North; longitude 106-34 East, in the Tonkin Gulf.
>
> The attacking boats launched three torpedoes and used 37 millimeter gunfire. The *Maddox* answered with 5-inch gunfire. Shortly thereafter four F-8 (Crusader) aircraft joined in the defense of *Maddox,* using Zuni rockets and 20 millimeter strafing attacks. The PT boats were driven off, with one seen to be badly damaged and not moving, and the other two damaged and retreating slowly.
>
> No casualties or damage were sustained by *Maddox* or the aircraft.

Various Administration press officers during the day gave a sketchy account of the Washington phase of the episode*: The National Military Command Center in the Pentagon received a flash on the attack at 4:08 A.M. Washington time, seconds after it began, and by dawn the basic details were known. President Johnson, as he dressed for church, was briefed by McGeorge Bundy, the White House national security adviser. Secretary of Defense Robert S. McNamara, enjoying a rare weekend holiday in Newport, Rhode Island, sped back to Washington by military jet for a midmorning meeting with the President, Secretary of State Dean Rusk, Undersecretary of State George Ball, Deputy Defense Secretary Cyrus Vance, and General Earle G. Wheeler, chairman of the Joint Chiefs of Staff. The meeting lasted

---

* Except for several designated instances, this chapter and the succeeding one are confined to information available in August 1964 to the public, via the press, and to the Congress, via testimony of Johnson Administration officials. Occasional footnotes will alert the reader to await elaboration.

45 minutes and, according to background accounts given newsmen, most of the time was spent in "puzzled discussion" of what could have caused North Vietnam's puny navy to challenge the mighty Pacific Fleet. The reported consensus was that either a local commander had acted on his own initiative, without the express approval of higher authorities in Hanoi, or that the government itself had become momentarily aberrant. The reported decision was not to magnify the attack into anything more than a local incident—hence the low-key Pentagon statement, discussed during the meeting and issued soon after it ended. (The announcement, it will be noted, did not even identify the attackers as North Vietnamese.)

Rusk went to New York in the early afternoon to keep a date to address the 50th anniversary celebration of the American Field Service. To reporters who pressed for comment on the Tonkin incident, he said simply: "The other side got a sting out of this. If they do it again, they'll get another sting." The United States, he said, is "going to use and insist on using international waters." And in answer to a question, he said that the attacking craft were North Vietnam's. (Without naming Barry Goldwater, Rusk's formal speech was an oblique rebuke to the Republican presidential nominee: Many incidents since 1945 could have mushroomed into a third world war "if sobriety had not exercised a restraining influence," Rusk said, in a theme repeated time and again during the campaign.)

In Honolulu, Admiral Sharp declared: "If they are so bold as to shoot at us, it is a change. We have always had a policy that if someone shoots at us, we will shoot back at them. Our ships will go wherever they need to in international waters. This incident may well be a change in the present situation and may heighten the seriousness of the present crisis in Vietnam, but I do not know whether this will be temporary or not."

Pentagon press officers added little detail to the formal announcement, stating only that the patrol boats were picked up by radar, continued to close in on the *Maddox,* and opened fire. The *Maddox* made no attempt to pursue them when the engagement ended "because the fleet was not at war."[1] State Department and White House officials spent the late morning briefing congressional leaders on the incident. According to the Congressmen, they were told little that was not contained in the three-paragraph public announcement. And they felt that the Administration did not anticipate a crisis or a repetition of the attack.

Senator Hubert H. Humphrey of Minnesota, only three weeks away from nomination as Johnson's running mate, was among those briefed. On "Face the Nation" he reported: "Our navy defended itself in an admirable, creditable manner." The real test of crisis management, Humphrey said, "is being able to sustain ourselves . . . without emotional reaction." Senator Everett Dirksen of Illinois, the minority leader, said the attacks warranted a "new hard look" at Asian policy. "We must lay all of the cards on the table so that the American people will be fully informed and then take action to correct the situation," Dirksen said. Senator Richard Russell of Georgia, chairman of the Senate Armed Services Committee, said that enemy ships attacking United States vessels "can be certain of instant retaliation." Senator Thomas Kuchel of California was the only Congressman commenting, that Sunday, who sensed the potential outcome of the incident: "If this contemptible gunboat attack was something more than an isolated, undirected foray, then it constitutes a grave and serious development."

Monday's *Washington Post,* in its main story on the Tonkin incident, made passing reference to North Vietnamese claims of raids by the South Vietnamese on two offshore islands the night of July 30–31, and of air attacks on North Vietnamese settlements near the Laotian frontier. A separate Associated Press story from Tokyo, tucked away on page 13, quoted briefly from the Radio Hanoi broadcast in which the charges were made. The *Post's* story said, "In Washington, Administration officials *denied there was any shelling of North Vietnamese islands* and said they had no knowledge of any air raids on any North Vietnamese villages."

The broadcast upon which the Post's *story on the island raids was based was made over Radio Hanoi's international service in English at about midday on August 2, before the episode in the Gulf of Tonkin. Western news agencies monitor the Hanoi broadcasts in Tokyo, Hong Kong, and Saigon. The Central Intelligence Agency's monitoring service picked up both the English-language version and an earlier Vietnamese-language version directed at South Vietnam, at 0400 (Greenwich time) on August 1. Routinely, important broadcast intelligence gathered by CIA monitors is flashed back to Washington immediately in a form similar to wire service bulletins, and the ticker copy is photostated and circulated within the CIA, the State Department, the Pentagon, and the White House national security office. However, the unclassified compilation of monitoring reports is published only five days weekly, skipping Saturday and Sunday. Therefore it was not until the morning of Tuesday, August 4, that the full text of the broadcasts was generally available in Washington. Staffs of the Senate Armed Services and Foreign Relations committees receive the compilation, the "White Book" of the CIA's monitoring service.*

The Vietnamese-language version of the complaint, available to the White House, and to the State and Defense departments by late afternoon on August 1, stated:

On 31 July the Vietnamese People's Army liaison mission addressed a telegram to the International Control Commission protesting against an extremely serious violation of the Geneva agreements by the Americans and the South Vietnamese administration. The telegram reads:

'At 2430 hours on 30 July, the Americans and their henchmen in South Vietnam sent two warships to bombard Hon Ngu Island off Gua Hoi Hoi, Nghe An Province. This island is four kilometers from the coast. At the same time, another warship was sent to bombard Hon Me Island off Ba Lang, Thanh Hoa Province. This island is twelve kilometers from the coast.'

The telegram called the acts a 'serious violation' of the Geneva agreements, and a 'shameless provocation' of North Vietnam. 'Obviously, these are not individual acts, but are part of the premeditated common plan of the Americans and their henchmen to carry out schemes to intensify the provocative and destructive acts against the DRV [Democratic Republic of Vietnam, or North Vietnam] while striving to step up their aggressive war in South Vietnam.'

The English-language broadcast repeated the basic complaint and added a protest, in the name of the DRV foreign ministry, against "intensifications of incursions on the air space and territorial waters of the DRV and of sabotage and commando activities against it." It said that Johnson could not continue talking about peace while his "henchmen" in South Vietnam were "raving about attacking and bombing the North. It is a cunning and well-known behind-the-scenes trick of the United States imperialists . . . [who] are precisely the chief authors who have mapped out and organized the carrying out of the plan of provocation and sabotage toward the DRV. The United States Government must bear full responsibility. . . ."

On Monday, August 3—one day after the attack on the *Maddox*—Rusk and McNamara met privately with the combined Senate Armed Services and Foreign Relations committees, with Senator Mike Mansfield of Montana, the majority leader, and minority leader Dirksen sitting in. Their review was general: a slightly more detailed recitation of the *Maddox's* battle report; puzzlement at North Vietnam's motivation (both secretaries calling the attack "entirely unprovoked"); and a belief within the Administration that the incident was a miscalculation or misunderstanding by the North Vietnamese, and that it would not be repeated. No record of this meeting was made; however, both Senate and Pentagon sources say McNamara's presentation was almost exactly what he repeated to the same committees three days later in formal hearings on the Gulf of Tonkin Resolution; it is from those hearings that the following language comes. The account matches in every respect a public chronology of the event released by the Pentagon around noon on Monday, August 3. McNamara outlined the engagement itself as follows:

The *Maddox* was "engaged in a routine patrol in international waters . . . about thirty miles from the coast . . . [when] she reported that three torpedo boats were on a southerly course heading towards the ship at a range of over ten miles." This was "about noon."

"Two hours later, at approximately 2:40 P.M., the *Maddox* was approached by a high speed—45 to 50 knot—craft. She reported that the apparent intention of this craft was to conduct a torpedo attack and that she intended to open fire in self-defense if necessary. She was attacked by the three PT craft at 3:08 P.M. She opened fire with her five-inch battery after three warning shots failed to slow down the attackers. The PTs continued their closing maneuvers, and two of the PTs closed to 5,000 yards, each firing one torpedo. The *Maddox* changed course in an evasive move and the two torpedoes passed on the starboard [right] side at a distance of 100 to 200 yards.

"The *USS Ticonderoga,* which was operating in waters to the southeast and which had been alerted to the impending attack, advised she was sending four already airborne F-8E (Crusader) fighters with rockets and 20 millimeter ammunition to provide air cover for the *Maddox.* At about 3:21 P.M., the third hostile PT moved up to the beam of the *Maddox* and received a direct hit by a five-inch round; at the same time it dropped a torpedo into the water which was not seen to run. Machine gun fire from the PTs was directed at the *Maddox.* However, there was no injury to personnel and no damage. The *Maddox* continued in a southerly direction to join with a sister destroyer, the *C. Turner Joy**,* as *Ticonderoga* aircraft commenced attacking the PTs. Zuni rocket runs and 20-millimeter strafing attacks were directed against two of the PTs, and they were damaged. The third PT remained dead in the water after the direct hit by the *Maddox.* At 3:29 P.M. the engagement terminated and the aircraft escorted the *Maddox* southward on its patrol course."

Twenty-four hours after the McNamara-Rusk testimony, at a press briefing that began at 12:03 P.M., August 4, Admiral William Mack, the Navy Chief of Information, indicated that the Pentagon still hadn't received a complete battle report on the Sunday incident. The transcript of the briefing quotes him as saying, "The *Maddox* is still up there where it's difficult" to send what "we might call routine things, so what we have is small bits of information which we did get from her. . . . It's rather sketchy still." Arthur Sylvester, the Pentagon's chief press officer, added, "We still don't have all the details . . . ." The briefing began almost three hours after Washington had received word that a second attack on the *Maddox* and the *Turner Joy* was underway; however, not a word was said of the reported second attack.[2]

Concurrent with the McNamara-Rusk appearance before the senators on Monday, Johnson made public some of the decisions reached at the Sunday meeting. To reporters summoned by press secretary George Reedy

* The vessel is named for the late Admiral Charles Turner Joy, who was chief United Nations delegate to the Korean Armistice Conference in 1951–52.

---

to the President's Oval Office at 11:30 A.M., Johnson announced that he had issued new instructions regarding future patrols and engagements with enemy craft: The Navy was to continue the patrol in the Gulf of Tonkin, with the *Turner Joy* joining the *Maddox,* and a combat air patrol was to be maintained over both vessels. Both the planes and the destroyers had orders "(a) to attack any force which attacked them in international waters, and (b) to attack with the objective of not only driving off the force, but of destroying it." No questions were permitted. After the President had read his statement, correspondents were ushered from his presence.

Later, McNamara explained[3] that the order of self-protection was among the normal "rules of engagement for our forces worldwide ... to protect yourself, defend yourself in any way necessary." But the pursue-and-destroy portion "was not necessary ... if their mission required them to take other action." He continued: "In this case this mission was a patrol mission and it was perfectly appropriate ... [that] they continued their patrol after they drove off the attacking force, but the President wanted them to go beyond that and not resume the patrol until they had endeavored to destroy the attacking force."

At the State Department's regular noon briefing for newsmen the same day, a reporter asked department spokesman Robert J. McCloskey what the Administration meant by saying that the *Maddox* was on a "routine patrol."

Q. Can you say what the American ships are doing there?
A. [by McCloskey] They are patrolling on those international waters. American ships patrol international waters around the world.
Q. Would it be fair to ask why?
A. It would be fair to ask, yes, sir. But I'm afraid I can't enlarge on my answer at this time.

Asked about the North Vietnamese charges of raids against their islands, and the alleged United States involvement, McCloskey rejected them as "without foundation." He professed to have "no knowledge of any such attacks being made by anyone." He added that the department was preparing a note of protest to North Vietnam.[4]

At this juncture the press and the public accepted the Administration's handling of the affair. All seemed equally bewildered that North Vietnam had launched a foolhardy assault upon a destroyer known to have far more deadly firepower than the PTs and to be under the protective air umbrella of the *Ticonderoga,* stationed permanently off the coast a short distance to the south. The North Vietnamese navy consisted of about 200 officers and 2,000 enlisted men. At their disposal were four 100-ton wooden PT boats, of Soviet design and capable of 40 knots, built in China and transferred to North Vietnam in 1957; twelve 50-ton aluminum PT boats, built in Russia and given to Hanoi in 1961, each 87½ feet long and capable of 42 knots; three subchaser patrol craft and three small gunboats. The *Maddox* alone weighed more than the combined North Vietnamese PT fleet, 2,200 tons to 1,000 tons.

Editorially, the *Washington Post* said that the Administration "has responded with a reassuring blend of firmness and balance," and hoped that the incident was not the "deliberate start of a campaign to tease the American navy or provoke a David-Goliath confrontation with the mighty Seventh Fleet." But the *Post* also noted that "the difficulty of reading Hanoi's mind on this score is enhanced by the peculiar half-light of 'signal' and security which shines on, but fails to illuminate, many moves by both sides in Vietnam." These moves included charges of attacks on North Vietnamese islands as well as brisk speculation (and official denial) since early spring that the United States would have to "go north" to win the war. "These accusations were promptly rebutted by American officials, but they contribute to the atmosphere of danger and ambiguity that enshrouds the attack on the *Maddox*," the *Post* concluded. The *New York Times* said Johnson's response "contained the right mixture of firmness and restraint," and added, "It is essential that Hanoi realize immediately that it has opened a Pandora's box."

In background briefings,* Administration officials offered five possible reasons for the attacks: The Chinese Communists really believed the United States was a "paper tiger" and prompted North Vietnam to make the attack as a test of Washington's will; North Vietnam's demonstrated ability to attack United States vessels would demoralize South Vietnam's Premier Nguyen Khanh, whose government would collapse; North Vietnam and China considered the Tonkin Gulf, about three-fourths enclosed by their land masses, a "Communist lake" not subject to international laws on territoriality; North Vietnam was willing to risk a predicament militarily to encourage the Chinese to supply more aid; and finally, an embarrassed Soviet Union would be forced to choose sides between the United States, with whom Premier Nikita Khrushchev was then seeking detente, and North Vietnam, a "Communist friend under fire." The Administration did not put its imprimatur on any of these reasons, simply offering them as possible explanations for the incident.

Barry Goldwater, resting at Newport Beach, California, before his presidential campaign, declined comment on Sunday, pleading a lack of information. But on Monday he served notice that the White House would hear more of the incident before November: "Does the presence of Ameri-

* At "background" press briefings the speaker may be identified neither by name nor by title, and stories arising from them must be attributed to "Administration sources" or "Administration officials" or variations thereof. One purpose of backgrounders is to air opinions which the Administration does not wish to endorse openly.

can destroyers in the area signify the possible landing of larger American ground forces? Does it mean medium bombers are going to be used to intercept supply lines? Does it mean a change is taking place in foreign policy at the White House and State Department levels?" His press secretary, Ed Mellor, asked for Goldwater's answers to the questions he posed, said, "The words speak for themselves."

Lyndon Johnson had not the slightest doubt he would overwhelm Goldwater in November; private polls taken for the White House immediately after the GOP convention showed the President obtaining as much as 75 percent of the vote. He knew this figure would diminish, but wished to approach it as a mandate for the Great Society. But Johnson also has a nagging fascination with history: What he has seen and experienced yesterday he expects to be repeated tomorrow, and Goldwater's taunt of "Why Not Victory?" unsettled him with memories of the Korean War torment suffered by the Democrats during the first Stevenson-Eisenhower campaign.

The Republican platform, dictated by Goldwater people, charged that the Johnson Administration "has encouraged an increase of aggression by appearing to set limits on America's willingness to act and then, in the deepening struggle, it has sacrificed the lives of Americans and allied fighting men by denial of modern weapons. . . . [I]t has abetted further Communist take-over in Laos, weakly accepted Communist violations of the Geneva agreement which the present Administration perpetrated, and increased Soviet influence in Southeast Asia." And in his acceptance speech Goldwater shoveled scorn upon Johnson: "Failures in the jungles of Vietnam . . . proclaim lost leadership, obscure purpose, weakening wills and the risk of inciting our sworn enemies to new aggressions and to new excesses." Goldwater credited the "strength and believable will of the Eisenhower years" with blunting the "thrust of Communist imperialism," then declared:

> And I needn't remind you, but I will, that it's been during Democratic years that our strength to deter war has been stilled and even gone into a planned decline. It has been during Democratic years that we have weakly stumbled into conflicts, timidly refusing to draw our own lines against aggression, deceitfully refusing to tell even our own people of our full participation and tragically letting our finest men die on battlefields unmarked by purpose, unmarked by pride or the prospect of victory.
>
> Yesterday it was Korea, tonight it is Vietnam. Make no bones of this. Don't try to sweep this under the rug. We are at war in Vietnam. And yet the President, who is commander-in-chief of our forces, refuses to say, refuses to say, mind you, whether or not the objective there is victory, and his Secretary of Defense continues to mislead and misinform the American people, and enough of this has gone by.

Johnson's campaign cabinet—Bill Moyers, Clark Clifford, James Rowe, and Lawrence O'Brien—concluded early that Goldwater's hard-line talk would scare nominal Republicans out of their wits (and into the Democratic ranks). Nonetheless Vietnam worried them, because it was a difficult and fluid war, difficult for the Administration to explain and for the people to understand. At several planning conferences the campaign cabinet discussed what should be done if the war "suddenly fell apart." Should the South Vietnam government totally collapse, or events compel the United States to make a sudden and massive commitment of manpower, Goldwater's dictum, "Let's win it!" could become an appealing alternative to the voters. To Democratic campaigners Johnson let it be known that he wanted to be depicted as the "candidate of restraint and moderation," but not as a weakling afraid to stand up to a fourth-rate power.

To handle the defense question, Cyrus Vance, McNamara's principal deputy, and Joseph Califano, Pentagon counsel (and later Johnson's domestic-programs overseer in the White House) created a special office which assembled material to rebut Goldwater's charges on Vietnam and other Defense Department matters. The office operated secretly. Six lawyers, civilian and military, were assigned to it. Twice daily a Navy chief petty officer, wearing civilian clothes, drove downtown to the Goldwater campaign headquarters, sauntered into the press office, and casually gathered up advance texts of the candidate's speeches and policy statements. Time and again the Vance-Califano office gave Johnson's "reply" to the press before Goldwater had delivered his accusation.

A lawyer who worked in the office recollected later, "Perhaps it was because we were so close to it, and had access to material unknown to the public, but we feared that Goldwater had a real issue in Vietnam, had he approached it properly. The bombing thing was no bother, because it had no popular appeal. But it was obvious to all of us that the Administration had not been candid about the war—take the Operation Farm Hand thing, for example—and that if Goldwater had had proper guidance, someone to bring up specific shortcomings, he could have given us a tumble. In a nutshell, the Viet Cong was shooting hell out of Americans, and we weren't shooting back (or admitting we were, anyway), and all we could offer in rebuttal was a bunch of malarkey about commitments." (Operation Farm Hand was an Administration decision, in early 1964, to permit United States pilots to fly combat missions, ostensibly to "advise" Vietnamese enlisted men who went along for the ride. The Administration told congressional leaders of the decision, but in secrecy. The new combat role was revealed in April when an Air Force captain complained of the duplicity in letters to his wife. She made them public via Dirksen and Representative Charles Halleck of Indiana, House minority leader, after her husband had died in a crash.)

Goldwater, however, was a peripheral nuisance when compared with Premier Khanh, who emerged as Vietnam's ranking politician after the fall of the Diem regime. The frustrated Khanh couldn't inspire the Vietnamese army to fight; he couldn't put together an effective national government; he couldn't tolerate the kibitzing of President Charles de Gaulle of France, who campaigned incessantly for neutralization of all of Indochina at a reconvened Geneva Convention of the powers involved there. For seven months Washington repeatedly assured Khanh: "We'll stick with you, and give you what it takes," yet despite recommendations of Khanh's good friend Ambassador Henry Cabot Lodge, Americans had not appeared in appreciable numbers.

Johnson confused Khanh. The Premier had a dangerous half-knowledge of American politics. Embassy officials told him that the President intended to do nothing drastic about the war until after the election; but Khanh apparently suspected Johnson's "no-wider-war" stumping pointed to a negotiated settlement after November, over Saigon's head or behind its back if necessary. Khanh argued repeatedly and heatedly for permission and arms to carry the war to Hanoi's homeland. An official of the Agency for International Development (AID) recalls a poignant scene when the Premier went into a hamlet near Saigon which the Viet Cong had raided with frightful and bloody loss of life. Khanh said something to this effect: "Just once, just once, we should do this to the North. Let them feel the pain and the agony." Khanh fumed, and read Goldwater's statements, and asked official Americans: "Does Johnson listen to this Goldwater? Will Goldwater force any change?"

Khanh erupted on July 19, at a rally marking what the South Vietnamese call their "national day of shame," the anniversary of the 1954 armistice dividing Vietnam along the demilitarized zone. A crowd of 100,000 persons, directed by government cheerleaders, shouted *Bac thien!* ("To the North!") as Khanh said:

We have often heard that the people have called for the war to be carried to the North. That is not only an urgent appeal of a million refugees from the North, nourishing their dream of liberating their native land. This is not only the ardent wish of thousands of families in the South with relatives who went to the North, who long for the day when they can be reunited with their loved ones.

This is also the fervent wish of the religious sects, of the Buddhist and Christian communities, who have always thought of the silent church suffering under Communist tyranny.

This still is the enthusiastic demand of the students, of this generation of youth who are eager for the destiny of the country to rise for the liberation of our oppressed compatriots.

The government cannot remain indifferent before the firm determination of all the people who are considering the push northward as an appropriate means to fulfill our national history.

The speech infuriated Johnson. "Can't this man shut up for awhile?" he fumed during a Vietnam conference in his office. "If Khanh marches north, Lyndon Johnson isn't marching with him." Johnson was also angry at press speculation about an expansion of the war. Moyers has said, "The President was furious, not because the stories were leaks of formulated policy but because he didn't believe we would have to get to that kind of policy. He plowed the bureaucracy until he thought he had uncovered the culprit [in a particularly irritating instance] and in a telephone call half across the country to where the fellow was vacationing, he gave him hell. 'If you want to plan a war,' the President told him, 'you make it clear it's your war you're planning. And you go and fight it, because I don't want to fight it for you.' " Moyers said that anyone who heard the President then "had to believe him."[5]

Air Marshal Nguyen Cao Ky inopportunely chose the week of Khanh's speech to reveal offhandedly in a chat with newsmen in Saigon that for some three years South Vietnamese "combat teams" had conducted hit-and-run raids against the North "by land, air, and sea." He also declared that 30 South Vietnamese pilots were "ready" to bomb the North. Pressured by the Saigon embassy, Khanh retreated slightly, saying the only differences in policies with the United States were of timing and of "what to announce publicly." Since the South Vietnamese "are already victims of North Vietnamese aggression," he declared, "any response from us would be a counterattack."

Johnson's attention was further concentrated on Vietnam in late July, when the Soviet Union and Great Britain, permanent cochairmen of the 1952 Geneva Convention, gave what was to Washington disturbingly close attention to De Gaulle's proposal for a reconvened conference on Indochina. Britain's Foreign Minister R. A. B. Butler flew to Moscow to confer with Soviet officials, followed quickly by United Nations Secretary-General U Thant. Johnson firmly put into the record his objection to any new formulae for Southeast Asia, declaring, "If others would keep the solemn agreements already signed, there would be no problem in South Vietnam."

Thus the pressures on Johnson at the time of the first Tonkin episode were: the uncertainties inherent in a political campaign; the unpredictable quality of the Khanh government in Saigon; the continued deterioration of the war; and finally, increasing world pressures on the United States to negotiate from a position of weakness.

The center of government in Washington is structured so that the existence of what officials consider a grave crisis can be kept from public view for days; thus the Johnson Administration entered the next phase of the Tonkin affair behind a surface calm. That it was able to do so is further evidence of an administration's ability to "control" events of great national import, and is in keeping with the modern pattern. For example, late on the afternoon of October 15, 1962, CIA photo interpreters, viewing U-2 espionage pictures taken the previous day over western Cuba, found the erectors, launchers, trucks, and radar vans of a battalion of Soviet medium-range ballistic missiles. By the night of October 21, many newsmen sensed that a crisis was building, and that it involved Cuba. The *New York Times* "had most of the story" then but, at the request of President Kennedy, did not publish it.[6] The situation was not made public until 7:00 P.M. on October 22, when President Kennedy went on television to announce the missiles' presence and to declare a quarantine on shipments of offensive military equipment to Cuba.

The second Tonkin incident did not approach in gravity the Cuban missile crisis, which the late Robert F. Kennedy has said "brought the world to the abyss of nuclear destruction and the end of mankind."[7] The Cuban situation demanded United States action lest the nation live under the shadow of Soviet offensive missiles; the Tonkin situation had no element of immediacy, for even by the most pessimistic analysis the episodes represented probes of United States determination, not a challenge to the Seventh Fleet to do battle. Nonetheless, the decision was to maintain official silence while the planners worked.

The period of secrecy on August 4 lasted from 9:20 A.M., when the National Military Command Center in the Pentagon—known both in the military and in the movies as "The War Room," or more simply, "The Tank"—received the first flash that another attack was thought to be under way, until 6:00 P.M., when the Defense Department issued another statement in the name of Assistant Secretary for Public Affairs Arthur Sylvester:

> A second deliberate attack was made during darkness by an undetermined number of North Vietnamese PT boats on the *USS Maddox* and *USS C. Turner Joy* while the two destroyers were cruising in company on routine patrol in the Tonkin Gulf in international waters about 65 miles from the nearest land. The attack came at 10:30 P.M.* local time (10:30 A.M., August 4, Washington time).
>
> The PT boats were taken under fire by the destroyers and thereafter by attack aircraft from the *Ticonderoga* and the *Constellation*.

---

* To convert Tonkin Gulf time to Washington (Eastern Daylight) time, subtract 12 hours —that is, 7:00 P.M., August 4, in the Gulf would be 7:00 A.M., August 4, in Washington. Between July 30 and August 5 the *Maddox* ventured several times into another time zone, 13 hours distant from Washington. But for consistency and convenience, incidents in the Gulf are stated in the so-called "golf" (not gulf) time zone—a military designation —in which most of the action occurred. Sylvester's announcement, because of a mix-up in time zones, put the incident an hour later than it occurred. Several hours later the Pentagon caught the error, and subsequent statements that night used the correct hour of 9:30 P.M. Communist media subsequently used the switch in time as "evidence" of Washington's confusion.

The attackers were driven off with no U.S. casualties, no hits, and no damage to either destroyer.

It is believed that at least two of the PT boats were sunk and two others damaged.

Later in the week the Administration revealed a highly selective chronology of what had happened during the period of secrecy. The press accounts (give or take an adjective or terse quotation) were similar, and to this effect:

Promptly upon receipt of the message announcing the attack, the Joint Chiefs of Staff convened in McNamara's office, Rusk joining them within minutes. They talked about the first flow of cables, and of possible responses. At 11:45 A.M. Rusk, McNamara, and Wheeler drove across the Potomac to the White House for a previously scheduled National Security Council meeting on a crisis simmering in Cyprus. The meeting didn't last long, for Johnson thought, as Kennedy had, that it was an unwieldy group for serious business. So he, Rusk, McNamara, Bundy, and CIA Director John McCone, went to lunch in a second-floor dining room, where the President said immediately that Hanoi must be punished. The only question for debate was how, and by whom, and with what severity. ("There were no 'doves' or 'hawks' at this meeting," *Time* said in its August 14 cover story on Tonkin.)

Johnson wanted the retaliation to be by American planes, lest the North Vietnamese and Chinese Communists think Washington was "afraid" to use its own forces against the North. He wanted the strikes to come as soon after dawn as possible, so as to impress upon Hanoi the "fact" that it could expect a swift sting in return for further attacks. And he wanted to avoid bombing any population centers. A suggestion that Haiphong be shelled by destroyers was discarded out of hand because civilians might be killed, and Johnson didn't want to send warships "into territorial waters" (*Time's* phrase). McNamara listed five targets—four PT bases, one oil refinery (*Time* again). Rusk suggested saving the three northernmost bases for a "possible second-stage attack" (*Time*). McCone wanted to clobber all five, "in view of the gravity of the North Vietnamese 'act of war' against the destroyers." (*Time* again.) "That was it. 'All right,' said the President, 'let's go.'" (And again.)

The *New York Times* reported the decisive action with less high drama. The *Times* recessed the luncheon meeting before the discussion of targets began, and reported an "*ad hoc* group for planning" which added Cyrus Vance, General Wheeler, George Ball, and Richard Helms, Deputy Director for Plans (DDP) of the CIA and number two man to McCone. The *Times* also permitted the *ad hoc* group to choose targets "all afternoon."

Sylvester's public announcement coincided with telephone calls to key

Congressmen to assemble at the White House at 6:45 P.M. for an important briefing.* The briefing was preceded by a second National Security Council meeting. The decision to strike was made then, McNamara said the next day in an interview with Peter Hackes of the National Broadcasting Company.[8] "I think everyone present recognized we are facing a very perilous situation, and a very serious situation," he said. "There was a soberness of mind and attitude in discussions, but a firmness of purpose and a unanimous recommendation to the President that we respond as we did."

The congressional meeting began at 6:45 P.M. Let us again rely upon *Time* for the Administration's version of its handling of the crisis: "The President was grim, decisive. He made it clear he was informing his old Capitol Hill colleagues, not asking their advice. 'These are our plans,' he snapped." The *New York Times'* Johnson was more courteous with the group. He "left no doubt" that the decision and responsibility were his, and he asked each man, in turn, for support. McCone, Wheeler, and McNamara briefed the Congressmen until 8:15 P.M., and strictly admonished them to say nothing. Representative Charles Halleck of Indiana, the minority leader, said that he was so fearful of leaking the secret of the bombing decision he wouldn't even answer his telephone that night. "We were told by the President that there would be no announcement of the air strike until our pilots were over the targets," he said.[9]

At 8:25 P.M. George Reedy told newsmen there would be a presidential statement on national television later that night. When? Reedy didn't know, but he advised reporters it was "not safe to go to dinner," which is the White House way of saying, "Don't stray too far, you might miss something." The TV networks were put on a standby basis, and a pool camera was set up in the Fish Room of the White House, just across the corridor from the President's Oval Office. The *Times'* Edwin A. Dale, frankly stating he didn't know for sure, "surmised" in an article later in the week that the strike order went out at this time. *Time,* however, sounded the trumpets in midafternoon: "Orders crackled through the Pacific as units of the Seventh Fleet were alerted . . . and the massive military machinery gathered its strength."

The American people, their attention snapped to Vietnam by the second "attack" announcement, had their prime-time television viewing interrupted with the bulletin that the President would be speaking later that night. With whetted anticipation (and foreboding), the nation sat and waited for Johnson.

Something peculiar happened that evening which escaped general public notice in the mounting excitement of the "crisis." The North Vietnamese, who had quickly claimed a victory in the Sunday encounter, flatly denied

* Once 16 Congressmen are given a hurry-up summons to the White House, secrets have a short life expectancy.

*its craft were involved in any engagement on Tuesday. Radio Hanoi said
in a broadcast several hours after the Sylvester announcement:*

*"The United States Pentagon has alleged . . . four torpedo boats of the
Democratic Republic of Vietnam attacked two United States warships in
international waters. Vietnam News Agency [the official government news
service] is authorized to declare that this is a sheer fabrication by the United
States imperialists, aimed at covering up their illegal acts which brazenly
violated the security of the DRV and are aggravating further the situation
in Southeast Asia."*

One person didn't have to await the television announcement. In early
evening White House telephone operators started attempting to locate
Goldwater, who was at sea on his yacht, the *Sundance*. Three times within
two hours Johnson contacted the *Sundance* by ship-to-shore phone; three
times the conversation faded into crackling static. Goldwater finally told
Johnson: "Look, it must be important, and we shouldn't be yelling over
this kind of phone. Let me get back to shore and I'll call you." At 10:07
P.M. (the White House released the exact time) Goldwater called the
President and was told what to happen. Goldwater shortly thereafter
issued a formal statement (which actually reached reporters before Johnson's TV appearance): "I am sure that every American will subscribe to
the action outlined in the President's statement. I believe it is the only
thing that he can do under the circumstances. We cannot allow the American flag to be shot at anywhere on earth if we are to retain our respect
and prestige."

Finally, at 11:37 P.M., a somber-faced President appeared before TV
cameras in the Fish Room. "My fellow Americans," he said, "as President
and Commander in Chief, it is my duty to the American people to report
that renewed hostile actions against United States ships on the high seas
have today required me to order the military forces of the United States
to take action in reply." He told of the Sunday attack, adding that it was
"repeated today by a number of hostile vessels attacking two United States
destroyers with torpedoes," and continued:

The destroyers and supporting aircraft acted at once on the orders I
gave after the initial act of aggression. We believe at least two of the attacking boats were sunk. There were no United States losses. The performance of commanders and crews in this engagement is in the highest
tradition of the United States Navy.

But repeated acts of violence against the armed forces of the United
States must be met not only with alert defense but with positive reply.

That reply is being given as I speak to you tonight. Air action is now
in execution against gunboats and certain supporting facilities in North
Vietnam which have been used in these hostile operations.

In the larger sense, this new act of aggression aimed directly at our forces again brings home to all of us in the United States the importance of the struggle for peace and security in Southeast Asia.

Aggression by terror against the peaceful villages of South Vietnam has now been joined by open aggression on the high seas against the United States of America.

The determination of all Americans to carry out our full commitment to the people and to the government of South Vietnam will be redoubled by this outrage. Yet our response for the present will be limited and fitting.

We Americans know—although others appear to forget—the risk of spreading conflict. We still seek no wider war. I have instructed the Secretary of State to make this position clear to friends and to adversaries, and, indeed, to all.

I have instructed Ambassador [Adlai] Stevenson to raise this matter immediately and urgently before the Security Council of the United Nations. Finally, I have today met with the leaders of both parties in the Congress of the United States and I have informed them that I shall immediately request the Congress to pass a resolution making it clear that our government is united in its determination to take all necessary measures in support of freedom and peace in Southeast Asia.

I have been given encouraging assurance by those leaders of both parties that such a resolution will be promptly introduced, freely and expeditiously debated, and passed with overwhelming support.

And, just a few minutes ago, I was able to reach Senator Goldwater, and I am glad to say that he has expressed his support of the statement that I am making tonight. It is a solemn responsibility to have to order even limited military action by the forces whose over-all strength is as vast and as awesome as those of the United States of America. But it is my considered conviction, shared throughout your government, that firmness in the right is indispensable today for peace.

That firmness will always be measured. Its mission is peace.

At two minutes after midnight the television networks switched from the White House to the cramped, low-ceilinged news briefing room on the Pentagon's E-ring. There McNamara faced the cameras from behind a lectern, surrounded by maps of Southeast Asia, Vietnam, and the Gulf of Tonkin. His role was to spell out the details of the second incident, and to detail the "air action" taken in response.

"I can tell you that some of the action has already taken place," McNamara said. "U.S. naval aircraft from the carriers *Ticonderoga* and *Constellation* . . . have already conducted air strikes against the North Vietnamese bases from which these PT boats have operated. Our naval aircraft have also conducted strikes against certain other targets which have directly supported the operation of the PT boats. Furthermore, in view of the unprovoked attacks, the deliberate attacks in international waters on U.S. naval forces, the United States has taken the precaution of moving substantial military reinforcements to Southeast Asia from our Pacific bases . . . [and] to the Western Pacific from bases here in the United States." Mc-Namara said it was "not wise at the present time" to identify the units or their strength, "but I can assure you that the movements are appropriate to the provocation." He then moved into a chronology* of the attacks, noting that since Sunday the *Maddox* and *Turner Joy* "have operated on patrol in those waters . . . 30, 40, 60 miles off the coast of North Vietnam in international waters. . . ."

At 7:40 P.M. . . . Vietnamese time . . . the *Maddox* reported radar contact with unidentified surface vessels who were paralleling its course, paralleling the track of both the *Turner Joy* and the *Maddox*.

At 8:36 P.M. . . . the *Maddox* established two new radar contacts with two unidentified surface and three unidentified aircraft. At this time U.S. fighter aircraft were launched from the carrier *Ticonderoga,* which was also operating in the Gulf of Tonkin . . . to rendezvous with the *Maddox* and *Turner Joy,* and provide air cover to them.

At 9:08 P.M. . . . the unidentified aircraft had disappeared from the destroyers' radar screens and the surface vessels were remaining at a distance. By that time, the aircraft from the *USS Ticonderoga* had arrived over the destroyers and they commenced defensive patrol over them.

[At] 9:30 P.M. . . . the initial attack occurred. Additional vessels had by now appeared on the *Maddox's* radar screen, and these vessels were observed to close very rapidly on the destroyers at speeds in excess of 40 knots. The attacking surface vessels continued to close rapidly from both the west and the south.

By 9:52 P.M. the *Maddox* and *Turner Joy* . . . reported they were under continuous torpedo attack and were engaged in defensive counterfire.

By 10:15 P.M. they . . . were reporting they were avoiding torpedoes and that they had sunk one of the attacking patrol craft.

At 10:42 the destroyers reported they had evaded torpedoes and had sunk a second of the attacking patrol craft. Other aircraft from the *Ticonderoga* had arrived overhead and joined the defensive patrol.

At 10:52 the *Maddox* reported the destroyers were again under attack. At midnight . . . the destroyers reported they had suffered no hits, no casualties, and that the defense aircraft from the *Ticonderoga* were illuminating the area and attacking the enemy surface craft.

At 12:32 . . . the patrol reported that an additional enemy craft was believed to have been sunk, and that low ceilings, poor weather, was beginning to hamper the aircraft operations.

At 12:54 the *Turner Joy* . . . reported that during the engagement, in addition to the torpedo attacks, the destroyer had been fired upon by automatic weapons while being illuminated by search lights.†

* McNamara made frequent use of the maps and a pointer in his presentation. For clarity I have deleted from the transcript parenthetical references to his pointing and indicating. On the maps he showed the general southward courses of the *Maddox* and *Turner Joy* during the night. The deletions do not alter his account of the engagement.
† This statement is a prime specimen of what the military calls "report magnification."

At 1:30 A.M. .... the destroyers ... reported the attacking craft had apparently broken off the engagement. The *Maddox* and *Turner Joy* were directed to resume their normal and routine patrol operations, and they are continuing them at the present time.

Questions followed, with McNamara replying that the unidentified aircraft seen at 8:36 P.M. "did not participate in the attack and at this moment, we have no further information on them"; the targets would be named "at a time appropriate to the safety of our forces. It would be inappropriate to name them at this time. The attack is continuing at present." Hanoi was not among the targets: "We are attacking only the patrol craft bases and certain associated logistical facilities." He would not reveal future orders of the *Maddox* and *Turner Joy,* citing security, nor the exact time of launch of the attack planes from the carriers. The incident covered a track of some 80 miles.

Some other exchanges:

> Q. Mr. Secretary, I am sure there is no doubt in your mind that these PT boats came from, in fact, North Vietnam?
>
> Secretary McNAMARA. There is none. The radar made it quite clear that they were coming from North Vietnamese bases.
>
> Q. Mr. Secretary, can you give us the basic reasons for the Gulf of Tonkin patrol?
>
> Secretary McNAMARA. It is a routine patrol of the type we carry out in international waters all over the world.
>
> Q. Does it have anything to do with movements of junks, or whatever it is, back and forth?
>
> Secretary McNAMARA. No. It has no special relationship to any operations in that area. We are carrying routine patrols of this kind on all over the world all the time.
>
> Q. Mr. Secretary, do you have any idea why the North Vietnamese may have done this?
>
> Secretary McNAMARA. None.
>
> Q. Mr. Secretary, you mentioned that the destroyer at one point was under attack by automatic weapons. Does that mean both destroyers, or just the *Maddox?*
>
> Secretary McNAMARA. The report was, I believe, that both destroyers had been attacked by automatic weapons.
>
> Q. What was the closest, roughly, that the attacking craft have come to the *Maddox* and *Joy?*
>
> Secretary McNAMARA. We have had reports of torpedoes 100 and 200 yards off the beam of these ships. I can't tell you how close the

attacking craft came to the vessels, although if they were firing automatic weapons they must have come closer than 800 yards at a minimum.

Q. Who opened fire first?

Secretary McNAMARA. It was quite clear that the PT boats initiated the attack.

Q. When was the last time that there were destroyers up there in the Tonkin Gulf?

Secretary McNAMARA. I prefer not to answer the question other than to say that we have been carrying on routine patrols in that area for months.

Q. How far up do you go, Mr. Secretary, before they turn back?

Secretary McNAMARA. I prefer not to answer that, either. We don't wish to identify the course of our operations in the area.

Q. Mr. Secretary, have there been any similar aggressive actions on the part of the North Vietnamese navy short of the torpedoing that we didn't bother to report before?

Secretary McNAMARA. No . . . I want to emphasize that these attacks both on Sunday and today . . . occurred in international waters. *These destroyers were operating between 30 and 60 miles off the North Vietnamese coast.*

McNamara was then asked by a reporter if the *Maddox* and *Turner Joy* "were sufficiently close to be illuminated by the PT boats, the question a reader will have is, how come the destroyers weren't able to nullify the PT boats?"

Secretary McNAMARA. They did. They sunk at least two.

Q. Two out of how many, sir?

Secretary McNAMARA. We can't be sure. It was a night attack. We can't be certain of the total number of boats that were engaged. I will give you an estimate, just for your own information, although I can't be absolutely certain of these numbers. I would say between three and six boats were engaged in the attack, of which at least two were sunk.*

Q. How did you know they were sunk, those two? . . . Were these sunk by destroyer fire or aircraft fire?

Secretary McNAMARA. I can't identify the source of the sinking. . . . This, let me emphasize, was a night action. You must expect certain restrictions in the amount of information available under night conditions. But the report to us from sources that we believe reliable

---

* *Time* wasn't satisfied with McNamara's estimate. Its August 14 cover story said "there were at *least* six of them."

indicate that at least two vessels were sunk .... Just five minutes before I came down, I received a report that they were sunk .... [The] report was that two PT boats at least were sunk, and a possible third.

Q. Can you tell us at all whether any of the damage was inflicted by five-inch guns?

Secretary McNAMARA. No. This was nighttime. I can't identify the type of shell that caused the damage, or even the source of damage as between destroyers on the one hand, and our aircraft on the other.

Q. Mr. Secretary, approximately how many hostile torpedoes were fired at our ships?

Secretary McNAMARA. It is very difficult to estimate. I don't wish to make a guess at them.*

The conference ended at 12:30 A.M., Wednesday, with McNamara stating he intended to remain in the Pentagon overnight so he could receive reports every half hour from the Pacific.

Secretary Rusk, meanwhile, had talked on a background basis to State Department correspondents, giving them guidance which the press next day attributed to "high Administration officials." Rusk said the North Vietnamese are "writing the scenario" and that further escalation "is up to them." He didn't expect any declaration of war by North Vietnam, nor a wider war with Chinese participation. But Rusk admitted that the "lack of rationality" in the attacks made the future uncertain. He said the United States, through its "measured response," was attempting to tell Hanoi: "It's up to you whether this is a one-shot deal that we all forget about or is part of a major war."

Over the next two days the Pentagon released details of the air strikes, beginning with another televised McNamara press conference at nine o'clock Wednesday morning in which he reported that 64 American air attack sorties had been launched at four patrol-boat bases (in Hon Gay, Loc Chao, Phuc Loi and Quang Khe) and at the oil storage depot at Vinh, "which is associated with the Swatow torpedo [boat] base." Twenty-five of 30 boats based at the target sites were destroyed or damaged, as was 90 percent of the Vinh facility. McNamara's comments on the time of the strike were imprecise: "The local times ranged from on the order of noon to four or five o'clock in the afternoon [Vietnam time]." Two United States aircraft were lost, two damaged. Lieutenant (jg) Richard Sather, 26, of Pomona, California, presumably died when his A-1 Skyraider crashed into the sea. Lieutenant (jg) Everett Alvarez, Jr., of San Jose, California, bailed

* *Time* counted ten.

---

out of his A-4 Skyhawk when it was hit by flak over Hon Gay, and was captured.

According to an official "strike summary" issued on Thursday, the first attack began at 1:15 P.M., Wednesday, Vietnam time—or 1:15 A.M., Wednesday, Washington time—when six *Ticonderoga* jets hit Quang Khe. At 1:25 P.M. 16 planes hit Phuc Loi and Vinh; 14 planes returned for a re-strike of Vinh at 4:45 P.M. McNamara said an estimated eight oil storage tanks were set ablaze by the first attack, two or four others the second time. "Smoke was observed rising to 14,000 feet." The strike summary added: "Moderate anti-aircraft fire was encountered during the first strike on Vinh and two anti-aircraft positions near the oil storage area were attacked and destroyed. During the re-strike, a heavier concentration of anti-aircraft was encountered and an estimated five guns of a six-gun position were subsequently destroyed." Planes from the *Constellation* didn't get into action until 3:45 P.M., when 16 craft hit Hon Gay and 12 hit Loc Chao. At Hon Gay, guns from positions overlooking the harbor, and from patrol craft, fired on the United States planes.

McNamara also revealed that day the extent of the reinforcements in the Pacific: transfer of an attack carrier group to the "western Pacific"; movement of interceptor and fighter-bomber aircraft into South Vietnam, and of fighter-bomber aircraft into Thailand; transfer of interceptor and fighter-bomber squadrons from the United States to "advance bases" in the Pacific, and of an antisubmarine task force into the South China Sea; and the "alerting and readying for movement of selected Army and Marine forces."

The retaliation complete, the next concern was what, if anything, the Chinese Communists would do in support of their ally. In CBS and NBC television interviews on Wednesday, August 5, Rusk said that the United States had responded quickly to prevent a "mistaken judgment of our intent, a basic miscalculation of where we stood." He professed to have "no satisfactory explanation" for the attacks because the Communists "see the world in wholly different terms" from the United States and it is "very difficult to enter each other's minds across that vast ideological gulf."[10]

The last major Chinese statement prior to the incidents had been on July 6, in the name of Foreign Minister Chen Yi.* It had warned that "should United States imperialism launch an attack on the DRV, thereby posing a threat to China's peace and security, the Chinese people naturally cannot be expected to look on with folded arms." Chen Yi said that "all socialist countries" have the "unshirkable proletarian international duty" to "protect all its members from any imperialist invasion." For the specialists

* This discussion of Chinese attitudes goes considerably beyond analyses publicized during the immediate Tonkin period.

at the CIA and the State Department's Bureau of Intelligence and Research who spend tedious hours poking through Chinese statements for nuances of phrasing, the Chen Yi pronouncement had several interesting features: The warning was issued in the name of "the Chinese *people*," not "the Chinese *government*," as statements immediately prior to the intervention in Korea had been; the words "cannot sit idly by" are broad enough to cover everything from political support to economic and military aid or the dispatch of troops; and "imperialist *invasion*" indicated that air strikes against North Vietnam would not in themselves constitute a threat to Chinese national security. In the course of a long official broadcast the preceding March, the North Vietnamese claimed that Peking had promised them military support in the event of an invasion. When the Chinese radio repeated this broadcast, the passage about military aid was deleted (an important subtlety of the type the CIA cites to Congress to justify the high costs of its monitoring service). The President apparently had received an estimate that China would tolerate the retaliatory strikes before he ordered the raids.*

The first Chinese statements following the Tonkin incidents were markedly similar to that made by Chen Yi a month earlier. On August 5 the New China News Agency (Peking's official voice) called China and the DRV "neighbors closely related to each other like the lips and the teeth," and said, "Aggression by the United States against the DRV means aggression against China. The Chinese *people* will absolutely not sit idly by without lending a helping hand. Since the United States has acted this way the DRV has gained the right of action to fight against aggression, and all the countries upholding the Geneva Agreements have gained the right of action to assist the DRV in its fight against aggression."

A *People's Daily* editorial on August 6 pledged that the "Chinese *people* will resolutely support all just actions of the Vietnamese people to resist U.S. aggression and defend their motherland. Should U.S. imperialism at any moment invade the DRV's territory or its territorial waters and air space, the Chinese people will be honor bound to give resolute support to the Vietnamese people."

In both instances, United States analysts noted a lack of any threat or pledge of *specific* action. No one in the government was sanguine enough to think that the Chinese would do nothing, but Washington clearly anticipated no massive intervention. At an August 6 press conference McNamara said, "I think it probable that the Communist Chinese will introduce some combat aircraft into North Vietnam in support of them [because] North Vietnam does not possess any combat aircraft of its own.... I would think that that would be a likely response." He said that he had "no indica-

* The national intelligence estimates of the CIA, prepared by its Board of National Estimates, are reviewed at least once monthly, and in times of crisis even hourly. The basic conclusions on Communist China vis-à-vis Vietnam, however, did not change materially from early 1964 through late 1968.

tion . . . [of] any substantial movements of Communist Chinese forces either by land or air"—this in response to claims by Nationalist China of large-scale troop movements on the Chinese mainland through Yunan province, which abuts North Vietnam.

From the military standpoint, the Johnson Administration stumbled only once in its handling of the crisis, but managed to scramble back to its feet before the Republicans could press it to earth. Early in his August 4 TV address to the nation, which began at 11:37 P.M., Johnson said that "air action is now in execution. . . ." McNamara, at his press conference which began at 12:02 A.M. August 5, said that Navy planes "have already conducted air strikes against North Vietnamese bases." But the strike summary issued by the Defense Department on Thursday, August 6, said that the first bombs did not fall until 1:15 A.M., or one hour and 40 minutes after Johnson went on national television.

Representative Ed Foreman, a blustery Goldwater Republican from west Texas, promptly picked up the discrepancy. "What is this?" he cried in a floor speech. "What is this when we give an hour and a half notice of our attack upon the Communists? What kind of responsibility is it when the President . . . appears on the television networks so that he can talk nationwide to the people to tell them one hour and a half ahead that our planes are coming in? Why, this is better notice to the enemy than they could get with an alert radar defense system."

Foreman called the television announcement "publicity-happy political irresponsibility," and said families of the two downed pilots could justifiably ask, "Would we have our son or husband or daddy if the Communists had not been warned an hour and a half ahead of time?"

The Administration dismissed Foreman's charges as bunk. McNamara said the United States planes "achieved complete surprise" when they swept over the North Vietnamese targets. He and Wheeler said that "it is inconceivable that a military force expecting an attack would have its boats lying dead in the water at the base, and this is exactly the way we found most of the North Vietnamese."

Why, then, the advance announcement? An obviously stung McNamara took full responsibility for the decision in a statement Friday shortly after Foreman's speech, saying he had recommended that Johnson schedule the speech for 11:40 P.M. because:

1. By that time U.S. naval aircraft had been in the air on their way to their targets approximately one hour.

2. Hanoi, through its radar, had then received indications of the attack.

3. The time remaining before the aircraft arrived over their targets would not permit the North Vietnamese to move their boats to sea or to alert their forces.

4. It was important that the people of our country learn of the manner in which their government was responding to the attacks on its vessels from their President rather than from Hanoi, which was expected to announce the attack at any' moment.

5. It was desirable that the North Vietnamese government and others be told as soon as possible the character of the attack—"Our response for the present will be limited and fitting. We . . . know . . . the risks of spreading conflict. We ,will seek no wider war." [Quoting Johnson's TV speech.]

As you know, the North Vietnamese government did not have time to move their forces; our attacking aircraft found the torpedo boats at their docks; the attack was highly successful.

Apropos of television timing, an incident during the railroad negotiations the previous spring was recalled. Late in the afternoon of April 22, Johnson had persuaded railroad unions and management to agree to a settlement which averted a national strike. The evening television news shows were about to begin, and Johnson wanted to announce his good fortune at once. But an hour's time was required to set up sound cameras in the White House. Johnson summoned a Presidential limousine and with union and company officials beside him sped two miles up Wisconsin Avenue at 55 miles an hour through rush-hour traffic to WTOP-TV, where CBS network facilities were available. The presidential penchant for television crossed several minds when the timing of the bombing was disclosed. As Representative Halleck put it later, "Of course, had the President waited, network stations in the Eastern time zone would have been off the air and his audience greatly reduced. . . ."[11]

There is some evidence that the Navy was not happy about the advance notice. During research for this book, I found, in files of the Pentagon's Directorate for Defense Information, a transcript of an undated interview between Rear Admiral R. B. Moore, commander of Task Force 77 of the Seventh Fleet, to which the *Ticonderoga* and *Constellation* were assigned, and an unidentified questioner. Moore gave a general review of the air action. Then he was asked:

Q. Were our planes identifiable by enemy radar by the time the President began speaking?

A. [by Admiral Moore] *No, I do not think so.*

Q. Any evidence that you caught the Communists by surprise or were they expecting you?

A. I think they would naturally be alert considering the fact there had been an engagement two days before, very close to their country. And from the reports of the pilots, I think their anti-aircraft batteries were manned and ready.

Moore said antiaircraft fire was "heavy and of immediate effect," but called United States losses "light in comparison with the damage done."

The Moore transcript then reflects a peculiar "correction." The interviewer said that "because of a misunderstanding" he wanted a repeat on the question about whether the planes were identifiable by radar at the start of the Johnson speech. Admiral Moore's answer this time conformed with the Administration's stated position that the early announcement did not jeopardize the planes:

> The answer to that comes in three parts. Number one, the planes would be identifiable if they were there and the radars were in operation. However, the planes were not in that area at that time, so they were not identifiable at that time. Number two, by the time the President did announce it and the time the planes were there, I do not think [there was] sufficient time for communications systems available to have alerted the [North Vietnamese] people. And number three, I think the people there would have been alerted anyway because of the engagement that had taken place within 50 to 60 miles of the locations off their coast within the past 48 hours.

The file does not reveal what use was made of the Moore interview, and there is no evidence it was ever distributed publicly.

Chapter Two

MR. JOHNSON'S RESOLUTION

The morning of Wednesday, August 5, while the final draft of the President's desired resolution on Southeast Asia was being written, Senator Morse received a telephone call from the Pentagon.

During his eight years on the Senate Armed Services Committee, Morse had forged close professional friendships with the career bureaucrats, unknown outside their immediate sphere of government, who provide the day-to-day expertise which keeps the mammoth Department of Defense grinding along its way. The normal tour of duty for a uniformed officer at the Pentagon is two years; the civilian bureaucracy is permanent, and little happens within the department of which it is unaware.

By charitable description, Morse is irascible—a man with a low toleration threshold for humbuggery and its practitioners, be they presidents of his own party (in either his Republican or Democratic phase) or fellow senators. Few persons are neutral on Wayne Morse; they either admire his gutsy penchant for battle in causes avoided by the squeamish, and join him; or they loathe his rasping, waspish righteousness. Even when he's on their side, Morse can offend people.

The man who called Morse on August 5 was one of the admirers. He suggested that Morse do two things: obtain the logbooks of the *Maddox,* which would detail its movements in the days immediately preceding the August 2 attack and put them definitely within North Vietnamese "territorial waters" of 12 miles; and ascertain the *Maddox's* actual mission in the Gulf of Tonkin. The caller said unequivocally that the *Maddox* was not on a routine patrol, as both President Johnson and Secretary McNamara had claimed on television Tuesday night, but was actually a spy ship and had some connection with the South Vietnamese raids on the islands. The caller said there was a "hell of a lot of confusion" surrounding the August 4 episode, but he didn't know any details.

The name of his informant Morse will carry to his grave. But it is an indication of his rank within the Defense Department and his reliability that Morse accepted his information unquestioningly. Through the staff of the Senate Foreign Relations Committee, of which he was the fourth-ranking Democratic member, Morse informed McNamara's office that McNamara should come to the Senate hearings prepared to answer questions about the *Maddox's* mission. He also learned that the logs would not be available for days.

Morse outlined his information to his colleagues, warning that Johnson intended to rush the resolution through Congress as rapidly, and with as few questions, as possible. Morse found other Senators mildly sympathetic but uncooperative. One of them says he told Morse: "Hell, Wayne, you can't get in a fight with the President at a time when the flags are waving and we're about to go to a national convention. All Lyndon wants is a piece of paper telling him he did right out there, and we support him, and he's the kind of president who follows the rules and won't get the country into war without coming back to Congress. That's all it is—don't be so excitable." This Senator, recounting his talk with Morse a few years later, stopped for a moment at this point and mused, "Lord, what boobs we mortals be."

Morse himself has said bitterly: "The chief trouble was that the United States Senate, despite its manifold horrible experiences with Lyndon Johnson as majority leader, still trusted Lyndon Johnson, or pretended that it did, anyway." But Morse emphasized his was not an anti-Johnson fight. "I have complete confidence in and high regard for President Johnson, and shall campaign with all my heart for his reelection [sic] in November," Morse said during the debate.[1] "The most loyal service I can render any President is to disagree with him when I think he is wrong and try to correct his mistaken course of action."

Morse had long held an antipathy to broadly worded resolutions such as Johnson had said he would give Congress on Tonkin. In 1955, when the nation was in what Morse calls a "give 'em the works" mood about Communist Chinese threats to Formosa and the adjacent Pescadores, President Eisenhower asked for a resolution approving the use of armed forces and the "taking of such other measures as he [the President] judges to be required or appropriate" in defending them. According to Morse, Secretary of State John Foster Dulles and Admiral Arthur W. Radford, chairman of the Joint Chiefs of Staff, had told the Foreign Relations Committee (in testimony which has never been published) that this language authorized a "preventive war" against China. In Dulles's view, if the Administration felt that a Chinese attack was imminent, the United States could strike the mainland. Morse objected that the resolution "amounts to giving the military establishment, without a declaration of war, the power to make war." He protested the "psychology of trigger-happy military men, and the psychology of diplomats who convince themselves that it is necessary to pull the trigger before an act of war has been committed against us."

Morse's protests were so vehement that the chairman, Senator Walter

George of Georgia, hastened to the White House to ask Eisenhower if Dulles had accurately stated the Administration's view of the resolution. Eisenhower said yes, whereupon George said that he would not support it. After considerable wrangling, Eisenhower issued a statement that he alone would decide how to implement the resolution. This satisfied George, but not Morse, who argued that Dulles, Radford, and other foreign policy advisers would still make the "preventive war" decision because "the President will follow their advice." He was one of three Senators to vote against the resolution.

In the Tonkin affair, Morse realized he had little time to arouse opposition to the Johnson resolution, or even to attract much attention to flaws in the Administration's story. He considered the resolution a "predated resolution of war," regardless of the patriotic and legalistic verbiage in which the White House wrapped it for shipment up Pennsylvania Avenue to Congress. So Morse decided to speak long, and to speak often, in the hope that the nation, if not the Senate, would heed him. He had little serious hope of blocking the resolution; indeed, he didn't even bother to take a head count of potential supporters. A colleague tells how, in 1962, he had jocularly chided Morse for helping to immobilize the Senate for three weeks during the filibuster against creation of the Communications Satellite Corporation. "At least I slept well last night—a man with a clean conscience often does," the Senator quotes Morse as replying. All Morse realistically expected from Tonkin was a clean conscience.

When a presidential messenger brought the Tonkin Resolution to the Senate at midday on Wednesday, August 5, its members were desultorily going through House Resolution 11296 ("making appropriations for sundry independent executive bureaus, boards, commissions, corporations, agencies, and offices"). Senator Hubert H. Humphrey asked for a pause to permit introduction "of this important executive message," and the resolution was read by the clerk:*

> Whereas naval units of the Communist regime in Vietnam, in violation of the Charter of the United Nations and of international law, have deliberately and repeatedly attacked United States naval vessels lawfully present in international waters, and have thereby created a serious threat to international peace; and
>
> Whereas these attacks are part of a deliberate and systematic campaign of aggression that the Communist regime in North Vietnam has been waging against its neighbors and the nations joined with them in the collective defense of their freedom; and
>
> Whereas the United States is assisting the peoples of Southeast Asia to

* The resolution was formally titled the Southeast Asia Resolution, but the more commonly used designation, "Tonkin Resolution," will be employed hereafter.

protect their freedom and has no territorial, military, or political ambitions in that area, but desires only that these people should be left in peace to work out their own destinies in their own way: Now, therefore, be it

Resolved by the Senate and House of Representatives of the United States of America in Congress assembled, That the Congress approves and supports the determination of the President, as Commander in Chief, to take all necessary measures to repel any armed attack against the forces of the United States and to prevent further aggression.

The United States regards as vital to its national interest and to world peace the maintenance of international peace and security in Southeast Asia. Consonant with the Constitution and the Charter of the United Nations and in accordance with its obligations under the Southeast Asia Collective Defense Treaty, the United States is, therefore, prepared, as the President determines, to take all necessary steps, including the use of armed force, to assist any member or protocol state* of the Southeast Asia Collective Defense Treaty requesting assistance in defense of its freedom.

This resolution shall expire when the President shall determine that the peace and security of the area is reasonably assured by international conditions created by action of the United Nations or otherwise, except that it may be terminated earlier by concurrent resolution of the Congress.

Congress was responsible for the final 13 words of the resolution, added at the suggestion of Senator Russell during the White House meeting of congressional leaders on Tuesday night. Russell, a canny Southern constitutionalist, wanted a mechanism through which Congress could withdraw its endorsement of the Executive. Concurrent resolutions are not subject to presidential veto. Except for the single clause, the resolution was the creation of the Executive.

Morse began his fight immediately, taking the floor to say he felt the President was "quite right in meeting the attack on the destroyers," but wrong in going beyond self-defense to bomb the mainland. "In my judgment that constituted an act of war—not an act of self-defense. We had an irrefutable case of violation of international law by North Vietnam in connection with their attack on our ships. We would have a hard time, under international law, supporting our subsequent attack on North Vietnam in the absence of a declaration of war. There are those who will say that is cutting the line pretty thin. Nevertheless the difference is between acting within the Constitution and acting outside of it."

Morse's speech that day was too long, tedious, and repetitious of his standard antiwar orations to make the impact he sought. With his limited

* The SEATO treaty, signed in 1954, provided that nonsignatory nations could be covered by its defense and economic provisions by protocol, which was done for South Vietnam, Laos, and Cambodia.

information, and no authority even to hint at his source, he could make only a circumstantial case that the United States had provoked the attacks and was forced to rely on rhetorical questions rather than documented evidence. But, to anyone accustomed to the circumlocutions of Senate oratory, Morse's speech had intriguing points. He charged that the South Vietnamese had bombarded islands "within three to five or six miles of the main coast of North Vietnam" while "U.S. vessels of war were patrolling Tonkin Bay *presumably within six to eleven miles off the shore. . . .*" The Administration, in its statements earlier in the week, had never put the ships within less than 30 miles of shore. Morse called the South's raids the "forerunner to the attack" on the *Maddox*, and asked: "Was the U.S. Navy standing guard while vessels of South Vietnam shelled North Vietnam? That is the clear implication of the incident."

Morse agreed with the Administration that the three-mile limit for territorial waters "has the better support under international law principles" than the greater limits claimed by many countries. But he noted that United States fishing boats are frequently impounded for venturing into the claimed international waters of friendly South American nations. Why, then, he asked, should the destroyers venture so close to North Vietnam, since the territorial limit was bound to be controversial? He declared:

> The United States . . . knew that the South Vietnamese vessels planned to bomb, and did bomb, two North Vietnamese islands within three to six miles of the coast of North Vietnam. Yet, these war vessels of the United States were in the vicinity of that bombing, some miles removed.
>
> Can anyone question that even their presence was a matter of great moral value to South Vietnam? Or the propaganda value to the military totalitarian tyrant and despot who rules South Vietnam as an American puppet—General Khanh? . . .
>
> It should be unnecessary to point out either to the Senate or to the American people what the position of the United States would be if the tables were reversed and Soviet warships or submarines were to patrol five to eleven miles at sea while Cuban naval vessels bombarded Key West. . . .

Senator J. William Fulbright, chairman of the Foreign Relations Committee and in that capacity floor manager for the resolution, proceeded to undercut Morse's protestations of Administration deception. He praised both the quantity and quality of information supplied to the key congressional committees: "Both the present Administration and the previous Administration have been very good about reporting to us about the situation. I do not believe there has been any tendency to withhold anything. I do not believe that at any time when representatives of the Administration came to brief us and we requested information they have refused to divulge it. In many cases, they themselves have initiated such a request as far as the information goes." (One visualizes a warm, friendly Johnson Administration, rummaging through its files to give the Senate Foreign Relations Committee anything it wanted, candid and complete in its answers, a trusted friend!)

The first-day telegram response to Morse's speech was overwhelmingly favorable. Out of hundreds received, only two were critical (both of them "questioning my human paternity," as he put it). "Bravo for seeing and describing the Emperor's clothes in Southeast Asia," wired Virginia Gerson of New York. "As Democrats we are humiliated and angered by President Johnson's knuckling under to Senator Goldwater," said a couple in Berkeley. "Your vision and courage in Vietnam stand out like a beacon among the blind yes-men in our public life. Why are there not more of you?" came from Springfield, Massachusetts. But a couple in Highland Park, Illinois, reminded Morse of his greatest handicap: "We agree with your North Vietnam position. However, your speech and position on this subject not carried by our local news media. . . ."

But most of official Washington—and the Senate—ignored Morse's charges about the *Maddox's* involvement in the raids. When he returned to his office late Wednesday, Morse realized he must bludgeon more information from Administration witnesses when they testified for the resolution.

Room S-116 of the Capitol building is the main office and hearing room of the Senate Foreign Relations Committee, a baroque cavern entered through a white wooden swinging door, with glistening chandeliers and an outsized oval table with green baize top onto which is riveted a brass nameplate for each member. On days when there are executive hearings a Capitol policeman guards the door, and the press and tourists cluster at a respectful distance. It was to this room that Secretaries Rusk and Mc-Namara and General Wheeler came on the morning of Thursday, August 6, with the President's resolution. The combined Foreign Relations and Armed Services committees (less absentees) awaited them, 25 members totaling one fourth of the entire Senate.

Rusk led off, with a statement giving the background of United States involvement in the war, from Geneva through a Johnson promise of June 23 that this country "is determined to use its strength to help those who are defending themselves against terror and aggression." But in the "interest of time," Rusk put the statement into the record and launched directly into an explanation of the resolution. His oral statement is quoted here at length, for it stands as the Administration's presentation of the political considerations and obligations of the resolution upon which Senate support was solicited:[2]

> The preamble I believe . . . speaks for itself. It spells out in the simplest and shortest terms possible the fact of North Vietnamese attacks, their relation to the overall campaign of aggression by North Vietnam, and the

purposes and objectives of the United States in Southeast Asia.

As to the operative sections of the resolution, section one declares the approval and support of the Congress for actions, in response to armed attack on U.S. forces, which the President has the authority and obligation to take in his capacity as Commander in Chief.

Turning next to section two ... let me make clear at the outset what the resolution does not embrace. It does not cover action to assist any nation not a member of the Southeast Asia Treaty Organization or a protocol state.

You will recall the protocol states were South Vietnam, Cambodia, and Laos. In the case of Cambodia they have publicly declared they will not utilize their privilege of calling for help as a protocol state under the Southeast [Asia] Treaty Organization.

In the case of Laos the 1962 accords contained a declaration by the Government of Laos they would not call upon any alliance, or group of nations, for assistance.

Therefore, so long as the 1962 accords are in effect, the Government of Laos would be barred from calling on that assistance unless the relevant portions of those particular agreements had in fact withered away.

This resolution does not cover any action in support of a nation unless such nation requests it. It does not cover any action to resist aggression that is not Communist in origin. The Southeast Asia Treaty includes a U.S. understanding that it is directed solely against 'Communist' aggression.

The language, 'to take all necessary steps, including the use of armed force', is similar to the authority embraced in the Formosa Resolution of 1955, the Middle East Resolution of 1957, and the Cuba Resolution of 1962. ... The Formosa Resolution authorized the President 'to employ the Armed Forces of the United States' [in defense of Formosa and the Pescadores]. The Middle East Resolution stated that the United States was 'prepared to use armed force'. The nearest parallel to the language of the present language is in the first clause of the Cuba Resolution that the United States is 'determined ... to prevent by whatever means may be necessary, including the use of arms', Cuban subversive activities extending to any part of the hemisphere.

I shall not take your time this morning to review the constitutional aspect of resolutions of this character. I believe it to be the generally accepted constitutional view that the President has the constitutional authority to take at least limited armed action in defense of American national interests; in at least 85 instances, Presidents ... have in fact taken such action.

As I have said before, we cannot now be sure what actions may be required. The Formosa Resolution of 1955 was followed by the use of U.S. warships to escort supply convoys to the offshore islands in 1958; the Middle East Resolution was followed by President Eisenhower's sending of troops to Lebanon in 1958; the Cuba Resolution was followed by the well-known events of October 1962.

I do not suggest that any of these actions may serve as a parallel for what may be required in Southeast Asia. There can be no doubt, however, that these previous resolutions form a solid legal precedent for the action now proposed. Such action is required to make the purposes of the United States clear and to protect our national interests.

Mr. Chairman, I would like to add one comment to this statement, and that is that this resolution, and this consultation which the executive and the legislative branches are now having in the course of today, will in no sense be the last contact between the executive and legislative branches on these problems in Southeast Asia. There will continue to be regular consultations not only with committees but between the President and the congressional leaders, and on a bi-partisan basis. That has been the practice of Presidents in this postwar period.

Therefore, as the Southeast Asia situation develops, and if it develops, in ways which we cannot now anticipate, of course there will be close and continuous consultation between the President and the leaders of the Congress.

. . . [T]he important aspect of this resolution is, I venture to suggest, not so much in the constitutional field as in the broad political field here and abroad. We have, since 1945, been engaged in an effort to bring about a peaceful world situation. The main thrust of that has necessarily been to bring to a halt the kind of armed aggression and subversion and infiltration which have come, both as a matter of doctrine and as a matter of practice, out of the Communist world.

We feel that it is very important that this country, on as unified a basis as possible, make it quite clear to the entire world that we are prepared to take the steps that may be required to insure the security of those to whom we are committed, and to bring such aggression to a halt. That is the primary purpose of this particular action today. And we very much appreciate the speed with which Congress has turned its attention to this problem and hope very much that a unified and prompt action can be taken.

Rusk's prepared statement contained another paragraph on the purpose of the Tonkin Resolution: "We have never doubted the support of the American people for the [Vietnam] policies that have been followed through three Administrations over a period of a decade. But in the face of the heightened aggression on the Communist side, exemplified by these latest North Vietnamese attacks, it has seemed clearly wise to seek in the most emphatic form a declaration of congressional support both for the defense of our armed forces against similar attacks and for the carrying forward of whatever steps may become necessary to assist the free nations covered by the Southeast Asia Treaty."

McNamara's description of the attacks themselves duplicated what he had told the committees on Monday about the first incident, and had stated in his televised news conference about the second. He put the complete document into the committee record (each member had a copy) and briefly gave the highlights. Then came the questions.

Chairman Fulbright (who presided over both committees) didn't ask a single question, although he was well aware of the doubts raised by Morse. "I only want to make a very brief statement," said Fulbright. "The promptness and decision which all of you exhibited on this occasion was commendable and I also think the restraint with which you used overwhelming power in the area is a new attitude on the part of a great power that is extremely beneficial and I think will be effective."*

Senator Russell satisfied himself that nothing further had been heard of the unidentified "aircraft" picked up by the *Maddox's* radar at the start of the August 4 episode, and that North Vietnam's supply of petroleum by sea "could be cut off." Senator John Stennis of Mississippi asked for an elaboration on the incidents themselves. "What do you know about it . . . who is involved?"

Secretary McNAMARA. I think it is very clear that the attack of August 2 and August 4 was carried out exclusively by patrol craft of North Vietnam. There was an allusion a moment ago to three unidentified aircraft which appeared on the radar screens. Whose aircraft these were, where they came from we don't know . . . we don't know whether they were transport aircraft, combat aircraft. We don't know their point of origin or their purpose.†

Senator STENNIS. Well, the background, what led up to all this. What do you think about the possibility of Red China's participation or prompting . . . ?
Secretary McNAMARA. We see no evidence of their direct participation. What their counsel may have been from North Vietnam I can't say.
Senator STENNIS. You don't have any intelligence on that?
Secretary McNAMARA. No, sir, we do not.
Secretary RUSK. Mr. Chairman, I might just add one comment on that.

The immediate action that was here does seem to be exclusively North Vietnamese, but the Chinese Communists have been giving strong public support to the position of North Vietnam, and they recently made a statement on the 6th of August:‡

Aggression by the United States against North Vietnam means aggression against China. The U.S. Government must stop its armed provocations against the [D]emocratic Republic of Vietnam. Otherwise it must be held responsible for all the grave consequences arising therefrom.

* Fulbright's comments in 1964, when put into juxtaposition with his pained outcries from late 1965 onward, make ironic reading.
† The duty radar operator on the *Maddox* who "saw" the "planes" had no doubts about what happened, as shall be revealed later.
‡ The day *after* the United States air raids.

It is our impression that the Chinese would give at least very strong political and public support to the North Vietnamese in this situation. We just frankly do not know whether they will translate that into action of any sort. [Deleted.]

Secretary McNAMARA. Senator Stennis, there are Chinese bases on Hainan Island. Our destroyers were operating in this area as were our aircraft.

During the period our destroyers and aircraft were operating on patrol in this area, during the time of the North Vietnamese attack on them, Chinese aircraft were operating out of Hainan Island in this direction. They did not approach our vessels or aircraft and they did not in any way attack.

Responding to further Stennis questions, General Wheeler said the North Vietnamese "have got about a dozen of these PT boats of the type that made these attacks. They have 30 slightly larger craft but they are also patrol craft known as Swatows and then they have, of course, the usual support installations, smaller craft, barges, and things of that kind. Their navy consisted of about 200 officers and 2,000 enlisted men. They have no combat aircraft at all."

Senator Bourke B. Hickenlooper of Iowa wanted to know why the strikes were not simultaneous "because manifestly a strike at one would alert the others." McNamara explained that since the *Constellation* was farther south than the *Ticonderoga,* "its aircraft were required to fly a longer distance . . . and we knew they would be picked up at time of launch by radar and as it turned out, they were; it was a simultaneous launch rather than a simultaneous attack which was the important point in relation to the disclosure of intent."

The answer satisfied Hickenlooper. "I only want to say that I think the United States had no other recourse. The decisions were sound. I certainly support the necessity of vigorous and immediate retaliation in this situation." With this comment, the ranking Republican on the Foreign Relations Committee concluded his interrogation of the Administration witnesses.

Senator Leverett Saltonstall of Massachusetts, ranking Republican on the Armed Services Committee, had no questions. Noting that the Tonkin Resolution was the fourth such request on which he had voted, Saltonstall said, "I believe the action of the President was essential to defend the prestige of our armed forces, and certainly the submission of this resolution is in accordance with our Constitution to have Congress support the President in these defensive actions and I intend to support this resolution whole-heartedly and with my best efforts."

Next came Morse, whose Pentagon source had supplied him enough information to ask broad questions about the incidents in the Gulf of Tonkin —but not in sufficient detail to enable him to conduct a thorough cross-examination of either McNamara or Rusk. Morse said he was "unalterably opposed" to the "aggressive course of action on the part of the United States," and accused the *Maddox* of acting as a shield for the South Vietnamese raids on Hon Me and the other islands.*

"I think what happened is that Khanh got us to backstop him in open aggression against the territorial integrity of North Vietnam," Morse said. "I have listened to briefing after briefing and there isn't a scintilla of evidence in any briefing yet that North Vietnam engaged in any military aggression against South Vietnam either with its ground troops or its navy."

Even in print, Rusk's retort is tinged with anger.

Secretary RUSK. Mr. Chairman, I feel compelled to make a brief comment on what the distinguished Senator from Oregon has just said.

Since 1954 the North Vietnamese have been undertaking to undermine and take over the Government of South Vietnam. There was some surcease from these depredations during the years about 1956 to 1958, but in 1959 the North Vietnamese again came back to it, made a decision to step up their activities, and in 1960 publicly proclaimed their purpose.

Now, the shape and form of armed attack and aggression have been changing in this postwar world. I cannot myself see any lack of aggressiveness or any lack of military action in the infiltration of parties of individuals, some of them running up to 150 and 200 at a time, infiltrating through Laos, contrary to agreements, into South Vietnam contrary to their obligations, for the purpose of carrying on armed action against the authorities and the people of South Vietnam.

So that I think we ought to try our best to keep very clear who is the aggressor here, and what the purposes of the United States and the Free World are. We have helped country after country, through the Marshall Plan and NATO right around the world in this postwar period in maintaining their security and independence, and we don't control any of them. We have none of them in any American empire.

The issue here, it seems to me, is a very clear one between a persistent course of aggression and an attempt on our side and the side of our friends in Southeast Asia to create independent, secure, and prosperous countries who have a chance to live their own lives without interference from their neighbors.†

* Morse's questions about these raids, and McNamara's responses, were deleted by Pentagon censors when the Foreign Relations Committee finally published testimony from the hearing in November 1966. The portion of the censored testimony obtained elsewhere is indicated by brackets.
† A cogent capsulization of Washington's rationale for its involvement in the war, and Rusk's standing answer to the oft-repeated question, "Just why ARE we in Vietnam?" By 1968 Rusk could deliver this 250-odd-word speech virtually without varying a syllable from day to day.

Senator MORSE. I don't propose to engage in a debate with the Secretary of State here. I disagree on the basis of the many replies presented, on the basis of his own testimony before this committee when we have asked time after time for evidence from the Secretary of State and the Pentagon Building of any proof of any organized military operation of North Vietnam going into South Vietnam. You have never been able to produce a scintilla of evidence. We have all recognized the vicious infiltration tactics of the Communist system trying to undermine South Vietnam, but it has been going back and forth across the borders. The sad thing is that we were in there all the time when, in my judgment, we shouldn't have been in there except to keep the peace. We ought to have been at the conference table.

Secretary McNAMARA. Mr. Chairman, may I respond to this? There have been several misstatements made and I would like to correct them for the record. . . . I would like to cover three points.

First [*our Navy played absolutely no part in, was not associated with, was not aware of any South Vietnamese actions, if there were any. I want to make that very clear.*] The *Maddox* was operating in international waters, was carrying out a routine patrol of the type we carry out all over the world at all times. [It was not informed of, was not aware, had no evidence of and, so far as I know today, has no knowledge of, any possible South Vietnamese actions in connection with the two islands that Senator Morse referred to.]*

I think it is extremely important that you understand this. If there is any misunderstanding on that we should discuss the point at some length.

Senator MORSE. I think we should.

Secretary McNAMARA. I say this flatly; this is the fact.

Morse and McNamara then had an exchange on the boundaries of North Vietnam's claimed territorial waters, based upon statements the Secretary had made at the off-the-record briefing of August 3. Pentagon censors skeletonized the section thus:

Senator MORSE. What was your testimony the other day, Mr. Secretary, on the record [deleted].

Secretary McNAMARA. I testified the other day that the American vessels were, or the American vessel was—it was the *Maddox* at that time—was operating on a southerly course in routine patrol in international waters in this area [deleted].

Senator MORSE. [Deleted.]

Secretary McNAMARA. [Deleted.]

Now if you want to discuss actions by South Vietnam I will discuss

* As we shall discover, this claim is perhaps the most questionable statement McNamara made during the hearing. Bracketed material, it will be recalled, was deleted from the published report of the hearings in November 1966.

them, but before doing so I want to make one other point. This Government has positive proof of the organized effort of North Vietnam to subvert the Government of South Vietnam. It has positive proof of the direction of the military actions in South Vietnam by North Vietnam. This proof has been available for a long time. I assume this committee is aware of it. If it isn't aware of it, I will be perfectly happy to expose it to a selected group of members of the committee. There should be no misunderstanding on the part of any of you of the direction of the attempt to subvert the Government of South Vietnam by North Vietnam, of a day-by-day command of that effort, of the continued support of it.

Senator MORSE. I want to make it perfectly clear I have never questioned the subversive activities of North Vietnam. But I also want to make perfectly clear, Mr. Secretary, that you have not put in the record of this committee any proof at any time of any overt military operations of North Vietnam into South Vietnam.

We have asked you time and time again; you people come before this committee, 'Well, we think a cadre now and then but there has been no organized military invasion of North Vietnam into South Vietnam,' that has been the testimony time and time again.

Secretary McNAMARA. I dispute that, Senator.

Senator MORSE. Well, the record will speak for itself.

Secretary McNAMARA. You said there has been none.

I don't know what the record shows because I am not familiar with the record of this committee but I do know there is an organized effort of North Vietnam using men and material to destroy the Government of South Vietnam, and we have ample evidence of that, and if this committee wishes to enter into a discussion of that evidence I am perfectly willing to supply it to you, although some of it is so highly classified that I would have to ask you to appoint a selected committee.

Secretary RUSK. Mr. Chairman, since I have been before the Foreign Relations Committee a number of times, I would like to point to the distinction between organized units of North Vietnamese in their own uniforms, flying their own flag, coming into South Vietnam, and groups of infiltrators trained and organized by North Vietnam, bearing arms, who come down into South Vietnam, organizing operations against the people of South Vietnam.

This is what I said, what I had in mind, when I said the shape of aggression is changing in the postwar world. That doesn't mean it is not just as much aggression as if they were flying their own flags. There are certain technical distinctions, but the aggression in fact is here.

Senator MORSE. [Deleted.]

That is what the Communists are going to play up, and I don't think we ought to let ourselves get into that position.*

Secretary McNAMARA. Mr. Chairman, may I respond again very briefly to this?

I think you should understand the infiltration of South Vietnam by sea that has taken place for two and a half years, and the degree to which South Vietnam has endeavored to respond to that, and I will cover it very briefly for you.

During July and December of 1961 there were 140 incidents of infiltration from North Vietnam into South Vietnam by sea. These included infiltration of bazookas. It included infiltration of groups as large as 65 [men] by single junks. There were 1,400 probable or confirmed infiltrations of personnel at that time.

Then South Vietnam had no organized force to combat these infiltrators. They had only 80 sailing junks. None of these were motorized, obviously an ineffective sea patrol. We assisted them in organizing a sea patrol starting in December 1961.

At that time we started their junk force. A portion of that force was financed by military assistance funds. About 500 junks were built. Using their own funds, the Vietnamese added about 60 more. . . . These junks fall in four categories.

There are command junks, about 28 of them, that have a crew of ten, carry automatic weapons and radios. There are about 240 sailing junks that carry out surveillance. These are in a sense pickets or patrols stationed in particular areas carrying out routine surveillance. . . .

There are several hundred motorized sailor junks or motorized junks carrying automatic weapons, patrolling an extended area of the sea. This patrol of some 600 or 700 junks in the eight months—of the last eight months of 1963—searched 130,000 junks, searched 350,000 people, discovered 140 Viet Cong agents among them.

In the first seven months of this year, they have searched 149,000 junks, some 570,000 people. This is a tremendous operation endeavoring to close the seacoasts of over 800 miles.

[*As part of that, as I reported earlier to you this week, we understand the South Vietnamese sea force carried out patrol action around these islands and actually shelled the points they felt were associated with this infiltration. Our ships had absolutely no knowledge of it, were not connected with it, and in no sense of the word can be considered to have backstopped the effort.*]†

---

* Morse's deleted statement again touched upon the South Vietnamese raids, and the presence of United States vessels in the target area.
† Thus for the third time in half an hour did McNamara unequivocally deny Navy "knowledge" of the South Vietnamese raids. Again, the denial was deleted from the November 1966 version of the hearings.

With Morse silenced, the remainder of the hearing presented no challenge to McNamara. At one point Senator Stuart Symington of Missouri felt compelled to say he spoke "not in any sense of criticism" when asking why ten percent of North Vietnam's petroleum facilities were left unbombed. "The remaining portions of their petroleum depots were associated with other parts of their economic system," McNamara said. To Senator Margaret Chase Smith of Maine, McNamara denied that "lack of intelligence or error in judgment" was responsible for his initial opinion that the first attack was isolated and would not be repeated. "I think it was because with hindsight I personally consider the action of the North Vietnamese a form of suicide and I didn't expect them to undertake it," he said. Senator Russell Long of Louisiana thought "it sounded from what you say here as though we achieved . . . about the kind of surprise on their navy as the Japanese achieved in Pearl Harbor." McNamara said, "I think that is exactly true. That applies to all of the four bases." (General Wheeler interjected, "In thinking this one over, I can't imagine any military commander putting his boats into this limited anchorage when he expected an attack on them.") *

Indeed, the only question about the chronology of the two incidents came from Senator Lausche of Ohio—not as a doubter but as a man who fervently sought from the Administration confirmation that it had acted properly.

Senator LAUSCHE. I want to get clear in the record and in my own mind exactly what happened on the 2d. The testimony given thus far indicates that the *Maddox* reported hostile patrol vessels to some superior office and that it believed that those patrol vessels were intent upon hostile action.

Do the records of the vessels show a communication from the *Maddox* to a superior officer stating that they are being followed and that it looked as if hostile action would take place?

General WHEELER. The records of higher headquarters do show a stream of communications, a continuous stream of reports, from the *Maddox* back to the task force commander who was on the *Ticonderoga*. What actually happened was that on 3:50, eastern daylight time on the 2d, the *Maddox* was approached by three North Vietnamese patrol boats with the apparent intention of launching a torpedo attack. That is when the *Maddox* retired to the east at 27 knots.

The torpedo boats came on after her and she got within 9,000 yards [5.1 miles] which was at 4:08 eastern standard time, the *Maddox* fired three warning shots from a five-inch battery.

* *Did* the North Vietnamese expect an attack? President Johnson had stated on August 3 that the United States would "pursue and destroy" any vessel which attacked its ships. His critics argue that the North Vietnamese would not have moored their PT fleet into such a compact and attractive target upon completion of just such an attack one day later.

Senator LAUSCHE. That is not what I want. I want to know if your records show a communication; that is, the *Maddox* reporting to the *Ticonderoga* that it looked as though they are going to be subjected to an attack.

General WHEELER. That is correct.

Senator LAUSCHE. That would prove [sic] the *Maddox* did not precipitate the thing but was waiting instructions from the *Ticonderoga*. [There is a period, not a question mark, after Lausche's statement.]

General WHEELER. That is correct, sir.

Not only that, Senator, we not only have a communication record, but the fact that the *Maddox* turned to the eastward and proceeded out to sea.

Senator LAUSCHE. To avoid?

General WHEELER. To avoid any contact with hostile PT boats.

Senator LAUSCHE. Then the *Maddox* did nothing until it was actually fired upon?

General WHEELER. Fired three warning shots when these PT boats approached within 9,000 yards. That was the first action, sir.

Secretary RUSK. Despite the warning shots, the PT boats continued to close at a high speed.

Senator LAUSCHE. Continued to close?

According to your reports the torpedoes were set into motion and it was then that you began your firing.

General WHEELER. That is correct, sir.* They came within 5,000 yards [2.8 miles], two of them, PT boats came up within 5,000 yards away and launched torpedoes which the *Maddox* evaded by changing her course.

Senator LAUSCHE. Now then, on August 3, the President made his statement. You appeared before us.

Secretary McNAMARA. Yes.

Senator LAUSCHE. But there was nothing of any consequence happen- in the area.

General WHEELER. That is right.†

Senator LAUSCHE. Now then, on August 4, you again have the *Maddox* supposedly reporting radar contact with unidentified surface vessels who were paralleling its track and the track of the *Turner Joy*. . . . To whom was that report made by the *Maddox?*

Secretary McNAMARA. That was made by the *Ticonderoga* and, of course, transmitted to higher headquarters, CINCPAC and Washington as well.

---

* In attempting to keep up with Lausche's questions, Wheeler stumbled here—his earlier answer that the warning shots *preceded* the firing of the torpedoes is the correct one.
† Remember this depiction of August 3, a date about which we shall hear more.

Senator LAUSCHE. Then at 7:40 P.M., the *Maddox* reported to head-quarters that from the actions being taken by those unidentified vessels an attack by them appeared imminent?

Secretary McNAMARA. That is correct.

Senator LAUSCHE. Now, at this time the *Maddox* was heading south-east near the center of the Gulf of Tonkin in international waters approxi-mately 65 miles from the nearest land; 8:36 *Maddox* again established radar contact with two items by vessels [sic]. It still did nothing, is that correct?

Secretary McNAMARA. That is correct.

Senator LAUSCHE. Were there shots fired by the North Vietnamese on the 4th before you went into these lands [sic]?

Secretary McNAMARA. Oh, yes; the *Maddox* was attacked as was the *Turner Joy* on the 4th.

Senator LAUSCHE. Do you know how many of the torpedoes were set into motion and what small arms were used?

Secretary McNAMARA. It is difficult to estimate. This was a very dark night. The attack was carried out during the night, the hours of darkness. It was a premeditated attack, a preplanned attack. It was described as an ambush in the reports from the commanders, but because it was night it is very difficult to estimate the total amount of fire.*

Senator LAUSCHE. The shots were again initiated by the North Viet-namese?

Secretary McNAMARA. Yes.

Senator LAUSCHE. The attacks upon us occurred in international waters?

General WHEELER. That is right. First one was 28 or 30 miles offshore and the second one was about 65 miles offshore.†

Senator LAUSCHE. Then our course would be to either maintain our honor and our security [sic] or drop tail and run for the ocean, I suppose?

General WHEELER. That is correct.

Senator Sam J. Ervin, Jr., of North Carolina, considered the Senate's most astute constitutional lawyer, was politely curious about the legal basis for what the United States was already doing in South Vietnam.

Senator ERVIN. Did we have any treaty obligation which imposed any duty in that respect on us [to help South Vietnam "maintain its indepen-dence"] prior to the making of the SEATO Treaty?

Secretary RUSK. No, sir; there was no treaty obligation. This was on

---

* This oblique statement is the nearest McNamara came to an admission there was any confusion about details of the August 4 incident.
† An accurate answer, but a grossly incomplete one: Wheeler did not mention where the *Maddox* and *Turner Joy* had been earlier in their mission.

the basis of a request from the Government of Vietnam to us, and our acceptance of that request and action under our aid programs for South Vietnam.

Senator ERVIN. Is it your position that we are now rendering such aid as we are rendering to Vietnam under an obligation assumed by us under the SEATO Treaty?

Secretary RUSK. Well, there are several aspects of this.

In the first place, the President, we believe, has authority under aid programs and under his own responsibility as President and Commander-in-Chief to give assistance of the sort we have been giving there.

Of course, all this assistance that is provided, the tangible assistance, is done on the basis of congressional appropriations which are fully discussed here. We do believe that the obligations of the SEATO Treaty are both joint and several, and that the SEATO Treaty is a substantiating basis for our presence there and our effort there, *although, however, we are not acting specifically under the SEATO Treaty.**

That the Administration contemplated using the Tonkin Resolution to justify sending a massive land army into Asia was never directly discussed at the hearing. And the only mention of troops was in a context suggesting there would be withdrawals, not reinforcements. The statements came in response to critical questions by Senator Strom Thurmond of South Carolina as to whether "we have a policy to win the Vietnam war . . . or are we going to stay in there indefinitely?" McNamara replied, "It is our objective to move our forces as rapidly out of Vietnam as that government can maintain its independence and as rapidly as the North Vietnamese stop their attempts to subvert it." To Thurmond's suggestion that the United States "get on the initiative there," Rusk said, "Well, Senator, I think a highly relevant factor here is that there are a billion and a half people of Asia, half of them in the Communist world and half of them in the free world. *I don't see how we are going to get a long-range solution to this problem on the basis of our trying to go in there, into this vast mass of people, and try to do a job as Americans in lieu of Asians."* He added, "We can't now say what the future is going to hold in Southeast Asia, because the other side is making

* Testifying before the Foreign Relations Committee in 1966, Rusk attached considerably greater importance to SEATO as legal justification for United States participation in Vietnam. He quoted treaty language that "each party recognizes that aggression by means of armed attack . . . would endanger its own peace and safety, and agrees that it will in that event act to meet the common danger in accordance with its constitutional processes." Rusk said, *"It is this fundamental SEATO obligation that has from the outset guided our actions in South Vietnam."*[3] The difference is that in 1964 Rusk and the Administration wanted the Tonkin Resolution as backstop authorization, and thus could denigrate SEATO as a "commitment"; by 1966, however, Senators were objecting to the Administration's use of the Tonkin Resolution as a blank check, which prompted Rusk and Johnson to resurrect SEATO and present it as a formal obligation of the United States. In 1966 the Tonkin Resolution was called useful but legally unnecessary.

its own decisions," but "I think there is much to be said for a persistence and a determination to put other people in a position to maintain their security."

Thurmond next turned to the "go north" speculation, saying he understood "that General Khanh wants to go above the 17th parallel and eliminate communism so that he can bring about stability and peace. But our government objects . . . to such course, is that true?" McNamara said he "specifically asked" Khanh, during visits to Saigon in March and May, "and he stated he did not believe that it would be in the interests of his country to undertake such action . . . that at some point in the future it might be necessary to supplement . . . action [against the Viet Cong] with action in the North . . . but he didn't think the situation at that time warranted such action."*

Well, Thurmond wanted to know, if Khanh did decide it was necessary "to go to the source" to win the war, "Then would our government object?" Rusk didn't think so, for "the steps which would be necessary as preparation for going North are very close to the very steps that are needed to make going North unnecessary"—security of cities and the countryside, among other things. "I don't myself believe that now is the time for us . . . on our side by our own initiative, to enlarge this way on the theory that that is the way to bring . . . peace in Southeast Asia."

But Thurmond was insistent, citing General Douglas MacArthur's woes in Korea and maintaining that the United States should "strike at the heart of the trouble . . . or get out." Senator Frank Church of Idaho firmly demurred. "I think it would be the height of folly to believe that American war on the Asian continent, particularly for a western nation against Asians, can have any durable result that would be tenable or successful."

The hearing then trailed off into trivia and generalities: the alert status of United States and South Vietnamese forces; world reaction ("The free world nations in that entire region have been strongly in support; we haven't heard from Sukarno yet," said Rusk); the presence of Communist Chinese submarines in the Tonkin Gulf ("They have nothing that I know of in that area," said General Wheeler); and changes in orders-of-engagement for United States forces ("The commanders have been instructed to defend themselves if there is an indication of hostile intent from opposition forces," said McNamara). Morse did manage one parting jab on his allegation that United States ships had violated North Vietnamese territorial waters.

* Here McNamara had the opportunity to confide in the two Senate committees having the greatest responsibility for national security matters that certain covert projects which did involve "action in the North," were then under way. Instead, he gave the Senators the false impression that *no* actions were being undertaken against North Vietnam. In his defense, let it be said that the Foreign Relations Committee has a reputation in Washington for leaking material that administrations would prefer to keep secret.

Here is how the exchange emerged from the blue pencils of Pentagon security censors:

Senator MORSE. I thought he [Secretary McNamara] ought to tell us in the establishment of patrols of our ships, how close they will come to the North Vietnam border. The other day the Secretary testified* that the ships at a time were within 11 miles, which shows we did not recognize their 12-mile limit, and the record will speak for itself. But I think it will show at some times we were less than 11 miles, but beyond three miles.

Are we taking the position of the three-mile limit, which has to be right, disputed by some? When you reestablish these patrols, how close do these ships come to the North Vietnam ports?

Secretary RUSK. [Deleted] miles.

General WHEELER. [Deleted] miles is the answer.

The answers: eight nautical miles to the mainland, four nautical miles to islands.

Morse concluded: "I just want to say it is too close if you want to keep yourself in position and not be subject to the charge of provocation."

With that, the hearing ended. Pat Holt, acting staff director for the Foreign Relations Committee, called that portion of the roll, Morse booming out his solitary "no." Then William H. Darden, chief of staff for the Armed Services Committee, went through that list, and by proxy and by voice got unanimous consent. And off went the Tonkin Resolution to the floor for a vote.†

The two committees had been in session from 9:05 A.M. until 10:45 A.M.—one hour and 40 minutes of discussion during which they had only the information supplied by the Johnson Administration and the sketchy and contradictory details from Morse's tipster in the Pentagon. That the Senators paid no more attention to Morse's dissent, nor to his protestations that the full story was not being told, reflects both the national mood and the Senate's inclination to trust the President.

Rusk, McNamara, and Wheeler had just begun their testimony before the House Armed Services Committee and House Foreign Affairs Committee, meeting in joint session on the other side of the Capitol, when an aide slipped in with a note. Rusk glanced at it, learned of the near-

---

* Morse's reference was to the off-the-record briefing given congressional leaders on August 2. No transcript has ever been published of this proceeding, although Senators say privately that it contained nothing of substance which did not come out on August 6.
† The aye votes were cast by Senators Sparkman, Humphrey, Mansfield, Russell Long, Church, Symington, Dodd, Smathers, Hickenlooper, Aiken, Gore, John Williams, Mundt, Fulbright, Robert C. Byrd, Stennis, Jackson, Ervin, Thurmond, Cannon, Harry F. Byrd, Jr., Young, Inouye, Saltonstall, Beall, Goldwater, Smith, and Russell.

unanimous Senate committee approval, grunted appreciatively, and slid it along the table to McNamara. This time the presentation of the Administration's case lasted considerably less than an hour, and this time there was not a single dissenting vote. President Johnson called leaders Mansfield and McCormack, repeated his plea that the Resolution be voted upon that day, and went upstairs for lunch. "Just about what we expected," he remarked to an aide later that afternoon. "Wayne is going to stir up some dust, but it's moving our way and we'll have it before dark."

The Senate, though it moved rapidly, didn't finish with the resolution "before dark." The committee's favorable report went to the floor almost immediately after the hearing ended, for Johnson's orders to Fulbright were direct; as the Senator has described them, ". . . . [T]here was a great sense of urgency and we were asked to pass it immediately. . . . I was told that it would be most unfortunate if there were any amendments allowed or any delay, because this would evidence a lack of confidence and unity within the Congress with our President. So we were requested not to accept amendment."[4]

Morse, however, wouldn't be hurried. He and Fulbright conferred briefly just before debate began. Morse gave Fulbright a choice: Either Fulbright would permit the discussion to run for two days, or Morse would filibuster. They agreed to bring up the resolution that afternoon, during which time Morse would speak; then to resume at 10:00 A.M. on Friday under a unanimous-consent agreement to vote at 1:00 P.M. Morse would have two hours, with Fulbright and Senator Dirksen, the minority leader, controlling the remaining hour.

McNamara's testimony that the *Maddox* and *Turner Joy* had been permitted to go within less than 12 miles of the North Vietnamese coast gave Morse slightly more material with which to work—although he could not disclose what the Secretary had said in executive session. Calling the South Vietnamese raids "not a matter of infiltration . . . [but] a well-thought-out military operation," Morse said:

Oh, Mr. President [referring to the Senate's presiding officer] the Pentagon and the State Department throw up their hands in aggrievement if anyone suggests, as I did in my speech yesterday, that their [the destroyers'] very presence there is subject to the interpretation that they were a backstop. All the protestations on the part of the State Department and the Pentagon cannot change a physical fact. The presence of those ships in that proximity to the North Vietnamese coast, while an act of war was being committed against North Vietnamese islands by the bombings . . . was bound to implicate us. We are implicated.

Morse admitted, "I do not know exactly the mileage location of the

American vessels while the bombing took place . . . whether it was four miles, 11 miles or 20 miles . . . . But I think I violate no privilege or no secrecy if I say that subsequent to the bombing, and apparently because there was concern about some intelligence that we are getting, our ships took out to sea . . ."

Senator Lausche interrupted with a roar: "The Senator just made the statement that, on the basis of certain intelligence received by, I assume, the commander of the *Maddox*———" It was Morse's time to interrupt: "I am not going to comment on that. I think I have said all that I have a right to say within the proprieties." Lausche argued that any changes of position by the *Maddox* had "no relationship to what had happened on the islands. It had a relationship to the pursuit that was being made by the PT boats of our *Maddox*." He also rejected Morse's charges about United States complicity in the raids.

Mr. LAUSCHE. I would like to state my judgment as to what the evidence shows. Our government *had no knowledge of any nature about the attacks* which were made upon the two islands by the [South] Vietnamese. The *Maddox* was miles—

Mr. MORSE. Do not talk about the *Maddox;* talk about our American officialdom in Saigon, and our American officialdom in the Pentagon and the State Department. I state categorically that they knew the bombardment was going to take place before the ships ever moved up there.

Mr. LAUSCHE. Let me state to the Senator from Oregon that there is not a syllable of such testimony in the record which has been taken in the several days* we have been listening to witnesses supporting the declaration made by the Senator from Oregon.

Mr. MORSE. There was complete admission that that was known.

Mr. LAUSCHE. It is the judgment of—

Mr. MORSE. It was written out in cold print.

Mr. LAUSCHE. It is the judgment of the Senator from Oregon, based in a measure upon his wish that that had happened, because that is in conformity with the position that he has taken. There is no testimony in the—

Mr. MORSE. I shall ignore the—

Mr. LAUSCHE. Of any kind that—

Mr. MORSE. I shall ignore the implications of that snide remark.

Mr. LAUSCHE. That is not a snide remark.

Mr. MORSE. It certainly is a snide remark, but I shall ignore the implications of it and state categorically that high officials of the govern-

* Actually, the Foreign Relations and Armed Services committees heard witnesses for "several hours," not "several days."

ment have admitted on the record that they were aware of plans for the bombardment, but that they had nothing to do with it, they said—but they were aware of it .

Mr. LAUSCHE. There is no testimony to that effect whatsoever. That is an inference made by the Senator from Oregon as to the...

Mr. MORSE. Get permission of the State Department or the Pentagon to publicly release the whole of the transcript without a single word deleted, and let the country know what they said.

As floor manager for the resolution, Fulbright had to present the formal rebuttal of Morse's charges about the raids. He did so on August 6 in an exchange with Senator George McGovern of South Dakota: "It is my understanding, as best I can interpret what actually happened, that there were some South Vietnamese raids, if they may be so-called—coastal raids —by South Vietnamese junks or naval vessels—the only kind of naval vessels they have. My information is that they have relatively small PT boats, comparable to those of North Vietnam, plus what are called motorized junks, and those from time to time have engaged in what are called hit-and-run raids, none of them of a major nature, by South Vietnamese boats with South Vietnamese crews.

"Our naval vessels, such as the *Maddox* and associated vessels, have never engaged in any attacks on those islands or anywhere else in North Vietnam. The best information that I have from high officials in our government in this field is to the effect that *our boats did not convoy or support or back up any South Vietnamese vessels there were engaged in such attacks.*"

Mr. McGOVERN. The Senator would say the implication... is probably in error?

Mr. FULBRIGHT. It has been asserted by others that the *Maddox* was backing up or convoying the smaller vessels of the Vietnamese. The testimony I am familiar with shows that this is not a fact. . . . [It] was asked whether or not the junks . . . had American personnel in the nature of advisers or otherwise. We were advised they did not, that they were manned by non-Americans in all cases. In other words, the patrol duty by the . . . *C. Turner Joy* and the *Maddox* was an operational patrol, to keep our own forces informed about the activities in this very critical area, and was entirely unconnected or unassociated with any coastal forays the South Vietnamese themselves may have conducted.

Senator Allen Ellender of Louisiana asked if Fulbright was satisfied that "our naval forces did nothing to invite the attack."

Mr. FULBRIGHT. Nothing that they are not entitled to do. Their very presence in the Gulf of Tonkin could be said by someone to invite an attack, but they had every reason to be there, and they were not shelling the coast or intervening in any of the legitimate operations of the government of North Vietnam. In an area in which there is tension and in which there has been this very bloody kind of guerrilla warfare or irregular warfare, one might say, broadly speaking, that their presence could be a provocation. I do not think so. They had every right to be there. . . . Whatever provocation there may have been arose, if it did arise, from the activity of the North Vietnamese ships.

Senator Daniel Brewster of Maryland, referring to his World War II service, said, "I have had the opportunity to see warfare not so very far from this area, and it was very mean. I would look with great dismay on a situation involving the landing of large land armies on the continent of Asia. So my question is whether there is anything in the resolution which would authorize or recommend or approve the landing of large American armies in Vietnam or in China."

Mr. FULBRIGHT. *There is nothing in the resolution, as I read it,* that contemplates it. I agree with the Senator that that is the last thing we would want to do. *However, the language of the resolution would not prevent it.* It would authorize what the commander-in-chief feels is necessary. It does not restrain the Executive from doing it. Whether or not that should ever be done is a matter of wisdom under the circumstances that exist at the particular time it is contemplated.

Senator Jacob Javits of New York wanted assurances that because "the President gets the resolution, we are not going to vote on that one proposal and make everything else perfunctory."

Mr. FULBRIGHT. We have had positive assurances from the Secretary of State about the very matter the Senator is discussing. . . .

Mr. JAVITS. With the thoughts and the principles I have laid out, can the Senator commit himself, as chairman of the Foreign Relations Committee, to being our 'sentinel', to follow through on these matters, after the joint resolution is passed?

Mr. FULBRIGHT. I shall do everything I can, within the limits of my capacity and my position on the Foreign Relations Committee, because I really agree with this philosophy.

Senator Gaylord Nelson of Wisconsin ticked off the rise in United States troops in Vietnam from 1,000 in 1960 to around 16,000, and expressed concern about whether the United States was beginning to "provide military forces to do battle in place of South Vietnamese forces," rather than merely to supply military cadre, equipment, and material. "Am I to understand that it is the sense of Congress that we are saying to the Executive branch: 'If it becomes necessary to prevent further aggression, we agree now, in advance, that you may land as many divisions as deemed necessary, and engage in a direct military assault on North Vietnam if it becomes the judgment of the Executive . . . that this is the only way to prevent further aggression'?"

Mr. FULBRIGHT. If the situation should deteriorate to such an extent that the only way to save it from going completely under to the Communists would be action such as the Senator suggests, then that would be a grave decision on the part of our country as to whether we should confine our activities to very limited personnel on land and the extensive use of naval and air power, or whether we should go further and use more manpower.

I personally feel it would be very unwise under any circumstances to put a large land army on the Asian continent.

It has been a sort of article of faith ever since I have been in the Senate, that we should never be bogged down. We particularly stated that after Korea. We are mobile, we are powerful on the land and on the sea. *But when we try to confine ourselves and say that this resolution either prohibits or authorizes such action by the Commander-in-Chief, I believe that is carrying it a little further than I would care to go.*

I do not know what the limits are. I do not think this resolution can be determinative of that fact. I think it would indicate that he [the President] would take reasonable means first to prevent any further aggression, or repel further aggression against our own forces, and that he will live up to our obligations under the SEATO treaty and with regard to the protocol states.

I do not know how to answer the Senator's question and give him an absolute assurance that large numbers of troops would not be put ashore. I would deplore it. And I hope the conditions do not justify it now.

Nelson felt his doubts deepen as he listened to Fulbright's answer. "We may very well not be able to nor attempt to control the discretion that is vested in the Commander-in-Chief," he replied. Since the Johnson Administration drafted the resolution "to ascertain the sense of the Congress" on Vietnam, he said, Congress' reply should be precise. "I do not think . . . that Congress should leave the impression that it consents to a radical change in our mission or objective in South Vietnam. That mission there for ten years, as I have understood it, has been to aid in the establishment of a viable, independent regime which can manage its own affairs, so that ultimately we can withdraw from South Vietnam." Nelson said he would be "most concerned" if Congress or anyone else interpreted the resolution as authorizing a departure from those objectives. Never, he said, had the United States felt committed "to engage in a direct land confrontation with our Army as a substitute for the South Vietnam army or as a substantially reinforced U.S. Army to be joined with the South Vietnam army in a war against North Vietnam and possibly China."

Fulbright said that it "seems to me" that the resolution *"would be consistent with what we have been doing."* Then he reiterated that presidential interpretation and implementation of the resolution was a murky area.

". . . [I]n all frankness I cannot say to the Senator that I think the joint resolution would in any way be a deterrent, a prohibition, a limitation, or an expansion of the President's power to use the armed forces in a different way or more extensively than he is now using them," Fulbright said. But nonetheless he argued that the resolution was "appropriate" because "it would put the Congress on record—and we are the most representative body that we have under our system—as supporting the action. If anything will deter aggression on the part of the North Vietnamese and the Chinese, I believe it would be the action taken together with the joint resolution supporting the action. That is the best I can do about justification of the resolution."

Fulbright repeated that the resolution would have no practical effect upon the President's power to use "whatever means seemed appropriate under the circumstances," although Congress did hold on the Executive a checkrein of dubious validity. "Our recourse in Congress would be that if the action were too inappropriate, we could terminate the joint resolution, and that would precipitate a great controversy between the Executive and the Congress. As a practical question, that could be done."

Nelson sought to elicit a plausible explanation for the vessels' presence off the Vietnam coast, and how close they came to the mainland.

Mr. FULBRIGHT. It was testified that they went in at least 11 miles in order to show that we do not recognize a 12-mile limit, which I believe North Vietnam had asserted.

Mr. NELSON. The patrolling was for the purpose of demonstrating to the North Vietnamese that we do not recognize a 12-mile limit?

Mr. FULBRIGHT. That was one reason given for going in to a point 11 miles from the coast. The patrolling as such was not for that purpose. That action was in execution of our mission and our responsibility in that area under the SEATO treaty. As said a moment ago, we had a right to go where we like on the high seas. The reason we are in this particular area is that we have assumed responsibilities under the treaty as well as bilaterally with South Vietnam.

Mr. NELSON. Recognizing, as we all do, the great sensitivity of all countries, especially enemies, or those hostile to each other, what purpose in the promotion of our mission in South Vietnam is served by having our ships go within 11 miles of the North Vietnam coast?

"That strikes me as a question that raises a difficult problem," Fulbright said. For years, he continued, the North Vietnamese have "been sending in trained personnel, materials, guns and ammunition, to attack their neighbors. Why should the United States be so careful about the sensitivities of North Vietnam? . . . I am sure that the presence of our ships there is bothersome and irritating to them, but they brought it on themselves. For my part, I do not apologize for it at all. I do not believe they are in any position to question our right to be in the Gulf of Tonkin, or in any position to question our right to assist South Vietnam, however irritating it may be to Ho Chi Minh."

Nelson retorted that he was not advocating that the United States surrender its right of passage through international waters. "I do suggest—and this is what I do not understand—if patrolling that close has no necessary bearing upon the mission we have insisted we have in South Vietnam, it would seem to me that perhaps it is not the exercise of our best judgment to do it. . . . I am wondering whether we should be taking the risk of the sinking of our ships."

Fulbright said that "from the best information I have" the patrols were relevant to the United States mission in South Vietnam—"to restrain the activities of North Vietnam, and . . . to be forewarned if there were a possibility of a major blow."

"[I]t would be mighty risky," Nelson said, "if Cuban PT boats were firing on Florida, for Russian armed ships or destroyers to be patrolling between us and Cuba, 11 miles out. It would be a grave risk for her to be testing our viewpoint about her patrolling that close when Cuban boats were firing on Florida. So the question was whether the patrolling that close was really necessary to the accomplishment of our mission. We are, after all, dealing with the possibility of incinerating the whole world."

Mr. FULBRIGHT. I do not deny that it is risky. The whole operation is risky. It is full of risks.

Mr. NELSON. I hope we do not take risks that are unnecessary for the achievement of an objective that we have asserted to be ours for the past 10 years.

Fulbright's answers on the implications of the resolution did not satisfy Nelson. He spoke privately with Fulbright, Humphrey, Russell, and other leaders, but no one could tell him exactly what the President intended to do with the resolution. Even the floor debate was ambiguous. Senator Hugh Scott of Pennsylvania (who was not on the committees that heard Administration witnesses) thought it meant "no more privileged sanctuaries" for North Vietnamese supporting the war in the South. Fulbright's own interpretation was that the resolution did not change the United States mission in South Vietnam.

So on August 7, with only 20 minutes of debate remaining, Nelson moved to clarify the resolution. "I have great confidence in the President," he said. "However, my concern is that we in Congress could give the impression to the public that we are prepared at this time to change our mission and substantially expand our commitment. If that is the sense of the Congress, I am opposed to the resolution." He offered an amendment:

The Congress also approves and supports the efforts of the President to bring the problems of peace in Southeast Asia to the Security Council of the United Nations, and the President's declaration that the United States, seeking no extension of the present military conflict, will respond to provocation that is 'limited and fitting.' Our continuing policy is to limit our role to the provision of aid, training assistance, and military advice, and it is the sense of Congress that, except when provoked to a greater response, we should continue to attempt to avoid a direct military involvement in the Southeastern Asia conflict.

Fulbright had informed the White House of Nelson's intentions, and he was told that Johnson wanted no tampering with the resolution. To permit one amendment, Fulbright was told, would encourage further tinkering with carefully tailored language and would give the impression that Congress' endorsement of the President was qualified.

There was no place in the scenario for the doubts of a Gaylord Nelson, especially in view of the fact that at the very moment he offered the amendment, the House of Representatives, after perfunctory discussion, began its own vote on the resolution. Fulbright said he found the Nelson amendment "unobjectionable," in that "it is an accurate reflection of what I believe is the President's policy, judging from his own statements." But to accept it, Fulbright said, "would delay matters. . . . It would cause confusion and require a conference, and present us with all the other difficulties that are involved in this kind of legislative action. I regret that I cannot do it, even though I do not disagree with the amendment as a general statement of policy."

Mr. NELSON. Judging by the [*Congressional*] *Record* of yesterday, many Senators do not interpret the resolution in the same way.

Mr. FULBRIGHT. Senators are entitled to have different views. However, most members of the committee, with one or two exceptions, interpret it the same way.

Proceedings thereafter were brisk. Senator Ernest Gruening of Alaska emotionally denounced the war as the "inevitable and foreseeable concomitant and consequence of U.S. unilateral military aggressive policy in Southeast Asia," calling the resolution "a predated declaration of war." Morse had the last word: "I believe that history will record that we have made a great mistake in subverting and circumventing the Constitution of the United States . . . by means of this resolution. As I argued earlier today at great length, we are in effect giving the President . . . warmaking powers in the absence of a declaration of war. I believe that to be a historic mistake."

The resolution passed 88-2, with only Morse and Gruening voting nay. (The ten absent senators all announced in favor.) The House vote was 416-0.

According to a compilation by the Foreign Relations Committee staff, Senate deliberations on the Tonkin Resolution totaled eight hours and 40 minutes, as follows: August 5, 30 minutes floor discussion; August 6, one hour and 40 minutes in the joint committee hearing, and four hours floor debate; and August 7, two hours and 30 minutes debate (30 minutes of the allotted three hours being taken for quorum calls and other interruptions). The United States Senate, it might be noted, can spend two days amending a fisheries bill. Commenting later on the speed, Fulbright said, "That gives you some perspective as to how thorough the discussion was."

During the week of the Tonkin incidents, the Administration, through high-level voices, contended repeatedly and without qualification that the *Maddox* and *Turner Joy* had not the slightest connection with the South Vietnamese raids. Their motive was twofold: North Vietnam's Communist friends had raised the charge in the United Nations, and Morse's Senate speeches had provided fodder for domestic war critics. Rusk discussed the issue with Elie Abel of NBC TV on August 5:

ABEL. Mr. Secretary, were our destroyers operating in support of South Vietnamese units in these same waters? Could this have been the cause of the North Vietnamese decision to attack our destroyers?

RUSK. Well, I saw a story to that effect from Hanoi, but Hanoi knows just as well as we do that our destroyers were not involved in any mission *other than that that was publicly announced.*

They knew that they were well at sea, they knew that they were on normal patrol operations, they knew that they were not doing any firing at anybody. . . . There is no misunderstanding on the part of Hanoi on this point.[5]

McNamara went even further on August 5, implanting the impression he had heard of no South Vietnamese raids. His press conference statement that day is archetypical of the misleading and partial answers which the Administration gave the public that week; asked a question on one Navy operation, McNamara gave a detailed description of an entirely separate project.

Q. Mr. Secretary, have there been any incidents that you know of involving the South Vietnamese vessels and North Vietnamese?

Secretary McNAMARA. *No, none that I know of,* although I think I should mention to you the South Vietnamese naval patrol activities that are carried on to prevent the infiltration of men and material from the North into the South. In the last seven months of 1961, for example, about 1,400 men were infiltrated across the 17th parallel. . . . To prevent further infiltration of that kind, the South Vietnamese, with our assistance, have set up a naval patrol which is very active in that area, which continues to inspect and examine junks and their personnel. In one eight-month period that I recall they discovered 140 Viet Cong infiltrators.

McNamara said that the United States helped South Vietnam establish the junk patrol in December 1961. Washington provided funds for 500 junks of four categories: motorized command junks, armed with automatic weapons; motorized armed sailor junks for coastal patrols; sailing junks for surveillance of particular areas; and motor junks without sails. He continued:

> They operate on their own. They are part of the South Vietnamese Navy . . . operating in the coastal waters, inspecting suspicious incoming junks, seeking to deter and prevent the infiltration of both men and material. . . .

> Q. Mr. Secretary, do these junks go North, into North Vietnam waters?

> Secretary McNAMARA. They have advanced closer and closer to the 17th parallel, *and in some cases I think* have moved beyond that in an effort to stop the infiltration closer to the point of origin.

> Q. Do our Navy vessels provide any cover for these junks in those operations?

> Secretary McNAMARA. Our naval vessels afford no cover whatsoever. Our naval personnel do not participate in the junk operations.[6]

One comment is appropriate here: McNamara's lucid description was of a project called "Operation Market Time," which had been openly discussed in the press for months; several weeks before the Tonkin incidents, for instance, the *Wall Street Journal* ran a lengthy description of it which had about as much detail as McNamara revealed. But the South Vietnamese *raids*—which is what the questioner had in mind—were an entirely different undertaking.

"In a single stroke, Mr. Johnson has, at least temporarily, turned his greatest political vulnerability in foreign policy into one of his strongest assets," pollster Louis Harris wrote in a survey published in the *Washington Post* on August 10, less than three months before Election Day. Eighty-five percent of the nation approved the reprisal raids. In July, 58 percent of the public had criticized Johnson's handling of the war; the immediate post-Tonkin reading was a 72 percent vote of confidence. Public opinion, according to Harris, "had been moving slowly" toward favoring the extension of the war to North Vietnam; but a plurality had opposed such a move for fear of bringing in the Chinese. Now, the sentiment was two to one for taking the war to the North.

Before the attacks, 59 percent had felt that Johnson could handle the war better than Goldwater (five percent less than the 64-36 public preference of Johnson for the presidency). Now, the margin was 71-29 for Johnson over Goldwater for conducting the war.

Press reaction was equally favorable. The *Los Angeles Times,* which was to endorse Goldwater, called Johnson's conduct "fitting in selectivity, proper in application, and—given the clear, long-standing statement of U.S. intentions—inevitable in delivery." The *Baltimore Sun* said the Communists "have been put on formal notice that American reprisal will be swift and devastating," if there were further attacks. The *Wall Street Jour-*

nal, while regretting that the United States "is once again so enmeshed in so unpromising a venture," concluded "if the President's order means the government is at last on the road to firmness and decisiveness, it may be the best hope the circumstances offer." The *New York Daily News* surmised that "Ho Chi Minh is obviously hopping mad over this unexpected singe dealt . . . to his wispy whiskers," and wondered if he and China would seek revenge. "In that event," said the *News,* "it may be our heaven-sent good fortune to liquidate not only Ho Chi Minh but Mao Tse-tung's Red Mob at Peking as well, presumably with an important assist from Generalissimo Chiang Kai-shek and his Nationalist Chinese forces on Taiwan." Walter Lippmann approved the Seventh Fleet's presence off North Vietnam (although he found it "not yet clear why the Hanoi government decided to attack"). The important point, Lippmann wrote in his August 6 column, is that "the more firmly the fact is established that our presence in Southeast Asia is primarily as a sea and air power, the safer it will be to enter the negotiations which is the only alternative to an endless and indecisive war in the jungle. It is necessary to prove to the Chinese, who probably do not really understand sea power because they have none, that the elephant cannot drive the whale out of the ocean."

Foreign press comment had a tinge of skepticism. The leftist British *New Statesman* said, "There is so little trust in official [United States] accounts about Vietnam that the suspicion is surely understandable. . . . Is it not possible that the destroyers could not count the attacking vessels because they could not be distinguished from South Vietnamese craft that were engaged in another raiding mission?" *Demokreten,* of Denmark, wrote, "To create a pretext for an attack on Poland, Hitler ordered the Germans to put on uniforms and attack a German guard. What the Americans did in North Vietnam was not the same. But the story sounds doubtful." The denial that U.S. ships enter territorial waters had been made so frequently, the account continued, "that people begin to doubt it. . . . Why was the vessel off North Vietnamese coasts? In any case its presence there could be interpreted as provocative."

Should the press—and the American public—have been more wary of accepting the Johnson Administration's account of the Tonkin incidents as offered?

The immediate past should have put the public and the Senate on guard. In June, Radio Hanoi broadcasts forced the Administration's reluctant admission that United States planes were bombing Pathet Lao antiaircraft installations in Laos. The same month the Administration was caught in another evasion, this time by none other than those purveyors of international virtue, the Chinese Communists. On June 14, the New China News Agency (NCNA) said that American pilots and planes were fighting in the Congo. On June 15, the State Department said it knew nothing of what the Chinese claimed. On June 16, NCNA was more specific: United States Air Force Hercules cargo transports had carried the 13th Battalion of the loyalist Congolese army from Katanga province to Bukavu to fight the secessionist forces of Moise Tshombe, and fighter planes had attacked rebel forces. On June 17, the Administration admitted that it had furnished "contract fliers"—a euphemism for CIA paramilitary forces—and transports to the Congo.

The deception prompted a sharp rebuke by the *Washington Post:*

> The country has come to a sad pass when it must turn to Communist China's New China News Agency for reports on covert military operations being conducted by the United States. Yet this incredible inversion has taken place twice within the last week.

The *Post* detailed the Laotian and Congolese incidents, then continued:

> What in heaven's name does the United States think it is doing by trying to keep these air strikes secret? Does the government really have the *naiveté* to believe its hands in these operations can be concealed?
> If it is to conduct or sponsor such raids, then let the matter be decided openly in terms of whether American interests require it. But let there be no repetition of the humiliating sequence whereby Communist China makes a fool, if not a liar, out of the United States.

Thus the circumstances of Tonkin: a nearly unanimous willingness of the public and the Congress to accept as established fact the Johnson Administration's version of the incidents (an account which contained not the barest hint of doubt that the events occurred as described by the White House and the military); the overwhelming passage of the resolution as a symbol of Congressional endorsement of the retaliatory raids, and of national support for a President who acted firmly, but not rashly, in a time of crisis; the skepticism so muted, so (apparently) unfounded as to be ignored.

INTERLUDE: North Vietnam's Version

North Vietnamese media promptly publicized the August 2 engagement, claiming its vessels "drove the intruder out of Vietnamese waters" and shot down two of the planes which came to its aid. And they just as promptly denied any involvement in any encounter on August 4.

In September 1964 Hanoi's Ministry of Foreign Affairs published a 51-page White Paper entitled "Memorandum Regarding the U.S. War Acts Against the Democratic Republic of Vietnam in the First Days of August

1964," which spelled out in considerable detail the incidents as seen (or reported) from the North. (See page 228 for map from White Paper.) The following account comes from the DRV White Paper:

"On July 30, 1964, at 23:40 (local time), U.S. and South Vietnamese warships intruded into the territorial waters of the Democratic Republic of Vietnam and simultaneously shelled:

"—Hon Ngu Island, four kilometers off the coast of Thanh Hoa Province.

"—Hon Me Island, twelve kilometers off the coast of Thanh Hoa Province.

"From July 31 to August 2, 1964, the destroyer *Maddox* of the U.S. Seventh Fleet operated very near the Vietnamese coasts in Quang Binh, Ha Tinh, Nghe An, and Thanh Hoa Provinces. . . .

"The *Maddox* repeatedly intruded into Vietnamese waters, and threatened and provoked fishing boats in the area:

"—At 0530 local time on July 31, it was sailing five miles off Vietnamese coasts, between Mui Doc and Hon Gio Island. . . . From the coast its registration number 731 could already be seen clearly through binoculars.

"—In the night of July 31 it closed, and directed its headlights at, fishing boats between Mui Doc and Mui Ron, in Vietnamese waters.

"—At 1430 local time on August 1, it chased three fishing boats south of Hon Mat Island, in Vietnamese waters.

"At about the same time, when sailing past Hon Mat Island in Vietnamese waters, it aimed its guns at the island by way of provocation.

"—In the night of August 1, it repeatedly directed its headlights at, or gave chase to, Vietnamese boats fishing in Vietnamese waters between Hon Mat and Hon Me Islands.

"—Finally, on August 2 at 1500 local time, while sailing between Hon Me Island and Lach Truong, about eight miles off the coast, the *Maddox* encountered and opened fire on Vietnamese patrol boats thus compelled to take a defensive action to drive the intruder off Vietnamese waters."

The White Paper quoted the Pentagon announcement of August 4, then commented:

". . . [T]his is an impudent fabrication inasmuch as in the day and night of August 4, 1964, no naval craft of the Democratic Republic of Vietnam was present in the area where the U.S. destroyers were allegedly 'attacked for a second time by North Vietnamese PT boats.'

"The alleged attack was deliberately staged by the United States to have a pretext for carrying out its criminal designs against the Democratic Republic of Vietnam.

"According to reports from various sources, a task group of the Seventh Fleet including the aircraft carrier *Ticonderoga* and the destroyers *Berkeley, Edson, Harry Hubbard,* and *Samuel Moore* were cruising on a permanent basis in the South China Sea off Da Nang.

"On August 4, 1964, the *Harry Hubbard* met with the HQ 609 and HQ 11* of the South Vietnam Navy 60 kilometers off Da Nang. Thereafter, the South Vietnamese ships did not return to their base . . . as usual. In the same night, from 2000 to 2200, at about the time when 'North Vietnamese PT boats' allegedly 'attacked the *Maddox* and the *Turner Joy*' gun shelling was heard, flares and planes were seen off the shores of the Democratic Republic of Vietnam on international waters.

"That is what the Pentagon termed the 'second deliberate attack' on the destroyers *Maddox* and *Turner Joy,* or the 'second Tonkin Gulf incident.' "

* The South Vietnamese boat bearing the number HQ 11 is the *Chi Linh,* until January 1964 the *USS Shelter,* an escort vessel.

Part Two

THE REALITY

An account of the Gulf of Tonkin incidents as not related to the United States Congress and the American people by the Johnson Administration between August 2 and August 9, 1964.

Chapter Three

PARAMILITARY OPERATIONS
BEFORE TONKIN

In 1961 a United States Air Force veteran whom we shall refer to as Smith, while working in the Congo as a contract flier for the United Nations peace-keeping mission, met a man who introduced himself as the recruiter for an organization named "Helioaircraft."* The recruiter told Smith that much better money was to be earned in a new war just getting under way in a place called Vietnam, of which Smith conceded he knew very little. But Smith was adventurous and wanted money, and, enterprising mercenary that he was, signed on with Helioaircraft and went to Saigon as a service representative. Helioaircraft had numerous United States government contracts, ferrying American diplomats, AID officials, and military advisers around the country and doing occasional jobs for the South Vietnamese. But as far as Smith could tell, Helioaircraft was privately owned.

After six months, however, Helioaircraft passed into the hands of new owners—Aviation Investors, Inc., 505 Landmark Building, Washington, D.C. As was explained to Smith, Aviation Investors, Inc., consisted of a group of "private businessmen," not connected with the United States government, who had the inside track on contracts with the regime of President Ngo Dinh Diem.

Smith listened, said nothing, and watched. High-ranking United States Air Force officers and embassy officials seemed to have an inordinate interest in Aviation Investors, and clustered around the operation. "Aviation Investors was free-spending; money meant nothing," Smith recollects. "We needed a building at Tan Son Nhut Airport in Saigon that belonged to a French businessman. There was a corrugated tin shack with a dirt floor, but we just wanted it for office space and storage, and it was OK. The Frenchman asked $13,000 a year for it. Hell, the whole building wasn't worth that much. But Aviation Investors paid for it unquestioningly."

* I was introduced to "Smith" in 1968 through the good offices of Ernest Gruening, then United States Senator from Alaska, who headed a subcommittee of the Government Operations Committee, which was investigating South Vietnamese corruption in handling the United States economic assistance program. "Smith" has broken all connections with the CIA and now works in private industry.

Aviation Investors' chief public activity in Vietnam was the operation of an airline, "Vietnam Air Transport," which ferried South Vietnamese and American officials around the country. But Smith wasn't deceived for long, for he had seen other covert activities in the Congo:

"Aviation Investors, of course, was a fictitious company set up by the CIA, and Vietnam Air Transport, in addition to its so-called 'legitimate aviation' stuff, was a blind for a program called 'Operation Haylift.'

" 'Operation Haylift' was flying [South] Vietnamese agents into North Vietnam for the purpose of sabotage . . . blowing up railroads, bridges, etc. At first they used a C-54 for runs over the North. When this was lost they switched to four C-123s, all unmarked, and used them for recon [reconnaissance] runs and drop missions over the North. There were also flights over the Gulf of Tonkin during the summer of 1964, for recon, as I recall.

"Haylift wasn't too successful because of the high casualties—80 percent for some missions. The South Vietnamese would be dropped north of the DMZ and then fight their way back south, supposedly. They wouldn't be too enthused about it. Sometimes we'd load all their gear aboard and then have to scrub the mission because the guerrillas wouldn't show up, they'd be too frightened. Or their officers would deliberately come in drunk, knowing they wouldn't be permitted to go. The CIA paras [the agency's name for "paramilitary" operatives] would raise hell and yell, but there wasn't anything that could be done about it."

Haylift's overseer was Willian E. Colby, later to become chief of the CIA's Asian Desk at the Langley, Virginia, headquarters, and still later to succeed Robert Komer, another CIA man, as head of the pacification program in Vietnam, by direct appointment of President Johnson.

One of the South Vietnamese officers working on Operation Haylift was Nguyen Cao Ky, a native of the North who had attended a French aviation school during the Indochinese war and had fought against the Viet Minh of Ho Chi Minh. In 1963–64 Ky was assigned to the South Vietnamese Air Force's 43rd Air Transport Group, cover designation for the pilots detailed to Operation Haylift.

Ky, who then had the rank of air marshal, had problems with the Americans working with Aviation Investors in the spring of 1964. He would fly from Tan Son Nhut to the U.S. base at Da Nang, pick up a group of Haylift guerrillas, and go on to the North. After the drop he would fly to another United States base in Laos (this one covert) before returning to Saigon, the indirect route permitting him to minimize air time over North Vietnam. However, the CIA received what it considered reliable information that Ky was bringing in opium from Laos and selling it in Saigon through intermediaries. So he and the South Vietnamese crews were removed, Smith states, and replaced with Turkish and Nationalist Chinese pilots, also recruited by the CIA.*

* Ky heatedly denied any involvement in opium smuggling when this allegation was made public by Gruening's subcommittee in 1968.

Smith recollects something else unusual about the late spring and early summer of 1964: Both CIA paramilitarys and Navy officers became regular passengers on Vietnam Air Transport's daily flights from Saigon to Da Nang. Sometimes, to relieve the boredom and tedium of the airborne hours, they would talk about something called "Swift boats," very fast crafts which were engaged in mysterious missions along the coast of North Vietnam. "When you work around the CIA," Smith says, "you learn not to ask direct questions. But there were relatively few Americans in Vietnam then, and we were all considered part of the same fraternity. And you'd get into a conversational situation and they'd tell you what was going on.

"I thought it rather peculiar that we never read anything in the papers about the Swift boat thing, because the *Saigon News* used to run all sorts of stories about sabotage missions and guerrillas working against the North. Operation Haylift was sort of an open secret—although of course nobody called it by name—if you had the sense to put two and two together. But nothing about the boats, and the week-long trips these Navy and CIA people would take.

"But, like I said before, you learn not to ask direct questions when you're working around the CIA."

The CIA, it should be said at this point, was the executor, not the architect, of national policy in affairs such as Operation Haylift. The sporadic loud debate over the wisdom of "taking the war to the North," intensified by Premier Khanh's "Day of Shame" speech, contained elements of charade, for North Vietnam's borders were transgressed regularly by land, by sea, and by air; by the South Vietnamese; by Special Forces teams working under direction of the CIA; and by the CIA's own paramilitarys. There is one major difference between their activities and those which North Vietnam directed against the South: The special operations in the North were short-term intelligence and sabotage missions, with guerrillas seldom staying in place more than one week, and not attempting to establish permanent base camps or to organize indigenous bands. The overthrow of Ho Chi Minh's government was not a stated war goal of the United States —hence the policy decision not to strike at his political structure. There is also one major similarity: Neither Washington nor Hanoi would admit publicly its involvement in or support of across-the-border operations.

The special operations against the North began in 1961, when President Kennedy dispatched Special Forces teams to Vietnam as counter-insurgency "advisers." From the outset the activities were varied—and tinged with illegality. The October 1962 Geneva accords of Laos, for example, decreed neutralization of that country; the withdrawal of all foreign troops, American and North Vietnamese alike; and the creation of a coalition government of Communist, neutralist, and rightist elements. The pseudonymous Robin Moore, who spent months with Special Forces and CIA paramilitary groups in Vietnam and Laos, writes, "Fortunately, a few highly placed Americans were wise enough to realize that the Communists might not abide with the agreements they had signed and the Communist Pathet Lao, with the assistance of their Uncle Ho Chi Minh in Hanoi, would again try to take over Laos." According to Moore, the CIA decided that hardy Meo tribesmen, "when properly led and supplied [would] carry on guerrilla warfare against the Communists. Thus, it was the Meos who were trained and armed by Special Forces teams to resist Communist aggression." Moore also relates the orders a CIA man gave one of the "advisers" who was about to assume command of a Meo base in Laos: "Don't let yourself get captured. All our good old play-it-straight-down-the-line government needs is to get caught violating the Geneva agreements. It's OK for the Communists to build up for a take-over and disregard the convention, but we have to live by the rules." [1]

Moore's book (see Sources) was extremely favorable to the Special Forces and the CIA. Though written in the form of fictionalized vignettes, the opening sentence declares, "*The Green Berets* is a book of truth." The Department of Defense first tried to have the book withdrawn, then pressured the publisher into putting a bright yellow band around the dust jacket clearly marking it "fiction." Moore says in his preface that to have written the book as fact, giving the names and places involved in the covert operations he described, "could only embarrass U.S. planners in Vietnam." Thus he doesn't identify the Laotian/Meo project by the code name, "Operation Hard Nose," which the CIA assigned to it.

Prior to 1964, the special operations in the North had an *ad hoc* quality, their object random harassment rather than accomplishment of long-range war goals. One Operation Haylift mission was directed against a municipal waterworks in a town just north of the demilitarized zone—scarcely the type of destruction to diminish North Vietnam's war-making potential. The Laotian activities against the Ho Chi Minh Trail were hit-and-miss (usually the latter) and did not materially reduce traffic. Moving arguments were advanced to fit the special operations into a formal war structure. Frank N. Trager, professor of international affairs at New York University and prominent among the outside consultants relied upon by the Pentagon and CIA for national strategic planning, summarized the case for punishing the North in a 1963 talk at the Center for Strategic Studies* in Washington:

> If the past fifteen years, that is, since George Kennan first advocated a policy of containment for Europe ... have demonstrated any one fact, it is that Communist ideology, power policy, and advancing strategy have not been contained, even when we had nuclear monopoly. It should be evident in terms of ... past and recent East, South and Southeast Asian

* Retired Admiral Arleigh Burke, former Chief of Naval Operations, is director of the center, a think-tank.

experience that even to maintain the *current* defensive perimeter we shall sooner or later have to make an effort at penetrating, undermining, threatening and possibly attacking the enemy at bases on his terrain. Americans will not be willing to suffer casualties over a long period of time in Vietnam for want of stopping Vietminh at the source. Sooner or later we shall have to face up to the strategy of defending 'Saigon' by seriously threatening or attacking Hanoi.[2]

The intensification of special operations had its genesis in Johnson's appointment, in December 1963, of a "Vietnam Working Group" to help guide day-to-day conduct of the war and to plan strategy. Its leader was William H. Sullivan, a 41-year-old foreign service officer whom Ambassador Averell Harriman plucked from obscurity and made his principal deputy. The working group, drawn from the State Department, CIA, and Pentagon, was first commissioned to put onto paper what could be done in the war politically, economically, and militarily. After its appointment was announced, the Sullivan group disappeared from sight and began a detailed analysis of (a) the immediate military capabilities of the National Liberation Front and the South Vietnamese army; (b) the prospects for meaningful improvement of the South soon enough to check the obvious battlefield superiority of the North; (c) the gradations of United States assistance and action required to reinforce the efforts of the South; (d) probable responses of Hanoi; and (e) what Communist China and the Soviet Union could be expected to do.

Operating with presidential fiat, Sullivan demanded and received unstinting cooperation from the upper echelons of the Pentagon, CIA, and his own State Department (through Walt Whitman Rostow, then chairman of State's Policy Planning Council, and later Johnson's special assistant for national security affairs). For weeks during that early winter, position papers, estimates, and background data swirled into the working group's offices, there to be distilled, debated, and often dispatched to the source for elaboration or revision. If the Defense Department predicted that X number of troops would be required to seal a certain portion of the Laotian-South Vietnamese frontier, Sullivan (or a subordinate) wanted to know, "Why?" If the CIA's Office of National Estimates said that Nikita Khrushchev (sulking and in near-disgrace because of his backing down in the Cuban missile crisis 16 months previously) would not dare to send antiaircraft missiles into Hanoi if American planes bombed the North Vietnamese capital, Sullivan asked, "Prove it. Are you guessing, estimating, or hoping?" Much is said in Washington about the imminent computerization of government, of the use of machines rather than humans in decision-making. But the Sullivan effort was a process involving flesh, blood, and brains—one of those exhilarating experiences that comes when men in government realize they are helping to mold national policy, with presidential *carte blanche* to draw upon the thinking, the talents, the resources of any agency, any official, in Washington or elsewhere, who can contribute.

A State Department man who says that his role in the Sullivan group was minor (and who quickly became disenchanted with Johnson's conduct of the war) could say three years later: "As an FSO-5* I could call a three-star general and say—in a nice way, of course—that I needed certain information by noon the following day, and it would be there. Rare are the moments when anyone at my level in State approaches the Pentagon on anything other than courteously bent knees, but it happened that winter. I became convinced that government could work—and even if I make ambassador before I am carted off to the grave, I'll look back at the Sullivan bunch as the high point of my career."

After six weeks' research the Sullivan group began writing a paper whose thrust, in the most essential respect, is extremely ironic: Sullivan, given prestige and authority by the good offices of Harriman, a dove, reached conclusions on the war as hawkish as the let's-bomb recommendations of the militant Rostow and the Bundy brothers (McGeorge and his elder brother, William P., a ten-year CIA veteran who was an assistant secretary first to McNamara and then to Rusk). Because Sullivan's mandate was to develop a plan to "win" the war, or to stabilize it, without resort to negotiation in the near future, any other outcome would have been surprising; nonetheless, even Harriman is reliably reported to have expressed shock at the product (although his close relationship with Sullivan was not affected).

Sullivan's paper, sent to the White House in an unbound loose-leaf folder to expedite revisions and updatings, began with the premise that nothing short of direct United States force would halt or even delay the Viet Cong. The strength of the VC infrastructure in both the cities and the countryside gave the National Liberation Front a "government" far more viable than that of Saigon. Further, despite Pentagon gripes that the VC flourished only because of the North Vietnamese "sanctuary" and supplies flowing from it, Sullivan argued that the VC for the immediate future could be considered a self-sustaining force.

What, then, should be done?

Sullivan's paper tacitly accepted the thesis that Hanoi guided the NLF; were North Vietnam to be held accountable for its "aggression" and punished, it would likely order the NLF to lessen the tempo of battle (and also slow its supply of men and arms). Sullivan addressed himself to possible methods of persuading Hanoi to cease-and-desist, within the format of a plan of gradually increasing pressures, beginning with psychological techniques and ranging upward into conventional warfare.

* FSO-5 is a category-five Foreign Service Officer, equivalent in prestige and pay to an Army major.

Certain of the lower-rung proposals appear at first consideration too childish to be a part of international strategic maneuvering. One suggestion was to have unmarked United States jets, manned by South Vietnamese pilots, sweep low over Hanoi, Haiphong, and other major cities, rocking them with sonic booms.* Khanh would be encouraged to talk belligerently about an invasion of North Vietnam, and the United States would comment so ambiguously that no one could be certain of its intentions. United States advisers would make themselves conspicuous during reconnaissance patrols along the southern fringe of the DMZ.

Through diplomatic contacts the United States would bluntly tell the North Vietnamese that she intended to get tough and would continue to do so, in ever-hardening gradations, unless Hanoi stopped supporting the National Liberation Front. Make a public fuss, the United States would say, and we'll reply that you don't know what you are talking about. We are going to be careful enough that you can't obtain any physical evidence of our participation in the sonic boom "raids" and no one outside the Communist world would ever believe that the United States, with its arsenal of missiles, nuclear warheads, and supersonic bombers, is "fighting" a fourth-rate Asian nation with noisemakers. The flights would demonstrate to Hanoi that the United States was capable of unrestricted air operations over North Vietnam, and that the next noise well could be the sounds of bombs, rather than sonic booms. The private boastings and public denials of responsibility for violations of Communist air space would convey the notion that the United States was ready to play dirty.

The next phase called for massing United States warships off the coast of North Vietnam, in international waters (that is, beyond a three-mile limit) but close enough to the mainland to be unnerving. Destroyers would make frequent feints at the shore. Powerful ship-based jamming transmitters would attempt to disrupt domestic Vietnamese broadcasts and communications between Hanoi and NLF military units in the South. A South Vietnamese "Saigon Rose"—the American answer to Hanoi Rose—would make propaganda broadcasts to the North Vietnamese military and civilian population, denouncing the Communist government, sympathizing with the economic and political misery of persons living under Ho Chi Minh, extolling the joys of non-Communist life in the South, and asking that Vietnamese not be forced to fight against Vietnamese.

Should sonic booms, verbal bombast, and the sight of warships fail to dissuade Hanoi, the United States would blockade the port of Haiphong and use force, if necessary, to halt shipping—even if it meant firing upon Soviet vessels. South Vietnamese torpedo boats and other small patrol

* No one in the government has ever admitted publicly that the United States indeed did try to frighten Hanoi out of the war by rattling its windows and disturbing Ho Chi Minh's sleep. But in the late spring and early summer of 1964, Hanoi Radio did complain frequently of violations of its air space.

craft would be permitted to raid North Vietnamese islands and coastal installations. (One island mentioned in a working paper drawn upon by the Sullivan group was Hon Me, site of a radar station and patrol boat base.) The CIA's active program of parachuting saboteurs and small guerrilla teams into the North would be expanded, and United States military personnel (as contrasted with the CIA's paramilitarys) would be permitted to accompany South Vietnamese across the border.

The United States would not actively seek combat—but pilots would be authorized to shoot back if they were fired upon during reconnaissance missions over Laos, or if the North Vietnamese attempted to break the proposed blockade of Haiphong. Finally, if all else failed, the United States would commence a "tit for tat" bombing of North Vietnam, striking first for military bases directly involved in the support of the NLF, next at war-connected industrial installations, finally at Hanoi and Haiphong proper.

Under one of several schemes studied by the Sullivan group, North Vietnam would be given a "bombing price list": If the Viet Cong destroyed a Southern village, United States bombers would obliterate a village in the North. If the Viet Cong killed a village official, a factory in the North would be bombed. Before each retaliation, the United States would broadcast a list of several hundred prospective targets, and give residents one week to clear them. (To single out the exact village or plant to be bombed would enable the North Vietnamese to mobilize their antiaircraft. The early warnings supposedly would disrupt the normal life of villagers and workers by the scores of thousands.)

Should this extreme be reached, the Sullivan group warned, the United States should be prepared for the eventuality of a massive open intervention by the North Vietnamese army, and substantially increased aid from the Soviet Union and Communist China. It was argued that the Sino-Soviet split had the Communist nations in such turmoil that neither Moscow nor Peking wanted involvement in the war; however, the Sullivan group's conclusion was that the rivalry for party leadership would compel both factions to send aid lest they be disgraced as traitors to the revolutionary cause. Were this to happen, Sullivan warned, the investment of a "substantial" number of United States troops could be required—as many as six divisions, meaning 100,000 men when support troops are included.

In conclusion, Sullivan said the United States should make abundantly clear to the world that it had no intention of destroying or occupying North Vietnam, and that any pressures would promptly end once Hanoi ceased its support of the NLF. But unless the United States gave North Vietnam painful incentive for doing so, he said, that support would continue.

Thus given the potential United States price for "saving" South Vietnam, Johnson wouldn't accept the package. Persons who watched him that spring concluded that he was stalling; that when suddenly brought against the hard decisions required to implement his broad policy goal, he was not so confident it was worth the effort. In the view of subordinates, Johnson raised procrastination to the level of an art form. "He wouldn't say 'No' to any part of the plan; he said 'Maybe' to others, and we'd go ahead with it. But mostly it was a matter of sending back pieces bit by bit and asking for proof for the conclusion that Phase X wouldn't bring the Chinese down on us," one man recollects. "I can certainly appreciate presidential caution, because we were talking about the possibility, even the likelihood, that the United States would go to war. But someone said one day, 'He's filibustering so that he won't have to make up his mind one way or another.' That seemed like a fair assessment."

However, Johnson did approve the expansion of special operations against the North—although in doing so he made plain to the White House national security staff that they shouldn't consider the Sullivan plan a firm blueprint for what he intended to do in the future. But the changes of tactics in the war were soon felt by the men in the field.

In the spring of 1964, Special Forces troops working in coordination with the CIA began a program entitled "Project Delta" to organize and train teams to infiltrate Laos by air. The initial purpose was reconnaissance and intelligence on the Ho Chi Minh Trail; however, the training was extensive enough that the South Vietnamese soldiers in the program would be able to establish more or less permanent guerrilla bases in Laos in the future. General William C. Westmoreland, new United States commander in Vietnam, wanted to take the Army's Special Forces from under CIA jurisdiction, and Project Delta was a means of doing so. However, in planning for Project Delta missions, Special Forces officers had to obtain CIA approval, to preclude unwitting interference with the agency's Operation Hard Nose (the harassment conducted by the Meos guided by CIA paramilitarys).

As conceived by the CIA and the Special Forces, each Project Delta team would consist of two Green Berets and four South Vietnamese. The American planners, having a low regard for Vietnamese ability in leadership, told Ambassador Henry Cabot Lodge and the Pentagon that success depended upon the active participation of American soldiers.

Special Forces Sergeant Donald Duncan was among the cadre who trained the South Vietnamese and prepared himself for the first mission into Laos. At the last minute, he says, "We received a firm 'no go' for the United States personnel." Why? "The answer was that it was an election year and it would cause great embarrassment if Americans were captured in Laos.

Anything of that nature would have to wait until after the election. The reaction to this decision on the part of Americans was one of anger, disappointment, and disgust."[3]

Career soldier Duncan says his disgust with the Vietnam War began at this point, when he realized that "the denial of American participation was not based on whether it was right or wrong for us to be going to Laos. The primary concern was the possible embarrassment to President Johnson during an election campaign. Towards this end we sent people on a mission that had little or no chance of success .... We sent 40 men who had become our friends. . . . These were exceptionally dedicated people, all volunteers. . . . Six returned, the rest were killed or captured."

In an English-language broadcast over Radio Hanoi's international service at 1625 GMT on August 6, 1964, the North Vietnamese News Agency, Hanoi's official press outlet, recounted the recently concluded trial of "spy commandos" who dropped into the Quy Chau district of Nghe An Province on May 19:

> Before the court the culprits declared that they had been carefully trained in intelligence and sabotage activities and in psychological warfare by the United States. At about 10 A.M. on 19 May they were ordered to gather in a numberless house in Nguyen Thai Hoc Street, Gia Dinh provincial capitol, and were entrusted with the task of sabotaging North Vietnam.
>
> Together with a United States officer they went by air from the Tan Son Nhut Airport, Saigon, to Da Nang Airport, Quang Nam Province. At 7 P.M. on the same day their plane left Da Nang and flew along the coast northward to Nghe An Province, where they were dropped in Quy Chau. But once landed they were spotted, encircled and then captured with all material evidence by local militiamen and self-defense groups.
>
> The court sentenced Nguyen Van Sinh, deputy leader of the group, who had 'shown stubbornness' when being captured, to death; Nguyen Ngoc Binh, the leader, to life imprisonment. [*Four other men received terms of from twenty years to life.*]
>
> This is the ninth spy-commando group of the United States and its stooges in South Vietnam tried by the DRV since early this year.

Meanwhile, during the first half of the year, special operations by sea gradually increased in scope. In January the United States gave the South Vietnamese permission to intensify coast patrols north of the DMZ, and to rely more heavily upon ships to transport sabotage and intelligence teams to targets near the sea. On January 16 the United States Navy transferred the escort vessels *USS Serene* and *USS Shelter* to South Vietnam—elderly vessels launched in 1943 by the Winslow Marine Railway and Shipbuilding Company, Winslow, Washington. Each is 180 feet long and carries seven officers and 83 enlisted men; the armament consists of one three-inch gun, two 40-mm. antiaircraft guns, and eight 20-mm. antiaircraft guns, all suitable for use against surface targets as well. Upon transfer the *Serene* and *Shelter* became, respectively, the *Nhut Tao* (with the operational number HQ 10) and the *Chi Linh* (HQ 11). The *Serene* and the *Shelter* joined two sister ships already in South Vietnamese hands. The *USS Gayety* had been transferred in June 1962 and renamed the *Chi Lang II* (HQ 08). The *USS Sentry* had been converted into a patrol vessel by the Sun Shipbuilding and Dry Dock Company, Chester, Pennsylvania—its minesweeping gear being removed to provide more deck space—and then transferred to South Vietnam from the United States Navy Base in Philadelphia in August 1962 as the *Kua Hoa* (HQ 09).

Once Navy officers had shown the Vietnamese how to sail the *Serene* and the *Shelter,* a six-man team of paramilitarys from the CIA commenced another type of training—seaborne infiltration. The sailors were a peppery group: They adopted as their motto the words "Sat Cong" ("Kill Communists"), an adaptation of the slogan "Sat Dat" ("Kill Mongols") used as a rallying cry centuries ago when the Vietnamese fought the half-million-man army of Kublai Khan. The South Vietnamese festooned their headquarters and decks with "Dat Cong" signs. When some even wanted to tattoo the slogan on their chests, the CIA paras managed to find two tattoo machines for them (purchased at $25 each with funds provided through the military assistance program).

In the first weeks, the crews concentrated on gunnery against coastal targets, working from the Navy base at Da Nang. Then South Vietnamese marines were brought aboard and operations shifted to a closely guarded installation near Mui Vung Ta, on the peninsula south of Saigon where the Saigon River flows into the South China Sea. The base there has a broad, wide beach, and soon the CIA paras were satisfied with the professionalism with which the South Vietnamese swung over the sides of the *Nhut Tao* and *Chi Linh* (née *Serene* and *Shelter*) onto rubber rafts and stole ashore. They also displayed skill with explosive charges. One of the CIA paras said to a friend over drinks in Saigon that spring: "They're so short they have to get fairly close to the beach before they leave the boat, but they're fearless. We could have used some of these little guys at Inchon."

But as is the case with many CIA training exercises, the missions for which the South Vietnamese were being schooled had not been approved— and no one could say with assurance that they ever would be. The agency frequently must operate on the premise that it might be called upon to do an unusual task in a hurry; therefore its planners try to anticipate assignments and prepare for them on a contingency basis—with the knowledge and approval of the Pentagon and the State Department.

During this period the naval special operations were of two broad types:

infiltration of saboteur teams for short-term missions, and inspection of suspicious craft in waters above and below the demilitarized zone. North Vietnamese broadcasts give a highly flavored version of the operations. Typical accounts of episodes prior to the Tonkin incidents also reveal the restiveness of the North Vietnamese with what was happening off their shores.

On July 21, 1964, Hanoi Radio's international service broadcast an English-language account of the trial, before a military court in Quang Binh province, of four "frogmen" captured at the mouth of the Gianh River the night of March 12. According to Hanoi, one man, Vu Van Gioi, was shot when he resisted capture. The surviving three men received sentences of life, eighteen years, and seven years. The North Vietnamese broadcast stated:

> At the court the commandos pleaded guilty of having wilfully served as commandos for the United States imperialists to sabotage North Vietnam. They declared that they had been trained at the My Khe training ground [Da Nang] by two American and puppet officers of the Special Forces since December 1962 [sic].
>
> On the night of March 11, under the direct command of an American* they sailed from Da Nang port to North Vietnam on board an armed vessel bearing the mark USA and painted silver. At 10 P.M. on March 12 the vessel stopped at a place off the Gianh River mouth and the four commandos were sent to shore in a pneumatic boat. One of them, in a diver's outfit, was caught immediately after landing. Vu Van Gioi was shot dead because he resisted. The two others fled in panic but did not escape the net of the People's Forces.

On July 27, Colonel Ha Van Lau, head of the liaison mission of the Vietnamese People's Army high command, sent a note to the International Control Commission protesting the "piratical moves of the United States and its henchmen in the coastal area of Quang Binh Province." A Hanoi Radio broadcast in English the next day gave this account:

> At 4:30 P.M. on 25 July 1964 four United States-South Vietnamese warships intruded into the territorial waters of the DRV at 106 degrees 43 [minutes] east longitude and 17 degrees 45 [minutes] north latitude and encircled two fishing boats belonging to inhabitants of Bao Ninh Commune in Quang Binh Province. The army men on board opened fire, forced the fishermen to board the ships, and looted all their property.

---

* That an American sailed above the DMZ in this particular time span is questionable, according to persons with knowledge of the naval operations. They say, however, that the CIA's paramilitary operatives, many of them naturalized citizens, are a highly individualistic group, and well might have accompanied raiding parties to evaluate their commandos' performances. The claim of the "USA marking" is patently silly, for the men conducting the agency's special operations had enough experience—and common sense— not to launch such missions from identifiable boats.

Thereafter, they took the two fishing boats in tow, heading for South Vietnam. But confronted with the resistance of the local people's armed forces, they were compelled to leave them [the boats] behind with one man, and they carried along eleven fishermen and all the property.

Colonel Ha Van Lau strongly protested to the ICC against this extremely serious violation of the territorial waters of the DRV by the United States and the South Vietnamese administration and their illegal piratical acts. These constitute encroachment on the people's life and property, and menace and hinder the normal occupations of the population of the DRV coastal areas. He requested the ICC to recommend without delay that the US and South Vietnamese administration stop such provocation and piratical acts and release the eleven above-mentioned fishermen.

In early summer Vice Admiral Roy L. Johnson, newly appointed commander of the Seventh Fleet, put into Saigon on his flagship, the *USS Oklahoma,* for discussions with Ambassador Maxwell D. Taylor, also new in his position, and with military commanders. The Navy professionals were restless: Here the United States was with a quietly expanding war, and all the Navy could do was post carriers off the coast on Yankee Station, while the Air Force, Army, and Marines got all the action—and the promotions. The Seventh Fleet had naval responsibility for one-fifth of the earth's surface—30 million square miles from the Bering Sea on the north to Antarctica in the south; from San Francisco to Asia—yet insofar as Vietnam was concerned, it was little more than an ignored bystander. The *Washington Star's* Asian correspondent, Richard Critchfield, wrote shortly after Admiral Johnson's visit: "He discussed with Ambassador Taylor the possibility of the fleet's playing an increased operational role in the Vietnam War, including stepped-up coastline patrols to block supplies and infiltration from Cambodia and North Vietnam."

Whether or not Admiral Johnson's visit was the precipitating factor, coincident with his talk with Taylor came a substantial change in the rules governing South Vietnamese naval incursions north of the demilitarized zone. Previously, the South Vietnamese were permitted to harass and impede coastal shipping, and to put saboteurs ashore. Now the Saigon embassy recommended (and Washington approved) that they be permitted to attack North Vietnamese coastal and island installations with heavy-weapons fire. About nine new craft were supplied to supplement the *Shelter, Serene, et al.,* whose 14-knot top speed was far too slow for attack missions. These were United States-manufactured Swift boats—aluminum craft with a speed above 50 knots, armed with 40-mm. cannon and lighter machine guns. United States personnel—CIA paramilitarys and naval officers on detached duty—began an intensified training program in June, drawing heavily upon the crews which earlier had gone through the CIA's "beach landing school" near Mui Vung Ta. United States military intelligence helped the South Vietnamese select targets from the many possibilities covered by the directive authorizing the new missions. Practice runs were made at the South Vietnamese coast. The training included voyages 60 to 70 miles out into the Gulf of Tonkin from Da Nang, for the American advisers knew that the boats, when on raiding missions, would be detected immediately if they attempted to sneak up the coast through concentrations of North Vietnamese junks, which doubled as military picket ships.

Sometime around mid-July, working from photographs taken by a United States reconnaissance plane, the advisers drafted operational orders for the first of the new raids.

The cover name for the activity: 34-Alpha Operations, the name that had been used for the other forays above the North Vietnamese border.

The first targets: a new radar station on Hon Me, and a communications transmitter on nearby Hon Ngu, both islands heavily involved in Hanoi's sea infiltration program.

The projected date: the end of July, training of the crews and the weather permitting.

The decision on the 34-A Operations was secret, of course, as was the Administration's reasoning for making yet another change in the rules under which it fought the war. The United States and North Vietnam had an unspoken agreement to keep the war in Laos within manageable bounds. The North Vietnamese slipped men and supplies along the Ho Chi Minh Trail; they were harassed by the CIA's Meo tribesmen, as well as occasional Special Forces units. But in mid-April the Communist Pathet Lao mounted battalion-sized attacks against government positions, prompting a brief rightist overthrow of Premier Souvanna Phouma (a neutralist) and sending shivers of panic through Washington. North Vietnamese regular army troops were suddenly conspicuous among the Pathet Lao, in direct and open violation of the 1962 agreement. When the United States protested, the Communist nations began a well-orchestrated clamor for a reconvening of the Geneva Convention. To the State Department, the ploy smacked of a trap: If Washington went into a conference, the Communists would insist on widening the agenda to include Vietnam and Cambodia. Because of the military and political chaos in South Vietnam, the United States simply did not feel ready to attempt to negotiate an end to the war.

The United States was also checkmated militarily. The 1962 agreement forbade the "introduction of foreign regular and irregular troops . . . and foreign military personnel in Laos." In the State Department's opinion, it was imperative that the United States maintain a semblance of legality in Laos. Therefore the possibility of openly introducing United States advisers to supplement the covert CIA operations was never seriously considered. (Too, military intervention would hamper the construction of a "peace president" image then under way.)

The decision was for an aerial show of force in Laos. Johnson ordered reconnaissance planes to fly missions over Pathet Lao positions on the Plaine des Jarres, at the "invitation" of Souvanna Phouma—in the words of the State Department, "because of the inability of the International Control Commission to check on Communist troop concentrations." When State Department correspondents inquired whether the United States had decided to end the two-sided fiction of "neutralization" of Laos with the flights, the Administration replied with a straight face: Since the missions started and ended outside Laos, the planes were not "introduced" into Laos, and thus did not violate the bans on "introduction" of military equipment and personnel. The Administration also told North Vietnam and China that it considered Laos and South Vietnam inseparable, and that piecemeal advances would not be permitted.

Persons who were in the Administration at the time offer conflicting views on whether the "reconnaissance flights" were in fact legitimate intelligence patrols, or a demonstration of United States capacity to bomb the Pathet Lao at will, or an attempt to provoke an incident to justify bombing (as an alternative to increased ground action). The pilots who flew the unarmed reconnaissance planes were puzzled about several things: Their mission orders brought them over Pathet Lao positions at altitudes and speeds which they considered dangerous, and they felt—and so informed superior officers—they could obtain photographs of equal quality if they were permitted to fly higher. The pilots' protests eventually reached Admiral David L. McDonald, the Chief of Naval Operations. McDonald's subordinates convinced him that the missions, as being flown, were needlessly risky; if the Joint Chiefs of Staff were interested in intelligence only, pictures would be taken from higher, safer altitudes; if the Pentagon simply wanted to cow the Laotians and North Vietnamese, armed planes should be sent along which could defend the patrols when they came under attack (as they frequently did) from ground fire. McDonald agreed, put his case before the President, and in mid-May armed planes did begin flying alongside the reconnaissance craft.

Johnson put one stricture on the self-defense order: Pilots could not bomb or strafe Laotian installations *until and unless* United States planes were damaged.

The frequency of the flights being what they were, such hits were inevitable. On June 6 an RF-8 piloted by Lieutenant Charles Klusman of San Diego, flying from the carrier *Kitty Hawk,* was shot down. The next day Commander Doyle W. Lynn, of La Mesa, California, was hit at 20,000 feet by radar-controlled antiaircraft fire. And on June 8 Johnson ordered strikes on Pathet Lao gun positions near Phongsavang. Communist broadcasts said that 12 bombs and two rockets hit in and around the town. A day later, Washington confirmed the attack, saying they were "an expression of the President's determination to help the coalition government."

Surprisingly, there was little intra-Administration debate on the decision to authorize warplanes to fire at targets in a foreign land where they were forbidden to enter by a formal international treaty which the President was unwilling to abrogate publicly. Some persons in the State Department's Bureau of East Asian and Pacific Affairs felt the decision could have been even stronger: Assistant Secretary William Bundy in May even sounded British sentiment on sending fighter planes to neighboring Thailand as a cover for Marine units which Washington contemplated sending into Laos. But to Johnson, the Laotian situation was an opportunity to test the "tit-for-tat" principle of retaliation discussed in William Sullivan's plan. And there was little discernible presidential agonizing or indecision in the brief discussions following the loss of the second Navy plane. A State Department official intimately involved with Laotian affairs during the period says, "I think that the President was privately relieved that he could take such a momentous first step somewhere other than in Vietnam. Laos wasn't getting the attention that the public gave to Vietnam, because we didn't have any people there—officially at least. By late spring we had decided it would take some bullets and bombs, and not just words, to impress upon the North Vietnamese the fact that we weren't going to run. Since they had to be fired, Johnson thought it best that it be off in the woods where it would escape notice."

Through oversight or design, the United States did not inform Souvanna Phouma of the decision to begin bombings in his country; he angrily summoned Ambassador Leonard Unger and threatened to resign from the coalition government unless the raids halted. Unger, after much cajolery and pleading, persuaded Souvanna to turn his protest into an "invitation" for the raids to continue. Thereafter missions were flown almost daily, the United States saying they were directed only against antiaircraft batteries that fired at reconnaissance planes, the Communist media alleging destruction of "border posts" and "villages" both in Laos and inside North Vietnam.

Two points deserve underlining:

First, the President accepted the "tit-for-tat" principle of escalatory warfare. The executive branch of the United States government, unlike the judiciary, does not operate under the doctrine of *stare decisis;* therefore Johnson was not obligated to respond similarly to armed attacks elsewhere on United States planes, personnel—or naval vessels. But that he chose to apply tit-for-tat for Laos is firm evidence that he was moving toward a similar decision in Vietnam.

Second, the bombings of the antiaircraft installations did not deter the Pathet Lao from firing upon other reconnaissance planes, nor did the Viet Cong diminish their use of the Laotian portion of the Ho Chi Minh Trail.

By the same token, the only North Vietnamese and Communist Chinese reaction to the Laotian bombings and strafing was verbal—loud, to be sure, but Washington dismissed it as expected billingsgate from countries militarily incapable of more forceful response.

Chapter Four

THE DANGEROUS BUSINESS
OF ELECTRONIC ESPIONAGE

The Mediterranean is a half-world distant from the Gulf of Tonkin, but let us detour there briefly to report the misadventure of a relative of the *USS Maddox*—a misadventure that resembles the events of August 2–4, 1964, in planning, execution, and embarrassing outcome.

This episode began early the morning of June 2, 1967, when the *USS Liberty,* a sometime cargo ship now so festooned with antennae and other conspicuous electronic gear that crew members jocularly called her the "floating canebrake," slipped anchor at the United States Navy Base in Rota, Spain, and sped eastward into the Mediterranean. The course was a familiar one for Commander William C. McGonagle, the commanding officer of the electronic reconnaissance ship, for the *Liberty* had spent leisurely months cruising the coasts of North Africa and the Arab states. Once it had even darted northward through the Ionian Sea into the Adriatic, within sight of the Communist nations of Albania and Yugoslavia, and circled the onetime Soviet submarine base on the Albanian island of Saseno, its sensitive receivers soaking up, spongelike, military and civilian radio communications on the shore. Again, the *Liberty* would loll in the wake of Soviet cruisers and other warships which from 1962 on proliferated in the Mediterranean, her technicians recording inter-ship radio messages, and photographing with telescopic lenses the antisubmarine-warfare devices visible on deck.

On June 2, however, the *Liberty* was in a hurry, and McGonagle didn't pause even to make an electronic sweep of the big Algerian naval base at Mers-al-Kebir, long eyed as a potential berth for the Soviet Mediterranean fleet,* and a standing target for electronic espionage.

Hundreds of miles away, Israel and the Arab states danced on the brink of war, and in a crisis Washington has learned it cannot always rely upon

---

* But never used by the Soviets as of this writing, numerous press reports notwithstanding. United States intelligence keeps abreast of traffic into Mers-al-Kebir through a fortunate happenstance: The base and its many berths are clearly visible from upper floors of the United States consulate in Oran.

its attachés for fast reporting. Any outbreak of hostilities in the Middle East posed a distinct threat of a United States-Soviet confrontation; in such circumstances Washington wanted reliable intelligence of what was happening, and wanted it in a hurry.

Thus the *Liberty's* orders: Take up a position north of the Sinai Peninsula and monitor Arab and Israeli radio traffic. Concentrate on the Israelis, for (although the orders didn't say so) Washington reckoned that President Gamal Abdal Nasser of the United Arab Republic intended to continue blustering, whereas the Israelis were displaying readiness for a preemptive first strike. Specifically, the *Liberty* was told to watch for Israeli planes leaving the airfields ringing Tel Aviv; United States intelligence knew enough about Israeli strategic planning to forecast that air strikes wouldn't be mounted directly across the land frontier. Instead, planes would swing out in a wide curve over the Mediterranean, beyond Alexandria, Egypt, then hook inland and pound the Soviet-supplied Mig-21s and Mig-19s at UAR air bases from Cairo to the Suez Canal Zone and then to the Red Sea.

This is exactly what the Israelis did, beginning at 7:30 A.M. on June 5, and, thanks to the *Liberty,* Washington knew the raids were coming even before the first bombs fell on Arab soil.

The *Liberty* remained on station two more days, cruising a rectangular course outside the 12½-mile territorial limit claimed by the Egyptians, which she had orders not to violate. The *Liberty* listened to Israeli army radio traffic as the attackers swept across Sinai, followed by the frenzied collapse and withdrawal of the Arab armies. The voices of Israeli pilots crackled through the *Liberty's* receivers as they hunted down survivors of the crushed UAR tank force. So great was the volume of message-intercepts that most technicians on the *Liberty* worked 18 hours daily; the officer directly in charge of the monitoring operation was at his post at one point for 37 consecutive hours.

Then things began to fall apart for the *Liberty.*

On June 7 Cairo Radio broadcast a communiqué from the UAR high command, admitting that Egyptian forces had withdrawn in some areas from the "Zionist enemy, *supported by foreign sources.*" United States intelligence, meanwhile, got access to a recording of a phone conversation between Nasser and King Hussein of Jordan in which they had fabricated a charge that British and United States planes had aided the Israelis. (The Israeli defense ministry released the recording; however, there is credible circumstantial evidence that the actual intercept of the conversation was made by the *Liberty* and given to the Israelis through intelligence channels.) In the interchange Nasser said: "I will make an announcement and you will make an announcement and we will see to it that the Syrians will make an announcement that American and British airplanes are taking part against us from aircraft carriers. . . ." A bit later Nasser asked Hussein: "Will we say the United States and England or just the U.S.?" "The U.S. and England," replied Hussein. Nasser then wanted to know, "Does Britain have aircraft carriers?" Hussein's reply was inaudible.

To Washington, the Arab attempt to blame the United States for the war was about as laughable as the Arab military prowess. Nonetheless, as a precaution, President Johnson ordered that any naval vessels which conceivably could be linked with the Israeli attacks be sent out of the area.

The Pentagon drafted a message—under the signature of the Joint Chiefs of Staff—implementing the President's order, and directing that all United States craft in the battle area withdraw at least 100 miles to sea. The Army Communications Center in the Pentagon transmitted the message early on June 8 as JCS 080110Z* addressed to CINCEUR (commander in chief, Europe), with an information copy to the *Liberty* and other ships.

But the message didn't go to the *Liberty*. Through what Air Force Lieutenant General Richard P. Klocko, director of the Defense Communications Agency, calls a "personnel failure," it went instead to the Naval Communications Station in the Philippines. A clerk there caught the error and relayed the message back to the Pentagon, which proceeded to err again. The *Liberty's* information copy this time was not dispatched to Commander McGonagle in the Mediterranean, but to the National Security Agency, 25 miles north of Washington at Fort Meade, Maryland. (That the National Security Agency could be considered a mailing address for the *Liberty* points up a fact which the Pentagon won't admit for the record: Electronic reconnaissance ships such as *Liberty* are not controlled directly by the Navy, but by NSA, the supersecret agency of which more will be said later in this chapter.)

Says Lieutenant General Klocko: "This information copy of JCS message 080110Z was never delivered to the *USS Liberty*."

While the JCS warning ricocheted between the Pentagon message center, the Philippines, and Maryland, there remained one fail-safe procedure that should have enabled the *Liberty* to move to safer waters. Following routine procedures, the communications officer aboard the *USS Little Rock,* flagship for the United States Sixth Fleet in the Mediterranean, started converting the JCS directive into "action messages" for the specific vessels affected by the order. He began the task at 4:45 A.M. But not until 9:17 A.M. was the *Liberty's* copy transmitted—a lapse of four hours, 32 minutes. The *Liberty* was receiving fleet messages via a Naval Communications Station at Asmara, Ethiopia. But a clerk on the *Little Rock,* through error,

---

* The first two digits in a message time-block are the date; the remaining four, the time, stated on the basis of a 24-hour clock. The final letter represents the time zone. Thus 080110Z means that the message was transmitted on June 8 at 0110 hours (or 1:10 A.M.) Zulu (or Washington) time.

sent the *Liberty's* message to another Naval Communications Station in Morocco.[1]

The *Liberty,* meanwhile, continued cruising off the Sinai Peninsula, not venturing more than 15 miles from the coast, oblivious to the Joint Chiefs of Staff order and the threat of attack. The Israelis, of course, knew the ship was in the area. Several of the bombers which participated in the initial June 5 raids flew over the *Liberty* en route to their targets in Egypt. Israeli reconnaissance planes encountered her frequently during the next two days, and early on the morning of June 8 two Israeli jets passed over the *Liberty.*

When reports of the sighting reached Tel Aviv, an official of the Israeli Defense Ministry contacted the United States military attaché and asked whether there were any American vessels in the area. The attaché, having seen an information copy of the JCS message, assumed the *Liberty* had withdrawn, and thus told the Israelis that the United States had no vessel in the area. The Israelis apparently made a similar check with the Soviet military attaché, who also denied ownership.

Versions differ as to what happened next. According to the Israelis' story, one of their patrol boats approached the *Liberty* and signaled for identification. The *Liberty* replied, "A-A," meaning, "Identify yourself" in the international sea code. Whereupon Israeli boats and planes raked the *Liberty* with fire, killing 34 crew members and wounding 75 more.

Washington's version is somewhat different. Commander McGonagle later told a board of inquiry that the Israeli planes attacked his ship before the torpedo boat approached, and that he could not detect signal lights because of the smoke and flames already engulfing the ship.

Just how close did the *Liberty's* spy mission—and the collapse of naval communications—bring the world to war?

Washington's first reaction was moderated by the fact that no one in the Pentagon knew exactly what had happened to the *Liberty,* nor who was responsible. As Secretary of Defense McNamara was to admit months later, "I thought the *Liberty* had been attacked by Soviet forces. Thank goodness, our carrier commanders did not launch directly against the Soviet forces who were operating in the Mediterranean at the time. I then thought it had been attacked by Egyptian forces. Who else could have done it? Thank goodness, we did not launch against the Egyptians. We took time to find out it was the Israelis."[3] Carrier-based planes did speed to the *Liberty,* but the Israeli attackers had finished their work and vanished by the time they arrived. And President Johnson prudently used the hot-line Teletype link with Moscow to advise Soviet Premier Aleksei Kosygin that the United States planes were only going to the aid of the stricken ship, and did not have any hostile intentions.

After the *contretemps* of near-war, the Pentagon, quite understandably, was not prepared to be overly candid about the reasons the *Liberty* had sauntered into a war zone. The cover story announced in Washington was that she took up station off Sinai "to assist in relaying information concerning the evacuation of American citizens from countries of the Middle East." Given the *Liberty's* equipment, personnel, and normal assignments, one can only recollect what former President Eisenhower said in May 1960 during the furor over the loss of a U-2 spy plane over the Soviet Union at a politically inopportune moment: "These activities have their own rules and methods of concealment which seek to mislead and obscure."

The story of the lamented *Liberty* is germane to a study of the Gulf of Tonkin episode for several reasons. First, and paramount, the *Liberty* and *Maddox* were cousins, albeit distant and part-time ones. The *Maddox's* normal assignment was not spying.* However, as is the case with perhaps 50 other United States destroyers, she is capable of rapid conversion into what the Navy calls an ELINT (electronic intelligence) ship. And, as we shall detail at the appropriate moment, the *Maddox* was on an electronic-intelligence mission in the Gulf of Tonkin when her many troubles began. Further, although United States officials at the highest level consistently maintain that mechanical spies are more efficient and run less risk of compromise to national security than do live agents, technological espionage is marred almost as much with mud as with medals. The U-2 incident abruptly ended a promising period of East-West detente. The capture of the *Pueblo* set war drums beating within a Vietnam-frustrated United States which President Johnson was able to muffle only with vigorous political effort in Congress. Finally, because of the very nature of their work, precise operating control of espionage ships (and manned planes and drone planes and satellites) is impossible. Just as the matador who works closest to the bull receives the greatest ovation, a spy must make his way into range of the target to receive meaningful information. Since January 1950, at least 225 United States personnel have been killed or captured while engaged in electronic espionage and other "ferret" missions—and, as the *Pueblo* seizure amply illustrated, there is little the United States can do about it. United States planes and ships have been fired upon in and over

---

* The *Pueblo* also experienced communications snafus on its ill-fated last mission, according to a House Armed Services subcommittee that investigated its seizure by the North Koreans. According to the chairman, Representative Otis Pike of New York, the National Security Agency directed a message to the Joint Chiefs of Staff "suggesting that the characterization of the mission as minimal risk might be wrong." Pike said on March 12, 1969: "The message was directed to the Joint Chiefs of Staff. No member of the Joint Chiefs of Staff received the message. The message was received at the staff level of the Joint Chiefs and redirected to the Commander in Chief, Pacific . . . [who] apparently never received the message. It was received at the staff level in his office, and not brought to his attention. At the same time that the message was redirected to the Commander in Chief, Pacific, an information copy was sent to the Chief of Naval Operations. The information copy was never delivered. This message, over the signature of the director of the National Security Agency, was sent by a member of his staff. The director never saw it until after the *Pueblo* was captured."

the Baltic Sea, East Germany, Hungary, Czechoslovakia, the Adriatic Sea, the Black Sea, Soviet Armenia, the Straits of Taiwan, the Gulf of Tonkin, the China Sea, Japan, Korea, and the Soviet Union itself.

Yet, on balance, Washington insists electronic espionage is worth the recognized risks. At White House briefings for Senators following the *Pueblo* seizure, Richard Helms, director of the CIA, said that "machine spies" such as satellites have inherent advantages over human agents: Catch one, and it doesn't sign confessions, or make propaganda broadcasts over a Communist national radio, or sit in the defendant's dock at a show trial (as did U-2 pilot Francis Gary Powers in 1960). Unfortunately, not even the superskilled CIA has developed an ELINT ship capable of sailing for three weeks without a human hand at the tiller through the Sea of Japan, skirting near the North Korean coast; hence the *Pueblo* incident. President Johnson, speaking off the cuff to a group of southern officials in Nashville, Tennessee, on March 14, 1965 (in remarks which the White House tried to keep out of the press on the grounds they were confidential) said that satellite reconnaissance alone produced enough hard intelligence to justify spending ten times the $35 billion to $40 billion which the United States had already invested in space programs. Because of the intelligence, Johnson said, the United States does not harbor fears about its national security which otherwise might arise.[4]

Although naval vessels detailed for electronic espionage missions remain under nominal ownership of the United States Navy, their ultimate master is the National Security Agency—a big, rich, but little-known empire which has the responsibility for spying on the communications of foreign powers, hostile and otherwise, and of keeping secret the United States' own communications. NSA is a lineal descendant of the old "Black Chamber" eavesdropping and code-breaking operation made famous during World War I and afterward by the State Department's Herbert O. Yardley. To oversimplify grossly: NSA, with 14,000 to 20,000 military and civilian personnel, and $1.2 billion a year to spend, has the same mission as did Yardley four decades ago with a platoon of civilians and less than $100,-000 annually. NSA's creation, however, stemmed from the disastrous mishandling of intercepted Japanese fleet messages before World War II started. Navy intelligence, through astute cryptanalysis (code breaking), learned of Japanese fleet intentions in late November, but was so selective in distributing the information that not even the White House was aware of all the findings.

During the defense reorganization hearings of the late 1940s, witnesses generally agreed on the need for a complete meshing of cryptanalytical activities, and the free interchange within the intelligence community of the information derived. In 1949 the Defense Department set up the Armed

Forces Security Agency, which assumed responsibility for strategic communications and intelligence, while leaving to the individual services the
function of tactical communications. Because of a growing overlap between
CIA and the military, however, President Truman on November 4, 1952,
signed an executive order creating the National Security Agency and trans-
ferring to it AFSA's manpower and missions—in effect, "civilizing" the
agency.[5]

Truman did so in secret, however, and for some five years the government never acknowledged publicly that NSA existed. (The 1952 executive
order, in fact, has *never* been published.) Washington newspapers told
about the construction of the NSA headquarters building on an 82-acre
tract at Fort Meade, between 1953 and 1954, for such a highly visible
enterprise deserved mention: a longish three-story building a few hundred
yards east of the Balitmore-Washington Parkway, seen by thousands of
motorists daily during the seasons when shielding trees are bare of foliage.
This is NSA's operations building, 980 feet long, with 560-foot wings jut-
ting from each end—even bigger than the CIA's elaborate establishment at
Langley, Virginia (1,400,000 square feet to 1,135,000).* A nine-story
annex constructed in 1963–65 added another half-million square feet.
Three rings of fences, one electrified and two topped with coils of barbed
wire, surround the complex, and Marines man the guardhouses. Because
of the extraordinary security possible at Fort Meade, the government uses
the NSA facility to house high-level defectors from Communist nations
while they are being debriefed by the CIA and the State Department's
Bureau of Intelligence and Research. Major General Jan Sejna, the Czech
defense ministry official who fled to the West in early 1968, spent several
months within NSA walls.

Despite the conspicuous quarters, the government said absolutely nothing
about what happened in them until 1957, when this lucid explanation
appeared in the Government Organization Manual:

> The NSA was established pursuant to Presidential directive in 1952.
> It is an element of the Department of Defense, and its activities are
> subject to the direction and control of the Secretary of Defense. The
> NSA performs highly specialized technical and coordinating functions
> relating to the national security.

Although it is an "element" of the Department of Defense, NSA falls
beyond the direct control of the Joint Chiefs of Staff. Its director, always
a military officer, reports to the deputy director of defense research and

---

* This comparison doesn't take into account the multitude of secret, quasi-secret, and more
or less public offices that the CIA maintains elsewhere in Washington and environs. The
CIA is so scattered that it operates its own bus line, a fleet of "bluebirds" (for their
color) which shuttle between Langley, the Pentagon, the State Department, the Rosslyn
annex in Arlington, and various downtown offices.

engineering, a civilian, who in turn reports to the secretary of defense. The secretary's briefings on NSA matters are given directly to the president or the White House national security staff. When NSA officials attend White House meetings, their names are omitted from published lists of participants. At the working level, NSA coordinates with the Pentagon through the Joint Chiefs' Directorate for Communications-Electronics (J-6), which has responsibility for communications and electronic warfare. In addition to the NSA director, the military supplies to the agency uncounted ("unrevealed" is perhaps the more exact word) thousands of servicemen who are detached as technicians. NSA itself has 15,000 to 17,000 personnel at Fort Meade and something more than a thousand abroad.

NSA's operating sections are the Office of Research and Development (RADE), whose 2,000 personnel refine techniques for intercepting communications; the Office of Communications Security (COMSEC), responsible for the cryptographic equipment and techniques used to transmit sensitive government messages; and the Office of Production (PROD), with 7,500 men. For administrative support, NSA has the Offices of Training Services, Personnel Services, and Security Services—the latter responsible for screening employees and maintaining the physical security of the agency.

If NSA can truly be called a "spy agency," the responsibility belongs to PROD. Literally, PROD's function is to eavesdrop when machines talk to machines, and to translate the codes which are the *lingua franca* of diplomatic and military intercourse. PROD has more than 2,500 listening stations around the world—on military bases; aboard such ships as the *Maddox, Liberty,* and *Pueblo;* aloft on one of the 20-odd "Flying Ear" planes which the Air Force has in the air at any given time; in United States embassies and consulates; in enclaves in friendly nations, the nature of which are concealed (often from the host, too) by cover activities.

An example of an NSA cover activity: The State Department, in a press release issued July 18, 1959, announced the following:

> The governments of Pakistan and of the United States on July 18 signed an agreement at Karachi formalizing previous arrangements between Pakistan and the United States for the establishment and operation of a communications unit at Peshawar, Pakistan.
> This facility is part of a worldwide United States command system and will provide a link between stations in the Middle East and the Pacific areas. It is located at sites outside the city of Peshawar and is staffed by personnel of the United States Air Force. Construction is currently underway to provide living and operating facilities for the members of this unit.[6]

Peshawar is in northern Pakistan near the fabled Khyber Pass. To call the station there a "communications unit" is as fully descriptive as saying,

"Douglas MacArthur was in the Army." Peshawar was an NSA base responsible for monitoring Soviet and Chinese Communist military communications—one which a ranking official in the Washington intelligence community has called "the most important installation we have" in that part of the world (or had—the government of President Ayub Khan in late 1968 refused to extend the ten-year lease on Peshawar, and the United States began looking for suitable quarters elsewhere). Peshawar is within easy eavesdropping range of a host of sensitive Soviet installations—the underground nuclear test site at Semipalatinski, in Soviet Central Asia; the missile test range at Tyuratam, near the Aral Sea; the Sary Shagan Air Defense Center, also near the Aral, which controls the alerting system for incoming missiles and aircraft. To the east is the Chinese nuclear facility in Sinkiang province, and the range where Peking is testing her crude intermediate-range ballistic missiles.

Electronic activity at these points was Peshawar's primary daily target, but technicians also picked up a tremendous volume of ground radio traffic between Soviet field units and their headquarters. This is important because Peshawar is adjacent to the frontier between the Soviet Union and the Sinkiang nuclear site; if the Sino-Soviet wrangling ever deteriorates into ground warfare, United States analysts think the first Russian strike would be for Sinkiang. Thus one Washington official in 1968 called Peshawar "a box seat that we'd be fools to relinquish." The intelligence community protests were to no avail; bargain as it could, the State Department could not persuade the nervous Ayub to permit the base to remain. He listened instead to Soviet warnings that its presence was dangerous (U-2 pilot Powers stopped there on his last, abortive mission) and decided that Moscow's friendship and military and economic aid were more important.

What categories of intelligence does PROD obtain from its installations at Peshawar and elsewhere? Any information which a foreign power transmits over the air, be it the voice interchange between a platoon commander and a higher headquarters; the encrpyted diplomatic traffic between the Soviet Embassy at 1125 16th Street Northwest in Washington and the Soviet Foreign Ministry or the KGB headquarters at 2 Dzezhinsky Street in Moscow; reports of the French ambassador to the president of France; the signals emitted by an air defense system; or the scientific (and espionage) data transmitted by a reconnaissance satellite.

How does PROD obtain its intelligence? Most of it in very unglamorous fashion indeed: from enlisted military men, working under NSA supervisors, who sit at typewriters for an eight-hour duty shift, earphones in place, transcribing code transmissions or operating tape recorders which collect voice communications. The bulk of this material eventually goes to Fort Meade for decoding, translation, and analysis, with the CIA delving heavily into both the raw data and completed summaries for items of interest. In critical areas, translators and analysts make flash evaluations of material (the *Liberty,* for instance, carried both Arab and Israeli linguists, and machines capable of breaking military ciphers used by both powers).

There is considerable overlap of function within the intelligence community in the field of electronics intercepts. A reconnaissance satellite developed by the CIA's research division might take photographs for the agency, and at the same time monitor communications for NSA. A listening station at a location such as Tabriz, Iran, near the Caspian Sea, would have the primary mission of watching Soviet missile shots and plotting Soviet radar defenses; at the same time, it monitors Soviet domestic radio for items of intelligence value, which are circulated to government officials and scholars by a CIA section specializing in foreign broadcast information.* And a ship such as the *Pueblo* searches for tactical naval intelligence as well as for evidence of troop movements on the North Korean mainland. Therefore Washington is technically correct when it denies that the *Liberty* or *Pueblo* are "*NSA* spy ships." But the operative word in both instances is "spy"—an adjective which can't be challenged.

SOMEWHERE DOWN THERE THEY DON'T LIKE US
From high in the sky or on the deck, radar homing and warning systems find the hostile radars . . . fingerprint them . . . provide the real-time intelligence that can mean the difference between mission success or failure.
—*Advertisement of Dalmo Victor Electronic Warfare Systems, Belmont, California, in* Aviation Week and Space Technology Magazine *for November 21, 1966.*

Intercepts of message traffic tell the United States the intentions of foreign powers, but the Pentagon relies upon another branch of electronic espionage to prepare for the actual business of fighting a war. Here the mission is to determine the location and workings of The Other Side's air and missile warning system, and to devise means of hoodwinking it in the event of a United States attack. Responsibility rests with the Defense Intelligence Agency (DIA), created by Secretary McNamara in October 1961 "to coordinate and integrate the finished intelligence that is needed . . . in the Washington area by the Joint Chiefs of Staff and by the Secretary of Defense, by the unified and specified commanders."[7] A separate Defense

---

* The CIA discourages publicity for its monitoring service. Through 1964 the booklets containing transcripts bore this cover notation:
Special Notice
It is requested that recipients of this report make no mention of the _____ _____ _____ _____ when referring by quotation or otherwise to information contained in this report.

The unclassified reports are available in the Library of Congress, and the Communist radio reports in this book came from the _____ _____ _____ _____. But, as the CIA requests, I shan't refer to the _____ _____ _____ _____ by name in chapter notes.

Department directive issued by McNamara on September 9, 1963, during a DIA reorganization, gave the DIA responsibility for developing "target materials," and listed among them the following: "target charts and mosaics; *area, radar prediction analysis graphics;* missile target data sheets and launch site data sheets; hydrographic-oceanographic data sheets; target illustrations; geodetic data sheets; graphic indexes and catalogues of such items; and similar items of target materials established by the unified and specified commanders."[8]

The ferret planes and ELINT ships that prowl the periphery of the Soviet Union and Communist China have equipment that can gather radar signals at distances greater than that from which discernible radar echoes can be returned. On so-called "passive patrols," the spy ship or spy plane will make a sweep down the Communist coast, staying well outside territorial waters, content to read radar signals at the normal volume. But the passive method is grossly time-consuming. The more sophisticated radar sensory equipment isn't activated unless the operators have reason to suspect that prowlers are abroad near the national frontier. A high-speed reconnaissance plane might record only fleeting seconds of a station's signal as it darts along the North Korean coast. Therefore, the intruders poke at the enemy as a schoolboy does at a hornet's nest, feinting toward the shoreline as if attacking, or employing equipment that gives a solitary destroyer the electronic profile of 20 incoming bombers or an armada of warships. The alarmed enemy activates all available warning systems, the intruder obtains readings from them, then quickly and discreetly withdraws.

The military calls this nervy business "electronic stimulation." The resultant data on radar defenses then becomes the raw material for an even nervier enterprise. A United States bomber is laden with electronic countermeasure (ECM) devices programmed to deceive the radar defenses, and runs simulated bombing missions that stop just shy of The Other Side's territory. If defending planes are slow leaving the ground, or impulses are not promptly received from guidance radars of surface-to-air missiles, the ECM is given high points, and the Strategic Air Command goes home with the happy knowledge that had the mission been a real one, Our Side would have won the first round of the war.

The British are assigned credit as the first wartime practitioners of what Sir Winston Churchill called the "queer and deadly game" of ECM, and the principles and techniques they employed against the Germans in 1940 remain valid today, although in highly advanced form. During the early phase of the Battle of Britain, British air intelligence discovered that navigators on German bombers relied upon radio beacon signals transmitted from stations scattered over the Continent. The navigators would lock their directional radio receivers onto the signals and fix their position and direction of travel by computing the angles from which either of the two signals came. The British countered with a device called the "meacom," which intercepted the German signals and retransmitted them, much amplified, from stations in England. German pilots depending upon one of these bogus signals for guidance would be sent scores of miles off course, dropping their bombs at sea or on the unoccupied countryside.

Churchill wrote smugly in his memoirs of the befuddled Luftwaffe pilot who landed a bomber in Devonshire, thinking he was safely back at his base in Nazi-occupied France. Describing British tampering with yet another German guidance system, Churchill wrote: "The success of our efforts was manifest from the acrimonious remarks heard passing between the pathfinding aircraft and their controlling ground stations by our listening instruments."[9]

Late in the war the Germans did come up with a beam guidance system which the British could neither jam nor deflect. But even then electronic intelligence was valuable: By intercepting the incoming beams, the British could forecast with reasonable accuracy the target and the route, time, and height of attack. The British didn't always have enough planes or antiaircraft to beat back the raiders, but fire-fighting and civil defense forces could be mobilized in advance, and the people evacuated. At the end of the war, British intelligence estimated that no more than one-fifth of the German bombs loosened in 1940–41 fell on target. Churchill regarded this as "the equivalent of a considerable victory," for the number that did strike home "was quite enough for our comfort and occupation."

The techniques of ECM are many: A multiple-target generator mounted in an incoming aircraft spews out signals which appear on the radar screen as blips representing other planes; a cast-off mechanism refuses to permit a radar to lock onto the target; a "signal holder" tampers with the echo time of the radar signal by delaying its bounce off the target, or by returning it at a spurious angle and speed.

Similar pranks are played on missile defenses. Here the goal is to (1) inundate the defense system with bogus warheads, so that nuclear weaponry slips through to target, or (2) conceal the trajectory and course of incoming missiles with deceptive devices. Persons knowledgeable in this highly classified area say that, as a general rule, any publicized device is outdated by at least five years. Assuming this rule's validity, the gadgetry of the past nonetheless reveals the intricacy of missile ECM. An early device developed by Sperry-Gyroscope Company consisted of a decoy warhead that emitted a minute-long burst of electronic noise when dropped from the reentry vehicle. The decoy was supposed to take radar's "mind" off anything else that came through the area during the period. Again, warheads were equipped with modernized versions of the old "retransmission" mechanism used by the British two decades ago, which tossed back radar signals at misleading intervals and angles. But any effective decoy must resemble the actual warhead and its behavior from the time it leaves the reentry vehicle until well toward the terminal phase of its flight, and it must return radar signatures matching those of a real warhead.

In the mid-1960s the art of building bogus warheads became so elaborate that someone in the Pentagon's Advanced Research Project Agency finally asked: If we are going to load a missile with all this weight, why not use a second—or third or fourth—*live* warhead, which has equal capacity for confusing defensive systems, and which could overwhelm them through saturation? Ergo, the Pentagon began development of the multiple individual reentry vehicle (MIRV), the so-called "space bus," capable of scattering up to six warheads from a single carrier.

Both qualitatively and quantitatively, aerial and satellite reconnaissance provides the United States with its most valued strategic electronic intelligence on the Soviets. The surveillance is virtually ceaseless: From January 1 through June 30, 1968, to cite a not untypical period, the United States had photo-satellites over the Soviet Union for 117 of 181 days. This included 41 consecutive days from January 18 through February 27, when the CIA suspected an imminent launching of the Soviet version of the MIRV. The longest blackout for the United States was the 20-day period May 16–June 5, occasioned by several launch mishaps at the Air Force's Western Test Range, at Vandenberg Air Force Base, California, from which the satellite spy craft are fired. The Soviets, during the same six-month period, had satellite coverage for 99 of 181 days. During June alone, when France was readying the Tahiti test site for the detonation of her first hydrogen bomb, the Soviets put up no fewer than five of their "Cosmos" series satellites, all programmed to cover the South Pacific. (United States coverage of the same area was intense, but not so continuous as the Soviets'.)

The workhorse among United States spy satellites is the Samos, an acronym for "Satellite and Missile Observation System," and little more is known about it than its name and mission (i.e., surveillance of enemy territory). The Air Force occasionally announces the launching of a Samos from Vandenberg Air Force Base—but says nothing further about flight data or intentions. According to electronic espionage expert John M. Carroll, Samos is so sophisticated that its scientists in 1967 were working on a system whereby photographic film could be developed in flight, with the information on it relayed to earth by radio. Carroll said that straightforward television didn't give the clear resolution required for "some intelligence purposes."[10]

During the early days of satellite reconnaissance, to use the analogy of a Pentagon official, a "good" picture would show the configuration of the greens area of a golf course. By 1960 the satellite camera could find the golf ball on the green; now, according to this official, "We can make out the trademark and the grass stains." The analogy is not completely unrealistic. Using a zoom-lens camera and swooping as close as 50 miles to earth, the satellites regularly snap such good pictures that analysts can read the unit designation letters on Soviet military vehicles (data incorporated into order-of-battle intelligence). A clear view of the subject is not essential. Aerojet General Corporation conducted a study for the U.S. Arms Control and Disarmament Agency in 1967 to determine "whether evidence of production activity going on inside a missile engine production plant can be detected externally. Some of the telltale signs investigated were rail and truck shipments, waste disposal, and multi-sensor observation of static test firings"—each subject to satellite observation.[11] In reporting on the research contract, ACDA never said publicly whether such production could be detected externally. Officials say privately the answer was affirmative.

Keen on-the-ground analysis is necessary to put the satellites' raw data to effective use. In 1961 United States intelligence knew well in advance that the Soviets planned a nuclear test at their Novaya Zemlya site just south of the Arctic Circle, a bleak, icy place with only a few hours of sunlight daily during the winter. On October 30 a 60-megaton blast was detonated there—and almost simultaneously the Soviets launched two satellites from the Archangel test site, adjacent to Novaya Zemlya. The orbital pattern was one which the Soviets had never used previously, with the satellites soaring southward over Novaya Zemlya towards Moscow. Analysts ultimately concluded that the Soviets were using the satellites to simulate incoming missiles, checking the effects of radioactivity on their guidance systems—information needed to engineer an anti-ballistic missile system. When the Soviets began preparing ABM sites near Moscow two years later, therefore, Washington was not surprised.

Both the United States and the Soviets shield aerial espionage behind semantics and euphemisms. In 1966 the Interior Department announced its EROS (for "Earth Resources Observation Satellite") program, in which a satellite would make 15 orbits daily "to complete data on natural resources," its recorders and cameras operating on command from the ground and dumping data to receiving stations. EROS's television camera was built with a keen eye, capable of transmitting images with 3,500 scan lines per picture—compared with only 525 lines for the commercial TV set in a citizen's living room. A civilian project? Few persons in official Washington (or embassies there) think EROS was intended to work solely for the Interior Department's Geological Survey, and, after considerable interagency wrangling, responsibility for the project was shifted to the National Aeronautical and Space Administration. A set of photos given relatively wide circulation in the government in 1968 showed details of the French nuclear test site at Landes, south of Bordeaux—and some of the people displaying them bragged that they came from the camera developed (by CIA researchers) for use in EROS.

Manned and drone planes supplement the satellites. Throughout 1964, spy planes watched the Chinese prepare for their first nuclear detonation in the Lop Nor Basin of Sinkiang province (even to photographing the manufacture of fissionable material for the device at a plutonium reactor in Pootaw, Inner Mongolia). Thus the United States announced in mid-1964 that the test was imminent, and gave an anticipated time just before the actual detonation—preventing surprise that could have panicked the public, and avoiding November embarrassment for Johnson. The YF-12A has supplanted the U-2. Johnson said in 1964 that it could fly higher than 70,000 feet at better than 2,000 miles an hour; more than a score are now in service. A close relative, the SR-71 long-range reconnaissance aircraft, is officially called "one of the highest-performance planes ever to enter service." It is capable of flying at more than three times the speed of sound at altitudes above 80,000 feet; the SR-71 went into service in early 1965 and has accomplished more than a dozen fly-over-the-Arctic reconnaissance missions from Beale Air Force Base, California.

The U-2s remaining in the United States stockpile are used primarily to keep watch on Fidel Castro's Cuba. Even allowing for exaggeration by Castro, the U-2s are very busy craft. In a letter to the United Nations on April 24, 1964, Cuba claimed U-2 flights had violated her territory 546 times between January 1, 1963, and April 20, 1964. The United States confirmed the flights, but not the number, saying that they were necessary "to avoid the deception" that permitted construction of missile bases in Cuba by the Soviets in 1962, and warning that any interference with the U-2s would create a "highly dangerous situation." President Johnson called the U-2s a substitute for on-site inspection, saying, "I do think it is essential that we . . . know whether any missiles are being shipped into Cuba. We will have to maintain our reconnaissance and overflights." Fidel was not mollified. "They [the United States] say they can make photos of Cuba with satellites. Then why do they make these flights? To humiliate Cuba? We shall consider these flights as armed aggression . . . and shall repel this aggression with arms." The Soviets didn't permit Castro to continue the argument. They withdrew an advanced radar system that the Cubans had used to guide their SAM-2 surface-to-air missiles, the only weapon on the island capable of touching the U-2s.

Similar bombast is heard frequently from the Communist Chinese about the overflights. A typical specimen is this New China News Agency broadcast of February 27, 1968:

A U.S. military plane intruded over China's territorial waters in the area east of Namoa Island in Kwangtung Province between 0840 and

0846 on 27 February. Between 1117 and 1121 on the same day another U.S. military plane intruded into China's territorial air space over the Yunghsing Island of the Hsish Islands in Kwangtung Province. A spokesman of the Chinese Foreign Ministry has been authorized in relation to these provocations by the U.S. military planes, to issue the 451st serious warning.

Try as they may, the Chinese have never succeeded in shooting down a manned reconnaissance aircraft—although the United States intelligence community does admit to the occasional loss of a drone plane.* In general terms, the drones concentrate on south and south central China, adjacent to North Vietnam, while the U-2s, SR-71s, and YF-12As snoop around the nuclear sites in Sinkiang province. The drones, which fly at a considerably lower altitude than the manned planes, are better suited for gathering tactical intelligence on movements of troops and supplies. The drones are dropped from mother planes (chiefly the C-130 Hercules), take aerial photographs of their target areas, and are guided back into friendly territory, where they either land or drop film cartridges.

The Soviet manned spy planes concentrate on China, and Washington knows (or has revealed) little about their intrusions into United States air space. In May 1963 two Soviet craft flew some 30 miles deep into Alaska and were quickly intercepted by F-102 fighters. Washington also received unconfirmable reports in 1964 of allegations by Soviet officers that in February of that year a new Soviet plane had flown over San Francisco, Oakland, New York, northern New Jersey, and Hawaii without being detected.[12] But no such claims by the Soviets—nor accusations by the United States—have ever been aired publicly, nor are any likely. They would constitute, first, an admission of violations of U.S. air space, and second, an admission that Washington could not do anything about the flights. So far as is known, the Soviets have never lost a spy plane to hostile gunfire.

Moscow boasts of planes with performances bettering those of the U-2 and YF-12A. "Modern Soviet aircraft are able to fly at the speed of 2,000 miles per hour at altitudes exceeding 100,000 feet," the information department of the Soviet Embassy in Washington said in a February 20, 1968, press release commemorating the 50th anniversary of the Soviet armed forces. (The United States is willing to accept the speed and altitude separately, but not in the same plane.)

The Soviet "spy plane" most familiar to United States intelligence is the Berieo Be-12 Mail, an amphibious antisubmarine patrol craft which often erratically lunges at NATO shorelines in apparent attempts to stimu-

* The last Chinese claim of bagging a U-2 came in 1964, when a New China News Agency broadcast said that "the air force of the Chinese People's Liberation Army" had shot down the third plane in as many years. CIA officials say flatly that the Chinese did no such thing.

late radar responses. The Mail in flight is as fat and awkward as a well-fed duck, but nonetheless can cruise for hours. Aside from harassing (and amusing) NATO radar, the Mail craft spend much of their time in the Bering Straits and off Scandinavia's North Cape, trying to detect Polaris submarines bound for the Arctic ice cap above the Soviet Union.

Soviet indifference to high-flying spy planes is perhaps attributable to former Premier Khrushchev (or to an early Soviet emphasis on satellite reconnaissance). When talking with former Senator William Benton in 1964, Khrushchev said that U-2 flights should be abandoned and more reliance placed in satellite photography. "If you wish, I can show you photos of military bases taken from outer space," Khrushchev told Benton. "I will show them to President Johnson if he wishes. Why don't we exchange such photographs?" Washington quickly replied that it didn't think space observation a suitable substitute, for satellite technology was then at the stage where mapping of target areas and measuring of distances were unreliable.

Spy ships are a sore subject with the U.S. Navy, and justifiably so. To the general public, the Navy behaved with peasant stupidity in permitting the *Liberty* to be shot to pieces by a "friendly power," and in losing the *Pueblo* to a fourth-rate power without firing a shot in response. In pained righteousness, the Navy states that these public impressions are erroneous ones.* "We're just like a cab driver," said a high Navy official during the *Pueblo* crisis. "A fare gets in and tells the cabbie where to go. There's no argument, and the cabbie has no say in the situation. Same thing in the *Pueblo*. NSA gets aboard, gives us a course, and off we sail. We're not a 'Navy vessel on a Navy mission'—we're hauling around spooks."

The lack of military operational control over spy vessels appalls Pentagon commanders (and also State Department officials who must help to solve the rhubarbs that result when one of them gets into trouble). At a background briefing for newsmen during the *Pueblo* crisis, a high State Department official (talking under ground rules which forbid his identification, then and now) conceded a part of the uncertainty over the vessel's route stemmed from some "purely technical messages"—messages that "did not come through command channels [i.e., military channels] at all" and were not "available to us" for about one week after the capture. He said they were finally located in an unnamed catacomb of the Federal bureaucracy—that is, at NSA, among the intelligence data which the *Pueblo*

* The week the *Pueblo* was seized, the Air Force lost four unarmed hydrogen bombs in a plane crash in Greenland, prompting the following authenticated conversation between an Air Force officer and a Navy officer in a Pentagon coffee shop:
  Air Force officer (patronizingly): "You fellows persuaded the North Koreans to give you back your boat yet?"
  Navy officer: "I haven't heard anything this morning. By the way, though, are y'all still digging in the snow for those bombs?"

had collected and sent to headquarters for analysis. The delay in locating the information should not be minimized, for the issue of whether the *Pueblo* had in fact violated North Korean waters guided United States policy planning during the first days after the capture.

Any mission, regardless of its nature, can be disguised under the catchall word "patrol." Such was the case long before the United States began dispatching ELINT ships through the world. President Roosevelt, in 1941, sent "patrol" ships with freighters carrying Lend-Lease shipments to Great Britain. Over presidential objections, congressional isolationists had put a provision into the Lend-Lease Act that "nothing in this act shall be construed to authorize or to permit the authorization of convoying vessels by naval vessels of the United States." Henry Stimson, Roosevelt's Secretary of War, objected to FDR's action after several of the destroyers were attacked by German raiders, with the loss of American lives. Stimson wrote in his diary on April 23, 1941, after a talk with Roosevelt:

> He kept reverting to the fact that the force in the Atlantic was merely going to be a patrol to watch for any aggressor and to report that to America. I answered there, with a smile on my face, saying, 'But you are not going to report the presence of the German fleet to the Americas. You are going to report it to the British fleet.' I wanted him to be honest with himself. To me it seems a clearly hostile act to the Germans, and I am prepared to take the responsibility of it. He seems to be trying to hide it into the character of a purely reconnaissance action which it really is not.[13]

On August 15, 1967, the Coast Guard craft *Edisto* and *East Wind,* both identified officially as "oceanographic research vessels," left Trondheim, Norway, for a scheduled 8,000-mile circumnavigation of the Arctic. The route originally announced would have taken them north of the Soviet islands of Novaya Zemlya and Severnaya Zemlya, which lie above the Soviet land mass. As the voyage progressed, however, the ships claimed that they encountered heavy ice north of Severnaya Zemlya. The United States Embassy in Moscow informed the Soviet foreign ministry that it would be necessary for them to change course and pass through the Vilkitsky Straits south of the island to proceed from the Kara Sea into the Laptev Sea and continue the mission. The straits are 22 nautical miles wide at their narrowest point; the Soviets claim a territorial limit of 12 miles. But the United States claimed the right of free passage on the grounds that the straits are international waters regardless of the overlap of territorial waters, because they connect two parts of the high seas.

The Soviets told the *Edisto* and the *East Wind* to keep out of the Vilkitsky Straits, asserting that any attempted passage through them would constitute a "violation of Soviet frontiers." Whereupon the United States withdrew the ships under strong protest and sent them elsewhere, saying that the Soviet position "has acted to frustrate a useful scientific endeavor and thus to deprive the international scientific community of research data of considerable significance."[14]

As stated earlier in this chapter, Novaya Zemlya and Severnaya Zemlya are highly secret nuclear test installations—the Soviet equivalent of Los Alamos, New Mexico, or Jackass Flats, Nevada. Why were the Soviets unwilling to permit the "oceanographic research" vessels to pass near the islands?

Officially, the *Edisto* and *East Wind* were checking "ice floe" patterns; water salinity, depth, and currents; and the type of ocean bottom beneath the Arctic. A more complete list of EEIs (Essential Elements of Information, in intelligence parlance) for the mission would include the following: (a) the capabilities and frequencies of the radar system guarding the Soviets' new anti-ballistic missile system, one anchor of which is south of Novaya Zemlya, the other slightly to the west of Severnaya Zemlya; (b) possible routes for Polaris submarines to follow during their frequent forays along the northern tier of the Soviet Union; (c) the conditions that submarines would encounter were they to attempt prolonged submergence in Arctic waters in the same area; and (d) any spare bits of information that might come along concerning the nuclear test site.

The U.S. Naval Oceanographic Office spent almost a quarter of a billion dollars in fiscal 1968, $100 million of it for oceanographic operations, which are defined officially as "direct support of operating forces through the collection of environmental data by specially equipped ships, submarines, aircraft, and buoys as well as other devices."[15] Covered by this definition are such mundane chores as maintaining nautical charts of bays and waterways. At the other extreme is a "Sonar Atlas" showing the sound track left by every submarine in the world as it passes through the water. When a Soviet sub encounters the "acoustical fence" built in 1964 along the continental shelf of the eastern United States, computers immediately establish its identity by checking its "electronic signature" against those on file in the Sonar Atlas.

The Navy intelligence mission most conspicuous to the target nation is the standing patrol which cruises back and forth across the entrance to Havana Harbor. The destroyer is visible from the upper floor of the Habana Libre (ex-Habana Hilton) Hotel, and the Cuban press routinely announces when one ship replaces another on the station. The excitable Cubans insist that the destroyer is capable of "tapping any telephone in Cuba, including Fidel's"—a feat which, while strategically attractive, is technologically impossible. But the destroyer does perform useful tasks. It keeps current the registry of Free World and Polish flag vessels which arrive in Cuba, and which are thereafter barred from carrying United States government-financed cargoes from American ports. (From January 1, 1963, through November 1, 1967, 216 ships went on the black list.)

Technicians on the destroyer monitor Cuban radio and watch Cuban television. A monitoring report on a Fidel Castro speech telecast August 11, 1967, from the Chaplin Theater in Havana begins with an editor's note: "On a large backdrop behind the two tables seating the [Latin American Solidarity Organization] conference dignitaries is a large picture of Ché Guevara and the slogan, in large letters, 'The duty of all revolutionaries is to make revolution!' " The editor's note said that the television camera "centers on each person as he is introduced"—ranging from President Osvaldo Dorticos to Stokely Carmichael, "the delegate of honor representing the people of the United States."*

The destroyer patrol off Havana has little tactical military value, although it does dissuade the Cubans from bringing any vessels of strategic importance into the port of Havana.

Conversely, the Cubans are very cooperative with the Soviets in "oceanographic research" in the Caribbean. In 1964 the Cuban Academy of Scientists issued an itinerary for a Cuban-Soviet expedition utilizing the Soviet vessels *Kovalivsky* and *Lomobosov*—from the Florida straits up to the west coast of the Florida peninsula, just off Panama City, Pensacola, and Mobile Bay; thence westward to New Orleans and Houston, and ending finally off Veracruz, Mexico. Coast Guard intelligence, commenting upon the route, noted its proximity to Tyndall Air. Force Base and Eglin Field, both sites of what were called "critical tests on material and defense equipment." The Cubans contributed two smaller vessels—the *Xiphias* and the *Delfin*—for work along the insular shelf of their island.[16] The vessels carried 22 Soviet scientists and 12 Cubans, augmented at mid-voyage by a group of Czechs. A defecting Cuban scientist later told the Coast Guard that the primary purpose of the expedition was to gain information on United States submarine and sub-chasing exercises.

Even legitimate scientific research can have strategic value. The Soviet vessel *Vladimir Obruchev* spent considerable time in 1965–67 on an "oil exploration survey" along the north coast of Cuba. Cuba subsequently announced its intentions to drill for oil in the area covered by the *Vladimir Obruchev,* which indicated that her mission perhaps was what the Cubans had claimed. But Coast Guard officers said that the vessel charted contours of the ocean bottom—valuable information for submarine commanders assigned to sneak up on the Gulf coast. The United States did not ignore the

---

* Monitoring reports from the destroyer must not be accepted as gospel. While researching this book I encountered a Havana Radio broadcast, circa July 1964, which chronicled the arrival of a "Joseph Kettles of the *Philadelphia Inquirer*" in Cuba for the 26th of July celebration. I was the *Inquirer* man in question, and I never remember traveling under such a name, drunk or sober.

"oil exploration" cruise: Coast Guard planes kept it under daily surveillance, making passes low enough to rattle the wardroom crockery. One photograph was made by a plane flying lower than the *Vladimir Obruchev's* radio mast.[17]

Elsewhere on United States coasts, the Soviets have expressed interest in the Cape Kennedy missile launch area, Vandenberg Air Force Base in central California, the Army electronic research center at Fort Monmouth, New Jersey, and the submarine bases at Norfolk, Virginia, and Portsmouth, New Hampshire. In 1960 the trawler *Vega* sat among United States ships off Long Island to watch the test firing of a dummy Polaris missile from the submarine *George Washington.* And, because the proceedings were in international waters, nothing could be done about the intrusion.

The well-organized Soviet spy fleet even has "command ships" for different areas of the world. The converted icebreaker *Navel,* for example, is overseer of the tracking and communications vessels which watch United States missile shots and satellite launches across the South Atlantic, relaying to Moscow information gathered by sister ships.

A NATO fleet exercise gives the Western allies a chance to survey the Soviet spy fleet and the planes which work in conjunction with them. In October 1966, British jet fighters intercepted no fewer than ten U.S.S.R. Bison and Bear reconnaissance planes 100 miles north of Scotland—apparently on a training exercise, with teams of trawlers, tugs, and submarines shadowing British and other NATO vessels in the North Sea. The United States makes similar deployments during Warsaw Pact and Soviet fleet maneuvers—individual commanders frequently fume about having to dodge spy ships which cut across their bows, but fleet brass welcome them as valuable live subjects for training exercises.

United States and Soviet submarines spend much of their underseas time trailing one another; according to leaks from a Navy court of inquiry, the last mission of the *SS Scorpion,* which vanished last May en route from Gibraltar to its home base in Norfolk, was to check on a Soviet nuclear-powered submarine not far from its course. The *Scorpion* completed the assignment May 21, radioed fleet headquarters that it was coming home, and was never heard from again.

If any credence is to be placed in Peking Radio, the Soviet spy ships are also busy around Communist China. On April 29, 1968, a New China News Agency international service broadcast in Mandarin complained, "In July 1967 alone the Soviet reconnaissance vessels *Gidrolog* and *Gidrograf* made six intrusions into East China coastal waters to engage in espionage activities, flagrantly encroaching on CPR [Chinese People's Republic] sovereignty and endangering its security." The charge was made during a protest against "espionage activities and serious violations of law" by the captain and crew of the Soviet vessel *Komsomolets Ukrainy* while in a

Chinese port on April 4. The captain and second mate were expelled, and the ship escorted from China under armed guard. According to NCNA: "In his deposition to the Chinese Whampoa frontier defense authorities, Soviet Captain Kosyakov explicitly admitted: 'While sailing along the navigation route in the Humen area on 23 March of this year' Ponomarchuk, second mate, 'took photographs of the military vessels of the CPR.' He also admitted that the photographs had been stealthily 'taken from the cabin of the first mate.' . . . Kosyakov's deposition was written in black and white and the evidence cannot be disputed. Furthermore, the camera . . . and the negatives, which he twice vainly tried to expose for the purpose of destroying the evidence, were all confiscated. . . ." The statement indicated that the Soviet interest was in a "fortress" at Humen.

So goes the chronicle. The major world powers spy upon one another incessantly by land, by sea, and by air, and complain loudly and publicly when a rival's operation aborts and is exposed. The American public fills its bookshelves with spy books, true and fictional, and vicariously shares the espionage adventures and erotic activities of James Bond. A studious reader of congressional appropriations hearings, and of the electronic trade press, is soon disabused of any notion that "Gentlemen do not read each other's mail," as Henry L. Stimson stormed in 1929, when, after becoming Secretary of State, he learned of (and promptly disbanded) the Department's cryptanalytical division.* Yet for reasons incomprehensible to the outside observer, Administrations persist in taking the White House version of the Fifth Amendment when Congress asks for information on specific espionage undertakings—a policy which no amount of past embarrassment has affected in the slightest.

Which brings us back to the *Maddox,* and the Gulf of Tonkin incidents.

---

* Stimson's latter-day successor, Dean Rusk, was once heard to say most jovially: "The hell we don't—we read anything we can put our hands on."

Chapter Five

WHAT REALLY HAPPENED ON THE "MADDOX"

In late June 1964 the United States intelligence community* received reports that the North Vietnamese were installing Soviet antiaircraft defenses along their coast, and around the cities of Hanoi, Vinh, Haiphong, and Thai Nguyen, among others. There was also discussion—but no firm information—of the possibility that the Communist Chinese would supply Hanoi with one of their crude submarines for a suicide attack against the American aircraft carrier *Ticonderoga,* an attractive and more or less stationary target on Yankee Station off Da Nang, as a gnat-versus-elephant propaganda coup. The intelligence agencies produced a flood of reports about suspicious Chinese troop and plane movements in Kwangtung and Kwangsi provinces, southernmost in the country, and of aircraft deployments to Chinese-owned Hainan Island, in the Gulf of Tonkin. On June 28 the Chinese imposed severe restrictions on foreign shipping using the 15-mile-wide strait between Hainan and the Luichow Peninsula, which juts into the Gulf from Kwangtung Province. The orders, issued in the name of Premier Chou En-lai, forbade ships to use photographic or radar equipment, restricted them to the middle of the channel, and said they must obey any challenge. The Chinese demanded 48 hours' notice from vessels entering the straits, as well as full disclosure of their nationality, tonnage, cargo, and destination.

With strategic bombing of North Vietnam high on the list of contingency plans before President Johnson, and with fears of Chinese intentions a great imponderable, the intelligence community, through an inter-agency reconnaissance target selection committee, began working up orders in early July for a multi-purpose mission in the Gulf of Tonkin for a United States ship.

The patrol was to be the fourth in the Gulf since United States involve-

* The community includes, in no particular order, the CIA, the National Security Agency, the State Department's Bureau of Intelligence and Research, the Defense Intelligence Agency, and the intelligence sections of the Atomic Energy Commission and the FBI (although the latter seldom has a role in strategic intelligence of the type involved here).

ment became major—one patrol in 1962, one in 1963, and the third in March 1964. All were a part of the intelligence community's "DeSoto" series—one-ship patrols along the Sino-Soviet coasts to collect information on both "military and civil activity of the Asiatic Communist bloc," as stated in the formal orders establishing the series. Ships were to patrol on a random basis, carrying a communications van, a mobile photography unit, and a photographer. Specific instructions varied from mission to mission, depending upon intelligence requirements.

The Defense Intelligence Agency had primary responsibility for drafting this particular mission plan, through its offices of collection, production, and special activities. DIA coordinated requests through a permanent inter-agency committee on reconnaissance target selection which meets daily at the Pentagon. NSA made recommendations on what was needed to update its "electronic profile" of the North Vietnamese coastal and air defenses. Persons with knowledge of electronic intelligence say that the period when new radar defenses are being installed is critical. Once they are in place, and identified, all that is needed is a periodic "inventory" to see what has been added or removed. What NSA wants to avoid is suddenly being called upon to produce an electronic profile of an area and having to admit that its files are barren, or outdated. Thus NSA maintains profiles even of United States allies. The CIA, which is responsible for amassing "geographic intelligence," wanted detailed photographs of coastal and island installations—taken from sea level—for use in planning special operations.* To a lesser degree, CIA wanted information on any changes in ports or harbors that could be detected from the sea.

The mission plan was completed the first week of July and reviewed and approved by the director of Central Intelligence, John McCone; by Dr. Eugene G. Fubini, who as deputy director of defense research and engineering, working directly under McNamara, was responsible for NSA; and, routinely, by the White House national security staff and State's Bureau of Intelligence and Research. The Joint Chiefs of Staff on July 15 transmitted the order for the patrol to Admiral Ulysses Grant Sharp, Jr., United States commander in the Pacific (CINPAC, by military abbreviation), who passed it down the chain of command to Admiral Thomas H. Moorer, commander in chief of the Pacific fleet (and later Chief of Naval Operations), and Vice Admiral Roy L. Johnson, commander of the Seventh Fleet. As operational commander, Johnson assigned the mission to Destroyer Division 192, commanded by Captain John J. Herrick.

* There was no shortage of geographic intelligence on North Vietnam. When the French left Indochina, the CIA obtained the maps, charts, and other minutiæ that the French military had accumulated by the ton during its years in Vietnam. Mundane stuff, for the most part, but an army operating in a foreign country needs to know whether a bridge on a remote rural road can support an armored personnel carrier; the grid pattern of the power system (the better to plan strategic bombing, or sabotage); and the berthing capacity of its ports.

The division consisted of three destroyers; Herrick chose as the patrol vessel the somewhat venerable *Maddox,* built by the Bath Iron Works Corporation, Bath, Maine, and commissioned at the Boston Navy Yard June 2, 1944. Her most exciting moment had come on January 21, 1945, when a Japanese *Kamikaze* pilot crashed into her wardroom in the western Pacific, killing one officer and seven men. Herrick wasn't particularly fond of the *Maddox,* and since assuming command of the division had "kept his flag" (i.e., his command and his living quarters) on another of the destroyers, the *USS Pickering.* But the *Pickering* was plagued with electrical problems that summer, and so Herrick switched to the *Maddox.*

The order from Washington, in its general guidance section, referred to the original JCS directive establishing the DeSoto patrol series. It repeated the geographic limitations: "The CPA [closest point of approach] to the Chicom [Chinese Communist] coast is 15NM [nautical miles]. CPA to the North Vietnamese coast is 8NM. CPA to North Vietnamese islands is 4NM." The order continued:

> The primary purpose of this patrol is to determine DRV [Democratic Republic of Vietnam] coastal activity along the full extent of the patrol track.
> Other specific intelligence requirements are as follows:
> a. Location and identification of all radar transmitters, and estimate of range capabilities;
> b. Navigational and hydro information along the routes traversed and particular navigational light characteristics, landmarks, buoys, currents, and tidal information, river mouths and channel accessibility;
> c. Monitoring junk force with density of surface traffic pattern;
> d. Sampling electronic environment radars and navigation aids;
> e. Photography of opportunities in support of above.* In addition, include photographs as best detail track would permit of all prominent landmarks and islands, particularly in vicinity of rivers and built-up areas; conduct coastal radarscope photography by ship which is transmitting from Point A, which is the end of the mission.

At another point the orders directed the *Maddox* to "stimulate Chicom-North Vietnamese electronic reaction." McNamara told the Senate Foreign Relations Committee on February 20, 1968, that the language "means they turn on certain kinds of equipment on board the *Maddox* which, in turn, leads the Chicoms or the North Vietnamese to turn on the radars so that we can measure the radar frequencies, that was clearly one of their objectives."†[1]

---

* In essence, take any pictures possible.
† The Chicoms and North Vietnamese would turn on their radars because the "electronic stimulation" gear would make the *Maddox* appear to be an incoming squadron of attacking aircraft or naval vessels.

The Joint Chiefs of Staff, in approving the patrol, recognized the tenseness of the situation in the Gulf of Tonkin and elsewhere in Southeast Asia. The directive to Admiral Sharp included these paragraphs:

A. Last DeSoto patrol in Gulf of Tonkin was made in March. Weather at that time greatly precluded visual intelligence collection.
B. U.S. has stepped up assistance to RVN [Republic of Vietnam] including stationing of CVA TG [the task group including the carrier *Ticonderoga*] at mouth of Gulf of Tonkin.
C. There have been considerable articles in news media discussing possibility of action against NVN [North Vietnam].
D. *Activity in 34-A operations has increased.*

The last sentence referred to the South Vietnamese sea raids above the DMZ. No further explanation of "34-A Operations" was given in the order, for none was needed—CINPAC and the Seventh Fleet knew the term well, for they were fully apprised of both the planning and the execution of the raids.

The existence of the 34-A activities was mentioned in at least one other cable involving DeSoto patrols in this period. On July 10, Admiral Sharp's command authorized his fleet units involved in DeSoto patrols to "contact COMUSMACV [Commander, United States Military Assistance, Vietnam] for any additional intelligence required for prevention of mutual interference with 34-A Operations and such communications arrangements as may be desired."

Herrick received information copies of all the orders mentioning the 34-A Operations along with his directive on the DeSoto patrol.

Hoots of disappointment and disbelief resounded through the *Maddox* when the crew learned she was leaving her comfortable patrol duty off Japan for a mission in other waters. For the single men, it meant farewell to what one of them called "the R & R delights of Tokyo, which is the reason most of us chose the Navy anyway." For the many married men aboard, it meant the death of a promising rumor. "There had been all sorts of speculation that we were going to cut off our voyage early and go back to the States," recollects Californian Patrick N. Park, then a Sonarman Second Class. As the *Maddox* headed south from Japan, Park noted a peculiar reticence among officers. "For the first time in my career there wasn't any good scuttlebutt as to where we were going. Very unusual."[2]

The *Maddox* stopped first at Keelung, the Formosan port that is also an extremely busy listening station for the National Security Agency, responsible for monitoring the Chinese mainland in the immediate vicinity, as well as coastal traffic. Just as the *Maddox* berthed, there was another unusual occurrence. Division officers collected cameras from all crewmen and put them under lock and key. "The order was pretty direct," says Park. "If you were caught with one after the order, you would go on report. I'd never heard of anything like that before, even in combat during the second world war. The idea crossed my mind that I should keep it and see if I could get some pictures of whatever it was that we were going to do. Then I said, Don't be silly, and turned it in."

Soon after the *Maddox* docked, a crane hoisted up a box the size of a truck van and deposited it on the torpedo deck between the smokestacks. A complement of enlisted men (nine Navy, six Marines) and a Navy officer came aboard with it. Herrick has explained its content thus: "It looked just like a truck van, army type, khaki colored.* It just contained extra receivers, extra radio receivers."

Q. Stuff you normally don't have aboard a destroyer?

A. That's right . . . not for our own circuits. If you're going to listen to somebody else, you're going to have to have extra equipment.[3]

Several antennae jutted from the van. Its personnel strung wires between the *Maddox's* stacks. "The crew was ordered to stay clear of it," Park says. However, no guard was posted, and *Maddox* crewmen working in the area got frequent glimpses inside the door. They saw seats for three or four men, or standing room for perhaps eight men, with cabinets of electronic equipment jammed along all walls. Cooling units mounted on top of the van kept the interior temperature at a bearable level.

The enlisted men assigned to the van shared quarters with the *Maddox* crew, while their commander, Navy Lieutenant Gerrell Dean Moore, moved into "officers' country." Everyone on board soon knew the newcomers were highly skilled communications technicians, and many of them Vietnamese linguists as well. "Damned sharp, every one of them," a *Maddox* officer says. Moore and three of the communications technicians came from the Naval Security Activity, based at Taipei, Taiwan—a cover name for a unit which specializes in radio and other communications intercepts. Three of the Marines came from the First Composite Radio Company, whose home base then was listed at Kaneohe Bay, Hawaii—again, a cover name for intercept activity directed by the National Security Agency. Another Navy communications technician came from the Naval Security Activity at Kamiseya, Japan, also an NSA operation. The remainder were all from the Naval Communications Station at San Miguel, the Philippines.

James Stankevitz, a radarman from Stevens Point, Wisconsin, was a little uneasy about the newcomers. While in Keelung he talked with a sailor from another destroyer who said that his ship had carried "The Black Box" earlier in the year. "He told me his tin can had been buzzed

---

* Recollections of the color of what came to be known as "The Black Box" vary, with some crewmen avowing it was deck-gray, others "hazy gray," others dapple gray. Since Herrick was custodian of The Box, let's call it khaki.

by planes and boats during the mission." (The sailor didn't tell Stankevitz the target of the mission; Communist China is probable, for the March DeSoto patrol did not encounter North Vietnamese naval or air surveillance.) But Stankevitz says the crew was more curious than nervous: "We still didn't know where we were going."[4]

Varying stories went around ship about the purpose of the van. One man got the idea "we were supposed to be photographing the coast for mapping purposes." Another man who talked with one of the Marines in the chow line says he was told that the crew was "picking up locations and frequencies of radio stations and other sorts of transmitters." Yet another said, "I thought they were going to try and track a satellite, or missile launch, and keep it away from China if it got off course."

While in Keelung, Herrick and other officers on the *Maddox* received thorough briefings on the mission. The officer with direct command over the *Maddox* was the captain, Commander Herbert L. Ogier, a 41-year-old native of Baltimore and an Annapolis graduate. However, as commander of the destroyer division, Herrick had overall authority over the mission. Herrick says he was aware of the DeSoto patrols and similar intelligence missions, although this was to be his first. But of the 34-A Operations, he avows, "It was hinted at in our briefings but nothing—no specifics. We were pretty much in the dark as to these things . . . no specifics as to where . . . they [the briefing officers] said there might be '34-Alpha Operations' and we were to stay clear of them."

The *Maddox* left Keelung and steamed directly to Yankee Station to take on fuel from a tanker. The refueling was in progress on July 31 and Park had the "forward line watch"—that is, to the front of the vessel. "I saw a bunch of 'rooster tails' [wakes] of patrol boats on the horizon. They were so far away I couldn't tell their nationality." Ogier simply told the crew, "They're not our patrol boats," and the first radio report dispatched by the *Maddox* surmised that they were Soviet-made P-6 patrol boats manned by North Vietnamese. Herrick now says, "We were somewhat surprised at first, but later assured ourselves that these were South Vietnamese patrol boats and that they were just exercising."

The patrol boats were South Vietnamese, but they were not "just exercising." What the *Maddox* crew saw was the return voyage of a 34-Alpha Operation.

At approximately 2:00 P.M. on July 30, four South Vietnamese patrol craft—the Swift boats supplied by the United States—left the naval base at Da Nang, put out to sea to avoid North Vietnamese junks posted above the DMZ as a screen, and proceeded north.

About midnight, the group divided. Two boats headed directly for Hon Me, 145 miles north of the DMZ, and 12 kilometers (7.3 miles) offshore;

the others sailed for Hon Ngu, another island 30 miles south of Hon Me,
four kilometers (2.4 miles) off the busy port city of Vinh.

At 12:21 A.M. on July 31, the South Vietnamese attacked Hon Me. The
battle plan called for South Vietnamese marines—the ones trained by the
United States Navy and the CIA paramilitary advisers during the preceding
months—to storm ashore with satchel charges of explosives and destroy
the radar station. However, because of unexpectedly heavy return fire from
the North Vietnamese, no landing attempt was made. The raiders had to
be content wtih raining fire onto the island with an unmounted 55-mm.
recoilless rifle, brought aboard especially for the mission, and with 40-mm.
and 20-mm. guns, part of the vessel's normal armament.

Meanwhile, the other two boats bombarded Hon Ngu, starting a series
of explosions along the beach. For at least half an hour the fire continued,
then the South Vietnamese put back to sea and regrouped for the return
voyage to Da Nang. In late morning they passed within sight of the Maddox
refueling.

The July 31 raids marked the first time South Vietnamese vessels bom-
barded North Vietnamese islands. In previous forays the 34-A Operations
had put ashore saboteurs and intelligence agents and had stopped and
searched suspicious craft, taking an occasional prisoner believed to be a
Viet Cong infiltrator—but never had they directed gunfire at islands.

The sight of the patrol boat sent shivers of excitement through Park.
"I suddenly got the idea we were going to be in for something," he remembers. The word was passed that mail could be given to the tanker, so he
jotted a quick note to his wife that "we still don't know where we are going,
but I think it's a mission off the coast of Russia [sic]." The mailbag was
passed, and the *Maddox* turned north.

During the afternoon, the *Maddox's* crew's last contact with the outside
world ended. Commander Ogier spoke over the public address system:
The *Maddox* was going into the Gulf of Tonkin. Ogier said the vessel would
stay in international waters, and "it shouldn't be dangerous." The *Maddox*
would be doing "observation by radio of the coast, and also observation
of water conditions." (One crewman says he had never heard of the Gulf
of Tonkin. "First thing I did was run find a map to see where the hell it
was.")

Herrick, however, recognized the mission as something less than a jolly
summer outing. With the veteran sailor's eye for position, he notes that
the Gulf is a "fairly enclosed body of water and once you're inside, you're
surrounded on three sides by what could be considered even at those times
rather unfriendly territory."

The route outlined by the intelligence people was to be covered over nine days, extending "almost to Kwangsi province in the south of China, then around a little island named Weichou-Tao and back down and out of the Gulf again," Herrick said. Weichou-Tao is 40 miles due south of the Pei-Hai Peninsula. Under his orders Herrick could not come within 15 nautical miles of Chinese territory; thus, on his pass above Weichou-Tao, he would pass within about 25 miles of the mainland. The *Maddox* was given checkpoints which it was to touch at appointed times during the mission (apparently because NSA and DIA wanted a sampling of the hours when North Vietnamese radar was operating at full capacity, and because of the desire to find a traffic pattern for the junks). Herrick says the patrol plan "gave us plenty of time. We didn't have to speed at any great speed, and we had time to loiter here and there, to circle or go back and forth, or whatever we wanted to do." The first check point, Alpha (others followed in alphabetical sequence) was a "little island right above the 17th parallel called 'Tiger Island', or Hon Gio," seven miles off the North Vietnamese mainland. "We passed within sight of it, heading north, always remaining in international waters"—that is, more than three miles offshore. Several times during daylight on July 31 and August 1, the *Maddox* went past fishing boats and junks, the crews exchanging curious waves and stares.

The North Vietnamese coastal radar detected the *Maddox* almost immediately after she passed north of the 17th parallel.

The personnel in the communications van enjoyed a leisurely three days during the cruise from Taiwan, inspecting their equipment and making electronic sweeps of the eastern side of Hainan Island as the *Maddox* headed for Yankee Station. But the monitors went on an intensive watch schedule on July 31. Routinely they sorted out the North Vietnamese naval communications channels, found those controlling craft in the area where the *Maddox* was operating, and listened to messages pass to and fro.

And there was much to listen to. The South Vietnamese raids of the previous night had the Hanoi military in an uproar, and the *Maddox* monitors heard orders positioning a defensive ring of PT boats to prevent a repetition. By late August 1 or early August 2, the *Maddox's* number (DD-731), painted on her side, was heard with increasing frequency, as the North Vietnamese watched her northward course and wondered about her possible connection with the raids and her intentions in the Gulf.

By early morning of August 2, the *Maddox* had come up to a point near Hon Mat, several kilometers to sea from Hon Ngu, shelled by South Vietnamese raiders at about the same time of night two days before. "We noticed numerous junks massing ahead of us," Herrick said. "We became rather suspicious because we had been informed that these junks could be manned by North Vietnamese military personnel and could very easily be brought alongside, since there were hundreds of them in the area, and we had to pass very close alongside many of them. They could have been used to mine us or bring explosives alongside."

The weather was stifling hot that night, and most of the off-duty crewmen dragged their mattresses on deck to sleep. "There was tremendous humidity down below, and we just couldn't take it," Park said. The *Maddox* played its searchlight over the junks, trying to find a navigable path through them, and the North Vietnamese shouted angrily. The concerned Herrick saw the lighthouse on Hon Mat suddenly go dark, and that was enough.

Fearing a trap, Herrick sounded a general-quarters alarm, and ordered the decks cleared. Awakening crewmen got glimpses of the junks as they ran to their stations, and Herrick radioed a report, at approximately 3:45 A.M. August 2, that he anticipated "possible hostile action." The *Maddox* steamed to sea "20 to 25 miles and skirted the edge of the junk concentration," he said. The monitors now were receiving a constant flow of chatter from the North Vietnamese, and just before dawn came an intercept which confirmed Herrick's suspicions: The North Vietnamese planned an attack on the *Maddox* (as one crewman remembers the order) "to see what we would do, what our reaction would be."

At 6:45 A.M.* Herrick cabled: "Consider continuance of patrol presents an unacceptable risk," and told why. The *Maddox* continued eastward to sea.

In response, Vice Admiral Johnson, the Seventh Fleet commander, "noted" Herrick's request, and directed: "When considered prudent, resume itinerary. . . . You are authorized deviate from itinerary at any time you consider unacceptable risk to exist." As interpreted by Herrick and other officers on the *Maddox* bridge, the import of Johnson's order was clear, despite its phrasing: The fears felt for the *Maddox's* safety by Herrick, the commander on the scene, were not shared by fleet headquarters in Hawaii.

Herrick ordered the *Maddox* north to pick up the former patrol route, passing Hon Mat again toward the Red River delta. She spent the morning in the delta area, then, he says, "decided to look back towards the Hon Me island area"—this being one of the South Vietnamese targets of the night of July 30–31. As the *Maddox* turned for Hon Me, "We saw three torpedo boats emerging from one of the rivers of the delta, followed by a small oiler or tanker heading towards Hon Me. We were not too excited because we knew the North Vietnamese had PT boats. We knew that some of them were kept in that area, and, therefore, it was not too surprising

---

* Cables quoting the exact language of messages are given in approximate times. The Soviet Union and other Communist nations have their code-breaking equivalents of NSA, and a cryptanalyst with the "in-clear" text of a message can work backward from the encrypted version and determine the cipher used. NSA maintains recordings of intercepted code messages for years—and suspects that hostile powers do the same. Knowing the exact time a cable was sent would permit a quick matching of the clear version with the coded one.

to see them moving there. We were in international waters and therefore expected nothing."

But even as Herrick watched the boats disappear behind Hon Me, the monitoring crews intercepted a startling message: A North Vietnamese commander, apparently speaking from the base on Hon Me, ordered the three boats to attack the *Maddox* as soon as they finished refueling, to test the destroyer's reaction. The information was immediately relayed to Herrick on the bridge. The *Maddox* was now approximately 16 miles offshore, proceeding north; Herrick ordered a turn southward out of the area so that he would have more room for maneuver.

Ogier ran below to the combat information center (CIC), which is a naval vessel's nerve center, controlling the radar and coordinating the firing of its guns. "Ogier told us to keep a close watch on the scope, that we were in for some problems," says Stankevitz, the ranking enlisted man on duty there. Thereafter, Stankevitz said, "We kept a tight watch, and we picked up all kinds of junks, oodles of them." About 3:00 P.M. Stankevitz found three contacts "more or less paralleling our course."

Herrick said that the three PT craft came out of a cove on Hon Me while the *Maddox* was some 16 miles distant. "They were heading in our direction and finally attained a speed of about 50 knots. These presented an entirely different aspect to a peaceful Sunday afternoon. PT boats normally don't do 50 knots unless they are attacking."

"We wanted to determine whether they were after us or not, so we turned to a southeasterly course, tracked them on our radar, and increased our speed. We went up finally to about 30 knots. The PTs continued to follow us and were apparently on an intercept course—in other words, a course that would intercept us, even at our speed of 30 knots, within an hour or so, because their speed was at least 50 knots."*

Ogier sounded battle stations and spoke to the crew over the public address system. "This is not a drill," he said. All hands donned flak vests and life jackets, and the officers got pistols and helmets. "This was the first time I had had to order this, other than a drill, since the Korean War, but it seemed it was going to be the real thing," Herrick says.

Park was at once queasy and excited: "Slam! Down comes the hatch, shutting off the sonar room from the outside, and you knew you weren't going to escape from below decks if anything happened—and here we were in peacetime." Park said the sonar room was "suddenly filled with white faces."

Herrick and Ogier planned their strategy. "We decided that if the PT boats approached to within 10,000 yards, [5.8 miles] that we would fire warning shots across their bow," Herrick said. Then he went below to CIC,

---

* A nautical mile is equal to 1.15 statute miles—thus the PT boats, at 50 knots, were traveling 57.5 miles per hour.

where Stankevitz' radar said the PTs "kept closing a right steady bearing." From the bridge, Ogier requested permission from Herrick to fire. "Fire," Herrick said, and two of the *Maddox's* six five-inch guns roared, plumes of water rising in front of the incoming boats.

The *Maddox's* log doesn't reflect that Herrick or Ogier considered these shots "warning," although Stankevitz, who was standing alongside Herrick in CIC when the fire-order was authorized, says he specifically remembers hearing the words, "warning shots." Lieutenant Raymond Connell, the *Maddox* weapons officer, has been quoted as saying he was "shooting to hit them" [the North Vietnamese] and that calling the first salvo "warning shots" is a hair-splitting definition.[5] That the *Maddox* could have hit the PTs with the first salvo is highly unlikely, even had it tried to do so. Gunnery officers, when firing at such a long range, consider the first shots to be "sightings"; corrections are then made to bring the shots on target.

The log entry is as follows, with times stated military fashion (that is, 1630 is 4:30 P.M.).

1430—Went to general quarters. . . . This ship is being closed by three patrol craft.

1442—CS [changed speed] to 25 knots.

1508—MT [mount] 52 and MT 53 [each with three five-inch guns] open fire with one round apiece on patrol craft bearing 270, range 9800 yards.

Thus the first shots of the action came from the *Maddox,* and the log says nothing of their being "warning shots." A *Maddox* officer said later that had the North Vietnamese not continued the attack, "we could have been in one hell of a situation—first to fire, and in international waters, and that sort of thing."

The roar of the guns shook the *Maddox,* and then there was dead silence everywhere—on the bridge, in CIC, in the sonar room, on the gun mounts. Park thought, "Is this really happening? Are we in battle? What's going to happen now?"

Herrick says, "The PT boats kept coming, didn't veer one way or the other, but continued their intercept course. . . . We were certain that they couldn't *not* have seen our rounds falling in the water near them or in front of them." Herrick watched for three minutes; the *Maddox* log shows his decision:

1711—MT 52, 53, 31 and 32 [the latter three-inch gun mounts] open fire.

1712—Patrol craft returning the fire.

Earlier in the summer, the *Maddox's* gun crews had received the highest proficiency rating for the vessel in five years; for 20 furious minutes they blazed at the attackers. "We fired both mechanical and VT and time fuzed projectiles* near the PT boats. They were spread out in a line of three, I would guess 500 to 600 yards apart." The tenacity and discipline of the attackers impressed Herrick. "They came at us with blood in their eyes. They came on in, the forward one . . . being somewhat ignored by our gun-- ners, the other two . . . getting plenty of attention."

Considering the forward boat the most threatening for a torpedo attack, Herrick ordered fire shifted to it. There was a moment's confusion on the forward five-inch gun mount, with a relatively inexperienced director (an enlisted man) ordering it rotated in the direction opposite to that ordered by the bridge. A shipmate said of the mix-up: "That's a job where experience is required, and lots of practice—you're out there with a headset with all sorts of people shouting orders to you, which you are trying to relay; it can get damned hectic." To Stankevitz, "watching" the action on the radarscope in CIC, "it was like trying to swat mosquitoes with a big fly swatter." The *Maddox* radar kept a firm lock on the targets all the while, even though the ship raced south at full speed.

Herrick, meanwhile, radioed the *Ticonderoga* for air support. By coincidence, the *Ticonderoga* had three planes aloft at the time, taking target practice against a small rock which juts from the water at the mouth of the Gulf. They headed for the *Maddox*.

Herrick says the forward boat fired a torpedo which passed down the side of the *Maddox* at 100 to 200 yards' distance. "You can see a torpedo as it goes by if it is set fairly shallow, as these apparently were. You see a little wake going by and a sort of spray or smoke coming up in the wake. We felt they had each fired at least one [before they] then turned toward us. . . . We managed to avoid all the torpedoes."

At about 1700 yards [one mile] the North Vietnamese opened fire with machine guns. "They had large guns, about 25 mm. size, which is about a three-fourth-inch bullet, and as they passed down our side, you could hear them pump away at us. They were apparently pretty poor gunners or else our bullets were harassing them considerably, and their . . . bullets all went overhead except for one," Herrick said. The slug hit the after-gun director and three pieces of it flew into the three-inch gun magazine, whizzing past men working there but not striking them.

By now the *Maddox* magazine crews were excitedly flinging up every piece of ammunition they could find—star shells, intended for area illumination at night, antiaircraft shells, even some practice rounds with solid metal heads, rather than explosives. (For reasons of safety, naval vessels don't keep an abundance of ammunition topside.)

* A VT fuze is a proximity fuze which is triggered as it approaches within 50 to 75 feet of the target.

As the patrol boats passed under the *Maddox's* stern, one appeared to Herrick to be "going dead in the water." The other two turned toward it, "probably to take off the crew or give it assistance," Herrick thinks. As the *Maddox* turned in pursuit, the *Ticonderoga* aircraft arrived and made a number of rocket and gun attacks. "I am sure they got some hits," Herrick said. "One of the boats continued dead in the water, and I'm sure one other was damaged."

Herrick intended to finish off the boats, and started to close again. "Then one of the pilots gave us a trouble call. It seemed one of his control surfaces had been hit by machine-gun fire from one of the PT boats, and he thought he was going to have to ditch. He didn't think it would make it to the *Tico,* which was 165 miles away. We followed him down the Gulf for 15 or 20 minutes until he finally realized the damage wasn't as severe as he thought and that he could make it back to his carrier. We then released the aircraft and he proceeded home."

As it turned out, the plane was *not* hit by enemy gunfire, which the pilot discovered upon inspection after landing. One bullet hole in the after-gun director was the sole damage suffered by the United States in the encounter.

The engagement had broken off at 3:29 P.M. Shortly before 4:00 P.M. Rear Admiral R. B. Moore, commander of Task Force 77 (the *Ticonderoga* and its support fleet), and Herrick's immediate commander, radioed an order: "Do not pursue and proceed to the southeast and await further instructions."

Before dawn on Sunday, August 2, an anonymous functionary on overnight duty in the White House Situation Room read the Pacific Fleet's first report on the Tonkin encounter as it ticked onto the teleprinter relay from the Pentagon. He telephoned McGeorge Bundy, the White House national security adviser, who decided there was no reason to awaken the President until more information was available. Bundy dressed and drove through the first glimmer of morning light to the White House and his West Wing office. Elsewhere, other branches of the national security establishment stirred. In Room 7516 of the State Department building, which is the Operations Center, the watch officer called Assistant Secretary William Bundy, whose bureau has geographic jurisdiction over Vietnam; he in turn got Rusk out of bed.* The Pentagon's National Military Command Center was already alive, with a duty officer tracking the vacationing Robert McNamara to New England.

* An irreverent soul who served a year in State's Operations Center once told me, "Anyone with a thirst for power should never work there, for you can stir up the damnedest excitement, and get the biggest people out of bed, just with one phone call. The rule of thumb is, 'If you're in doubt as to whether a situation warrants calling the Secretary, you call him.' You don't miss often before you learn what he wants to hear about at 4:00 A.M., and what can damned well wait until morning, or be handled by someone else."

President Johnson made his first decision almost reflexively when Mc-George Bundy told him what had happened. I want that ship back up there, he said, because we are not going to be run out of places where we have a right to be. If we let them bother a destroyer and get away with it, next week they'll be down further south after the *Ticonderoga.**

Johnson announced this decision matter-of-factly to Rusk and McNamara when they arrived for the midmorning meeting, and they talked about ways to put the *Maddox* back on its patrol route without subjecting it to undue risks. According to accounts of this meeting which later circulated in the State Department, Rusk was adamant about the fact that a United States vessel had been fired on in international waters, and said not too flippantly that he was ready "to send the whole —————— Seventh Fleet up there if necessary."

Based on what Rusk and McNamara said to subordinates, it is fairly certain that retaliatory raids were suggested (by whom is not known) but rejected by Johnson, still unwilling to go so far as to bomb the North Vietnamese mainland. Nor did Johnson care to do anything to magnify the incident in the public mind. We didn't lose anything in this fight, he said, and we got some of their boats. Now what we have to do is show them we are going up there again and not let them run us out, and that we will shoot hell out of anybody who bothers us.

Discussion followed as to whether the attacks indicated heightened belligerency by the North Vietnamese or the Communist Chinese. McNamara said that if this indeed were the case, the United States should be ready for it, militarily. He and Rusk blocked out some shifts of aircraft and naval vessels that would improve the United States' strategic position.

Johnson had a second thought after approving the aircraft and naval movements: What interpretation would the Soviets put upon the deployments? Thus another decision. He drafted, with Rusk's aid, a personal message to Soviet Premier Nikita Khrushchev for transmission over the Washington-Moscow teleprinter link, stating that the United States did not want to widen the war in Vietnam—but that she intended to continue to conduct naval operations in international waters, and that the North Vietnamese would be well advised to leave American vessels alone.

The message was the first use of the so-called "hot line," other than for ceremonial and test purposes. Johnson was to turn to it on no less than three other occasions during the next two days.

Whether two other subjects were discussed that Sunday morning remains unknown: the submission of a resolution to Congress, and Herrick's cable

* Johnson statements for the remainder of this section are not in quotation marks because informants who furnished them were not always present at the meetings; they are intended to express the direction of the President's thinking, as evidenced in reports circulated later by McNamara, Rusk, and the two Bundys, among others.

early in the morning of August 2 (Tonkin time) that he considered continuance of the patrol "an unacceptable risk" in view of North Vietnamese sensitivities about the *Maddox's* movements.

However, when Rusk returned to the State Department in late morning, he directed that the Bureau of East Asian and Pacific Affairs "pull together" material for a draft of a congressional resolution to give the President broad powers to handle any contingency which might arise in Southeast Asia.

The bureau easily complied, for it had received a similar assignment in May—a full three months before the Tonkin episode. A man who worked on the project has recalled: "The President said we were preparing to enter an election situation during which Congress would be out of town, and during which God knows what could happen in the war. He felt he needed standby authority to deal with anything that arose. We compiled background papers on the need for a resolution, and researched what had been done earlier in the Middle East, Formosa, and Cuba resolutions. Some of the liaison people at the White House had conversations with the congressional leaders and decided against submitting the resolution. Morse and Gruening would have fought it, and stirred up a big debate about the war, and the President didn't want this to happen. In early June we dropped the project."

William Bundy, who wrote the draft resolution, later was to call it "a matter of normal contingency planning.... We had always anticipated, and as a matter of common prudence I think should have anticipated, the possibility that things might take a more drastic turn at any time and that it would be wise to seek an affirmation of the desires of and intent of the Congress. But that is normal planning. *I am not sure that my drafts were even known to others.*"[6] Bundy said "no serious thought" was given to submitting his resolution to Congress at the time he wrote it. But his subordinates at State, who were well aware of the project, simply do not accept his declaration that "no serious thought" accompanied it.

Rusk, once his staff work was under way, flew to New York for his speech to the American Field Service. McNamara and the Joint Chiefs of Staff had a far busier afternoon. Admiral Sharp had already ordered the carrier *Constellation* to leave Hong Kong and hurry south to join the *Ticonderoga.* The *USS Kearsarge,* a smaller carrier heading an anti-submarine warfare task force, was directed to the South China Sea to protect the *Ticonderoga* and *Constellation* from sneak attacks. Fighter-bomber aircraft were ordered into Thailand and South Vietnam, and various Army and Marine group troops put on alert for possible movement. (The movements were not announced by Johnson until Monday.) The JCS also put into formal orders Johnson's decision that any vessel or plane attacked in international waters should respond with the intention of not only repelling the enemy, but also destroying it.

The Joint Chiefs reviewed target folders on various North Vietnamese military installations and cities—compilations of such basic data as air defenses, characteristics of buildings, population, and purpose. The Pentagon maintains such folders on practically every locale in the world. In the discussions on August 2, the JCS and staff officers concentrated on North Vietnamese ports known to house and support patrol boats, and their folders were set aside for study and updating.

In the Pacific, meantime, Admiral Thomas H. Moorer, the Pacific fleet commander, relayed the presidential and JCS decisions to subordinate units. An order went out late the night of August 2, Tonkin time:

1. In view *Maddox* incident, consider it our best interest that we assert right of freedom of the seas and resume Gulf of Tonkin patrol earliest.

2. For COMSEVENTHFLT [Commander, Seventh Fleet] UNODIR [unless otherwise directed] conduct patrol with two destroyers, resuming ASAP [as soon as possible]. When ready, proceed to Point Charlie* arriving first day, thence patrol northward toward Point Delta during daylight hours. Retire to the east during hours of darkness. On second day proceed to Point Delta thence patrol south toward Point Charlie retiring to night as before. On third day proceed to Point Lima and patrol toward Point Mike, retiring to east at night. On fourth day proceed to Point Mike and patrol toward Point November, retiring night. On fifth day return to [Point] November and retire to south through Points Oscar and Papa and terminate patrol. CPA [closest point of approach] to North Vietnamese coast 8NM [nautical miles]. CPA to North Vietnamese islands 4NM. Above points as specified.

The new orders completely scrapped Herrick's old DeSoto patrol mission plan. What he now must do was to make direct runs toward the North Vietnamese coast during the daytime, to within eight miles of the shore, four miles of the islands, then retreat to sea at night and repeat the pattern the next day, gradually moving northward. Two successive days would be spent in each area, giving the North Vietnamese ample opportunity to challenge the *Maddox's* presence. Some of the DeSoto intelligence requirements were dropped: For instance, she was no longer required to make bathythermographic readings, a process in which instruments were lowered overboard to test the salinity, temperature, and other characteristics of the waters through which she passed.

The *Maddox* arrived on Yankee Station Sunday evening, met the tanker, refueled, and took on fresh supplies of ammunition. Awaiting there was the

* The various points mentioned are the checkpoints named in the *Maddox's* original orders. They progress northward up the coast in alphabetical order.

C. Turner Joy, which had been patrolling to the east of Hainan Island. The *Turner Joy,* launched in 1958, was larger than the *Maddox* (418 feet, 5 inches, and 3,990 tons, versus 376 feet and 2,200 tons) and faster ("30 knots plus," in an official Pentagon description, versus 34 knots maximum). The *Turner Joy* had less but more modern armament, using the extra deck space for what the Navy calls "classified modern antisubmarine weapons." The *Turner Joy's* skipper, Captain Robert C. Barnhart, a 43-year-old Pennsylvanian with 23 years' service, had been Herrick's neighbor in Annapolis when both men were assigned to the United States Naval Acadamy in the 1950s.

Herrick had not been certain when he met the tanker that he would be going back into the Gulf. "We asked for fuel since we suspected we would be asked to continue the patrol." The route he had been given earlier was a long one, and required "just about all the fuel the *Maddox* could carry . . . she's one of the older destroyers and had a small fuel capacity."

Before commencing the reinforced patrol, Rear Admiral R. B. Moore, commanding the *Ticonderoga's* Task Force 77, passed along a warning to Herrick. Moore (not to be confused with Admiral Thomas Moorer, the Pacific Fleet commander) cabled:

> It is apparent that DRV [Democratic Republic of Vietnam] has thrown down the gauntlet and now considers itself at war with the United States. It is felt that they will attack U.S. forces on sight with no regard for cost. U.S. ships in Gulf of Tonkin can no longer assume that they will be considered neutrals exercising the right of free transit. *They will be treated as belligerents from first detection and must consider themselves as such.* DRV PTs [patrol craft] have advantage, especially at night, of being able to hide in junk concentrations all across the Gulf of Tonkin. This would allow attack from short range with little or no early warning.

Herrick instructed Ogier and Barnhart that they should "consider situation not unlike war patrol and demanding of maximum alertness and readiness. If we are attacked, follow our general movements at 1,000 to 2,000 yards. Take your own action as required to unmask batteries or avoid torpedoes." After an exchange of messages with Moore, it was agreed that planes from the *Ticonderoga* and *Constellation* would remain airborne constantly so they could speed to the aid of the destroyers, should attack come.

Then the *Maddox* and *Turner Joy* moved north, Herrick remembering: "It was very nice to have another destroyer along, one with the more modern five-inch, .54-caliber guns." The first order of business was to search for debris of the previous day's battle. "We did, but nothing was there," Herrick said. So the vessels went into their new patrol track, the *Turner Joy* trailing a thousand yards astern of the *Maddox.*

The reappearance of the United States vessels set the North Vietnamese naval radios abuzz. *Maddox* radar detected one vessel over the horizon at midday August 3, and Herrick called for air support. But the craft could not be found. According to electronic sensors aboard the *Maddox,* the North Vietnamese radar surveillance of her track was constant.

Word began to seep around the *Maddox* of the South Vietnamese 34-A Operations, and of the opinion of some officers that they had prompted the Sunday attack. "We didn't even know this South Vietnamese deal had taken place," Stankevitz says. "We thought it was kind of a shady deal to be pulling on us, setting us up as ducks. The crew was very resentful of it."

The *Maddox* and *Turner Joy* made the ordered feints at Hon Me, then withdrew to sea for the night, cruising in a square with 24 miles to a side.

At 4:00 P.M. on August 3, another flotilla of South Vietnamese patrol boats left Da Nang. Destination: a mainland radar station on Cape Vinh Son, and a security station near Cua Ron, both well to the south of Hon Me. As they had on July 30, the craft went far to sea to avoid North Vietnamese coastal traffic—and in doing so they paralleled the route traveled earlier in the day by the two United States destroyers, now some 75 miles to the northeast.

The raids began around midnight, with the South Vietnamese firing heavy weapons at the island installations for half an hour. As the craft withdrew, a North Vietnamese patrol boat gave chase and followed them southward toward Da Nang for an hour. But the faster American-made raiding boats gradually pulled away, and all boats arrived safely at Da Nang about 7:00 A.M. on August 4.

News of this second series of attacks by the South Vietnamese did not reach Washington until sometime after August 6—that is to say, the decisions taken at the White House, the Pentagon, and the State Department during the frantic hours of August 4 were made without knowledge that an event which earlier had stirred the wrath of the North Vietnamese had been repeated. Further, the attacks came within a day of Washington's stern warning of the consequences Hanoi would suffer if anything further were done to American warships, and within eight hours of the destroyers' feints at the coast.

Why the attacks were not reported to Washington is puzzling, for high United States naval officers in the Pacific were certainly aware of them. In testimony before the Senate Foreign Relations Committee in February 1968, Secretary McNamara said, "At the time of the specific incidents of August 4, I did not know of the attack of August 3 by the South Viet-namese, but we knew of the operations, and some senior commanders above the level of the commanders of the task force did know the specific dates of the operation."[7] *McNamara made this comment in an opening statement, and was not questioned further on it. In the Pacific table-of-organization, the "senior commanders" outranking task force commanders were Admirals Sharp, Moorer, and Johnson.*

In his August 6, 1964, testimony before the Senate Armed Services and Foreign Relations Committees, McNamara was to describe August 3, 1964, as "uneventful."

Herrick thought otherwise—indeed, so much so that he wanted to take both ships out of the Gulf, and keep them out. Even before the second round of 34-A raids, the North Vietnamese had reacted angrily, and Herrick was uncertain as to what could happen the next day when he made his scheduled feint at the coast. Thus, sometime late on August 3, he suggested that the DeSoto patrol be terminated. Admiral Sharp's reply was swift:

> 1. Termination of DeSoto patrol after two days of patrol ops [operations] subsequent to *Maddox* incident does not in my view adequately demonstrate United States resolve to assert our legitimate rights in these international waters.
> 2. Accordingly, recommend following adjustments in remainder of patrol schedule . . . in order to accommodate COMUSMACV [Commander, United States Military Assistance Command Vietnam] request that patrol ships remain north of LAT [latitude] 19-10 north* until [deleted time] to avoid interference with 34-A Ops. 4 August patrol from Point Delta to Charlie remain north of 19-10 North.

Sharp added: "The above patrol will: (a) clearly demonstrate our determination to continue these operations; (b) *possibly draw NVN [North Vietnamese Navy] PGMs [patrol boats] to northward away from area of 34-A Ops;* (c) eliminate DeSoto patrol interference with 34-A Ops."

As Senator Morse has stated, "This cable says one thing quite clearly and suggests another." The clear statement is that Sharp was disappointed with the results of the renewed mission—that although the *Maddox* had returned to the area of its first fight, the United States had yet to "demonstrate" its resolve. ("This seems to mean that we had not as yet had the opportunity to demonstrate this forcibly," said Morse.) And Sharp's suggestion that the *Maddox* and *Turner Joy* could "possibly draw" North Vietnamese vessels away from the 34-A Operations casts these ships as decoys, witting or unwitting. The *Maddox's* chronological and geographic separation from the July 30–31 raids made her no less suspect in the minds of the North Vietnamese—nor did the new limit on her movements.

* Latitude 19 degrees, 10 minutes north is in the vicinity of Cape Falaise—70 to 80 miles above Cua Ron and Cape Vinh Son, targets of the 34-A Operations of August 3–4. However, it is less than 20 miles south of Hon Me and Hon Ngu, attacked on July 30–31.

Based on Sharp's cables, Herrick accepted that the Navy (specifically, the Pacific command) was determined that the *Maddox* and *Turner Joy* "show the flag" in the Hon Me area, and that risks considered unacceptable three days previously must now be faced. Through the night of August 3–4, the monitors in the *Maddox* communications van listened to the new 34-A Operations, intercepting messages of both the attackers and the defenders. They heard radio messages of North Vietnamese patrol boats that swarmed out of Hon Me in pursuit of the South Vietnamese. They detected the incessant radar signals from the mainland as the North Vietnamese tracked the *Maddox*. And, once again, they heard their ship mentioned on the North Vietnamese radio—this time by name, not number, for the announcement of Sunday's battle had told Hanoi its adversary's identity. Finally, around 6:30 A.M., Herrick sent the fleet another estimate of his situation:

A. Evaluation of info from various sources* indicates that *DRV considers patrol directly involved with 34-A ops.* DRV considers United States ships present as enemies because of these ops and have [sic] already indicated readiness to treat us in that category.

B. DRV are very sensitive about Hon Me. Believe this is PT operating base, and the cove there presently contains numerous patrol and PT craft which have been repositioned from northerly bases.

Herrick concluded: "Under these conditions 15 min [minute] reaction time for operating air cover is unacceptable. Cover must be overhead and controlled by DDs [destroyers] at all times."

Shortly after 9:00 A.M. both the *Maddox* and the *Turner Joy* reported a radar contact paralleling the ships' movements, although out of sight over the horizon and unidentifiable. Admiral Moore, aboard the *Ticonderoga*, did not approve Herrick's request for continuous air cover, but did say in response to the radar sighting that aircraft were ready for "launch and support on short notice."

The *Maddox* at this time was cruising in some 60 feet of water, within sight of the North Vietnamese coast. Patrick Park, the sonarman, knew that submarines couldn't maneuver in such a shallow depth, and thus he wouldn't have much to do in the sonar room in case of another attack. Earlier in his career Park had spent many months on the five-inch gun mount. "This was all out of the ordinary, because it was none of my business, but I went to Mr. Connell [Lieutenant Raymond Connell, the weapons officer] and told him I wanted to be put back up on the gun mount because I had been on the ship almost four years, and I felt that if anything was going to happen, I'd be better there than the other kid, who didn't have my experience. I could tell the officers were very much concerned about our

* Even in encrypted ship-to-ship messages, Herrick did not dare refer to the fact that his vessel was intercepting tactical military messages of the North Vietnamese.

situation." Connell agreed. "He told me to come back as main battery director if we got into trouble again," Park said.

The operations departments of both vessels—radio, radar, and sonar—remained on a 50-50 alert throughout the day, half the crew sleeping, half at their stations. Park says there was a "high degree of anticipation." The stomach butterflies of Sunday had long departed. "The shots that day calmed us down just like after the kickoff and first contact in a football game."

August 4 was also a day of mechanical frustration for Herrick and his crew. In midmorning the *Maddox's* sonar equipment "went totally on the blink," according to one of the men attending it. Electronic specialists worked on the sonar for more than an hour, then gave it a qualified "operative" grade. But soon they were busy elsewhere on the ship, trying to repair the IFF (Identification Friend or Foe) device which enables the *Maddox* to tell whether nearby ships and aircraft are friendly or otherwise. In a combat situation, and especially at night, IFF is as important to a naval commander as a right arm is to a quarterback—and the equipment aboard the *Maddox* simply was not trustworthy on August 4, the earnest efforts of repairmen notwithstanding.

As night came the destroyers moved to sea, and Herrick said the CIC radar picked up "numerous skunks"—unidentified surface craft—in the center of the Gulf. "They seemed to be strategically placed so that they just about surrounded the area where we were night-cruising the night before." As a "precautionary measure," Herrick says, the *Maddox* went to general quarters and "put all the boilers on the line [in operation] so that we could make maximum speed."

Then another flash from the communications van: "We intercepted their attack orders," says Herrick. "We were continually tracking the skunks that we had previously observed. They seemed to be across the north and above us, and down to the south and east"—in other words, hostile boats forming three sides of a box, and the hostile coast the fourth. The weather rapidly deteriorated, with the *Maddox* and *Turner Joy* moving through rain squalls and high swells. Herrick remembers it as a "very disagreeable night . . . numerous thunderstorms, no moon, completely dark, ink dark—an ideal situation for an attack of this kind." Says Park: "It was as black as being three miles back in a cave without a candle. You could see the *Turner Joy's* running lights, and the phosphorescence of our wake, but only when you looked right down on it. That's all."

Stankevitz, watching the main radarscope in the CIC, at first thought the contacts were "low-flying aircraft." However, he and the officers there in the CIC decided this could not be the case. "They were too slow, they had to be in the water," he said. The "possible aircraft" were mentioned in one of the *Maddox's* early flash cables—but no one on board ever thought of them again. As Stankevitz explains, "It was a pretty poor night for radar. The atmosphere was bending the beams so they could go to land, or 80 or 90 miles away, rather than from antenna to horizon, or it would bend the signal around the earth, rather than bounce it back, or send it up in the air and you don't get doodle."* But Stankevitz is emphatic on one point: "I definitely saw at one time on the scope about four or five contacts at high speed." These contacts, he says, came at the very start of the evening.

Herrick talked with Ogier and Barnhart, and they decided that the two ships would "stay generally together, but act independently, so we could unmast [fire] our batteries on all targets that seemed to be threatening one or the other, and also to stay close enough together to give mutual support."

At approximately 9:00 P.M., Herrick says, the "boat which was closest to the *Turner Joy* approached to about 9,000 yards [about five miles] . . . then made a turnaway as it fired a torpedo or torpedoes. We immediately took it under fire." Both destroyers used star shells on the first volleys, hoping to illuminate the area enough to see the attackers. But the star shells didn't break the gloom.

Park, on the main gun director, disagrees with Herrick's statement that the *Maddox* took *anything* under fire, then or later. The main gun director radar, used for targeting the five-inch guns, has a narrower field of coverage than that in CIC. "When you narrow down to look for specific targets, you pick up everything out there—showers, cloud formations, water, even the coastline. It wasn't possible to follow specific targets. All we could do was to *estimate* when they were going to be where, based on their speed, direction, and those first spottings." Green blips constantly flitted across the scope before Park; under optimum conditions the radar can find a 55-gallon drum floating two miles away. "But there were rain squalls all over, and it was pretty hard to pick up anything. When you make a contact with the main battery director, it takes 30 to 45 seconds to lock on it; if it won't lock, what you have isn't metallic. It could be a swell, which will show until it rolls and goes under and breaks."

The main radar room, Park says, "was giving contacts it seemed like every five seconds. They were yelling, 'Try this one, why can't you get these things?' " But Park says he couldn't find anything to lock onto. "The whole two or three hours we were out there . . . we didn't pick up a single contact we could hold."

Herrick, in CIC, is equally convinced that one of the boats fired a torpedo and cut away—based upon the movements he saw on the radar there. "Torpedo in the water" was immediately flashed to the *Maddox* bridge,

* On June 16, 1968, United States planes, attacking what their radar showed to be helicopters in the Gulf of Tonkin, destroyed a United States patrol boat and severely damaged the cruiser *USS Boston* and the Australian destroyer *Hobart*. Seven men were killed.

where Ogier controlled the helm, and to Barnhart on the *Turner Joy*. Sonar rooms on both vessels were alerted to listen for torpedoes.

Several thousand yards away on the *Turner Joy,* Lieutenant (jg) John J. Barry, a young reservist, was acting as forward gun director. Barry saw what he later told Navy investigators looked like a "white streak" coming straight for the side of the boat.* The *Turner Joy* was in an evasive turn, and Barry says the torpedo passed off the side, submerged but distinct. Barry, who was trained as an antisubmarine warfare officer, had seen torpedo firing in training exercises. Seaman Larry O. Litton, standing alongside Barry, also reported later that he saw the torpedo, as did two other topside seamen: Edwin R. Sentel, the port lookout, and Roger N. Bergland, operator of the after-gun director.

Captain Herrick, it will be recalled, had described the night as "completely dark, ink black," with rain and high seas.

The torpedo reports sent both the *Maddox* and *Turner Joy* into wild evasive maneuvers—180 degrees for two minutes, then 45 degrees right for three minutes, then in the other direction, churning paths so erratic that the Navy has never been able to reconstruct anything other than a general outline of the tracks they followed that night.

The enlisted man in charge of the *Maddox* sonar that night was David Mallow, then 23 years old, who had been on the ship for less than a year and had very little experience. A former crewmate says, "On some of our earlier patrols, we'd lock on a submarine, and David might take over and listen while the regular operator took a coffee break or went to the head. But this was routine, 'passive' experience, when the target was already identified, and all you had to do was listen. Now when you get into a situation where you're trying to *find* something, Christ, that's all the difference in the world."

Sonar† is a device of highly variable reliability. The principle is the same as that of radar: A train of repeated sound signals, or "pings," is emitted by an underwater transducer and echoes are reflected back to the source from targets or submerged objects; they are electronically translated to give the distance and, to some extent, the shape of the reflector. Physically, Mallow had before him a viewing screen similar to a home television set, through which sonar impulses are reproduced visually. The return of the impulses themselves he heard over a headset. The sound emissions came from hydrophones mounted on each side of the ship, toward the front and below the waterline.

---

* Barry told David Wise, when interviewed for *Esquire,*[8] that the torpedo was "no more than a hundred feet away." Barnhart remembered the Barry report as "200 yards." McNamara's Senate testimony of February 20, 1968, was "approximately 300 feet." The Navy, for its own reasons, refuses to declassify the formal statements taken from Bergland, Litton, Sentel, Barry, and other crew members immediately after the incident.
† The word "sonar" is a contraction of the phrase, So(und) N(avigation) A(nd) R(anging). Radar comes from Ra(dio) D(irection) A(nd) R(anging).

Mallow's working conditions that hectic night were the poorest conceivable for a sonarman. J. Warren Horton writes, in the basic sonar textbook used at the United States Naval Academy in Annapolis:[9] "The impact of water against the hull is [a] . . . powerful source of self-noise interference. This is always serious for any hydrophone carried by a surface vessel. It is likely to be troublesome even when the vessel is lying to, and is usually a limiting factor for a vessel under way. It invariably increases with increasing speed, the intensity generally increasing as some power of the speed. Any attempt at search operations must take careful account of this factor. . . . Because of this type of interference a moving surface vessel is generally considered to be the worst possible support for a listening hydrophone. . . ." Another sonar expert, Robert A. Frosch—formerly director of the Navy's Project Artemis, which developed antisubmarine defenses, and more recently the Pentagon's director of nuclear test detection—has written that underwater noise and spurious sonar echoes come from such diverse sources as snapping shrimp, waves, air bubbles, masses of plankton, "the water itself." Frosch adds, "In the case of large simple objects such as whales, in fact, it is frequently difficult to make a meaningful distinction between reverberation and true target. Some responsible experts even claim that as many as 90 percent of the 'submarines' that have been contacted by sonar have probably been whales, or other large marine forms."[10]

But it was sonar upon which the speeding, weaving *Maddox* depended for "torpedo sightings" the remainder of the night.

And the "sightings" were frequent. To Park, listening to Mallow over the intra-ship phone from the main gun director, "It seemed like he was hollering all the time. I said to myself, Aw, God, if there are that many torpedoes in the water the whole Seventh Fleet would be blown up by now. I had an idea what was happening. At 30 knots there's a big pie-wedge of dead space behind the ship, with so much noise in it—a real roar—that an operator can't even keep his phones on it. Also, when you are making sharp turns, the effect on the hydrophone is exactly what a torpedo sounds like when it is passing you. I noticed the sequence would never vary: We'd make a turn, and Dave would call 'Torpedo' and give a range. So we would turn again, and sure enough, up would come another call, 'Torpedo'."

Mallow's immediate superior, Lieutenant John M. Leeman, was certain that night that the torpedoes were legitimate; four years later he wasn't as certain. "I don't know. I really don't know."[11] Herrick would not classify all the sightings as torpedoes, either on August 4 or later. "We heard numerous torpedo effects on our sonar. Some of them were later judged to be self-noises or boat noises, but the authenticity of several* were confirmed by visual torpedo wake sighting by *Turner Joy* personnel."

* Actually, *Turner Joy* personnel reported only one torpedo sighting, according to McNamara's 1968 testimony before the Senate Foreign Relations Committee.

All the while the *Turner Joy* fired furiously "on God knows what," in the words of a *Maddox* crewman. (One *Turner Joy* officer, who declined attribution during an interview in the summer of 1968, said, "We were getting blotches on the radar screen—nothing real firm, so we were whacking away at general areas with proximity fuzes, hoping to get something.") Herrick, however, is convinced that the *Turner Joy* scored hits. "I personally saw *Turner Joy's* bullets going out on the radar—I saw the pip from the bullets as they went out. I could see the target pip on the radar, see the bullet pip and the target pip merge, and then the target pip disappear. It was obvious to me that there were several boats, and that at least two of them had been sunk." The *Turner Joy* did most of the firing, Herrick said, because "she was second in column, and the attackers seemed to be coming from astern of her, approaching her and making turns away, after firing torpedoes."

Herrick had asked the *Ticonderoga*—25 minutes flying time to the south —for air cover upon the first radar contact, and eight planes came overhead at 9:08 P.M. When the radar contacts began to close, the A-4 Skyhawk attack jets dived through the cloud ceiling and dropped flares, trying to pick up targets. Several times the *Turner Joy* fired star shells at areas which it wished the planes to attack. The Skyhawks made rocket runs for about 40 minutes, then ran low on fuel and returned to the *Ticonderoga*.

Between 11:00 and 12:00 P.M., numerous flash messages (highest priority in naval communications) went out from the *Maddox:* The *Turner Joy* reported the firing of five torpedoes, and planned to "ram" one of the attacking PT boats; the *Turner Joy* reported, "We think a PT boat sank one of its own boats"; the *Maddox* said that "seven torpedoes" had already been fired, and two more were in the water; finally, the ships had counted a total of "22 torpedoes" fired during the engagement.

North Vietnamese patrol boats of the Swatow class—the ones the Navy says attacked the *Maddox* and *Turner Joy*—have a capacity of two torpedoes each.

For Stankevitz, the night was a radarman's horror. "We had a hard time even keeping the *Turner Joy* on the radar. We were running in the dark with lights out so the attackers couldn't see us. We were really sweating it out to avoid collision."

Around midnight Park, at the main gun director, was given a range on a target spotted by the main radar room, "the firmest target we've had all night." He directed his own radar toward the target. "It was a damned big one right on us, no doubt about this one. About 1,500 yards off to the side, a nice fat blip."

Park asked for the "firing key"—control of the triggering device on the five-inch gun mounts—and for permission to open fire. Park tells what happened next:

"*Just before I pushed the trigger, I suddenly realized—That's the* Turner Joy. *This came right with the order to open fire. I shouted back, 'Where's the* Turner Joy?' *There was a lot of yelling of 'Goddamn' back and forth, with the bridge telling me to 'fire before we lost the contact,' and me yelling right back at them. (I really wasn't thinking about what I was saying.)*

"*I finally told them, 'I'm not opening fire until I know where the* Turner Joy *is.' The bridge got on the phone and said, 'Turn on your lights,* Turner Joy.'

"*Sure enough, there she was, right in the cross hairs. I had six five-inch guns right at the* Turner Joy, *1,500 yards away. If I had fired, it would have blown it clear out of the water. All I had to do was squeeze the trigger. In fact, I could have been shot for* not *squeezing the trigger.*"

On the *Turner Joy,* Captain Barnhart saw a searchlight flicker skyward for a few seconds, then go out. He interpreted it as a recall signal, for it never touched his destroyer. There were no further contacts, suspected or otherwise, with targets felt to be North Vietnamese boats. The *Maddox* and *Turner Joy* continued south at full speed, out of the Gulf of Tonkin, the "battle" phase of the second incident at an end. It was just after midnight—or noon, Washington time.

And Washington was in turmoil, beginning with the arrival of the first flash-red cable from the Far East at 9:20 A.M., telling of the intercept of the order for the North Vietnamese to attack. Admiral Sharp requested—and was unhesitatingly granted—permission to ready planes on the *Ticonderoga* and *Constellation* for a possible retaliatory strike. Within half an hour Herrick cabled that the North Vietnamese attack was under way. And, after that, long periods of silence from the *Maddox,* broken only by sketchy flashes about torpedo "sightings" and of the destroyers "returning fire." But no reports of substance arrived in the National Military Command Center until well after 11:00 A.M., or two hours after Herrick had declared he was under attack.

There are several reasons for the delay. Herrick was busy fighting what he considered to be a naval engagement in bad weather at night—circumstances scarcely conducive to prompt and detailed report writing. More importantly, the *Maddox* was not equipped with encrypting machines which automatically put secret messages into code. Each time Herrick wanted to communicate with Admiral Moore on the *Ticonderoga*—his immediate superior and his communications relay point—an officer had to probe laboriously through code sheets and encrypt the message character by character. (Although communications is one area in which the Navy is particularly tight-lipped, comments of several crew members indicate that the *Maddox* and *Turner Joy* exchanged voice messages "in-clear"—that is, uncoded and unscrambled—during the engagement.) *Maddox* messages would go to the *Ticonderoga* for relay to the Naval Communications Station at San Miguel, the Philippines, thence to Hawaii, for further relay to Washington.

Message traffic through the Defense Special Security Communications System *in theory* is instantaneous, with a teleprinter operator at one end, typing the message onto a keyboard "in-clear." The message is encrypted automatically by machine, transmitted, and then decrypted by the receiving machine and printed out again in-clear. *In fact,* however, the system is far from perfect. A staff report for the Defense Appropriations Subcommittee of the House Appropriations Committee, prepared in 1968, stated that "approximately 20 percent of all incoming messages received are garbled . . . [due to] human error, equipment malfunction, or poor quality circuits." The report said a "significant amount of time of communicators is spent in editing, correcting, and servicing garbled messages."[12]

McNamara himself·admits that the first flash messages of the engagement were "ambiguous . . . and . . . confusing."[13] There were also delays in the distribution. The White House national security staff, for instance, supposedly obtains instant relays of crisis material via teleprinter from the Pentagon. Not until well after 11:00 A.M., however, did the staff realize that a new incident was being reported. One of these people recollects asking a superior, "What do we do now?" The superior replied, "Go to lunch. In situations like this one, the big boys take over, and we'll be told when we are needed."

The "big boys" to whom he referred were Johnson, Rusk, McNamara, and the Bundy brothers. The President learned of the first flash by phone from McNamara soon after a breakfast meeting with the congressional leadership. He told McGeorge Bundy to put together as much information as possible before a National Security Council meeting scheduled to discuss Cyprus at noon, then went ahead with a routine greeting of S. K. Patil, the Indian Minister of Railways.

Because the reports were coming through military channels, Dean Rusk couldn't learn enough at the State Department to satisfy himself, so his limousine whisked him across the Memorial Bridge into Virginia. He and McNamara rode the Secretary's private elevator three floors down into the Pentagon basement to the National Military Command Center—a maze of soundproof rooms walled with acoustic tile and protected by guards who inspect the identity cards of anyone who enters, McNamara included. The main conference room is dominated by an elliptical-shaped table with the ends squared, each position containing its own communications console of telephones, headsets, and switches. Loudspeakers on the wall permit officers at distant commands—such as Admiral Sharp in Hawaii—to be heard by everyone in the room; incoming teleprinter messages can be flashed quickly onto a viewing board which covers most of one wall.

The Joint Chiefs of Staff* awaited the two civilian secretaries with a host of options, in the form of contingency plans drafted since the Sunday incident. The swift consensus at this early stage was for a strike against bases of the PT boats, and preparatory orders began going to the Pacific. Rusk and McNamara gathered up a thick folder containing descriptions of recommended targets and went to the White House.

One of the distribution points for crisis cables was the "rebut Goldwater" office run by Deputy Defense Secretary Cyrus Vance and Pentagon counsel Joseph Califano. A young military lawyer on duty there recalls thinking at the time, "Oh, oh, if we are being shot at out there, there's going to be big trouble before dark."

At the State Department, the reaction in William Bundy's Bureau of East Asian and Pacific Affairs was angry outrage. A foreign service officer assigned there—a man who is by no means hawkish—says, "Hell, they were shooting at the American flag. Men were walking around the halls in our area saying, 'They can't get away with this.' We had no doubt at all that the response would be tough—our only question that afternoon was 'How tough?' In our particular office we didn't see a hint of any information that the existence of the attacks was questionable."

Rusk and McNamara slipped into Johnson's office before the NSC convened in the Cabinet Room and quickly outlined the cursory information they had. Let's take care of it at the luncheon, Johnson said. We'll have more facts by then, and it looks as though we're going to have to do something about this situation.

The NSC meeting was brief, with only cursory discussion of Tonkin. Like Kennedy, Johnson could never bring himself to consider such officials as Carl Rowan, the head of the United States Information Agency, and Edward McDermott, an amiable midwestern lawyer who was director of the Office of Emergency Planning, as serious foreign policy advisers, even though both were statutory NSC members. Johnson preferred the intimacy of an institution that became known as the "regular Tuesday luncheon." He, Rusk, McNamara, and McGeorge Bundy retired to the President's dining room on the second floor of the White House—a warm, sunlit room whose early nineteenth-century wallpaper depicts heroic battle scenes of the American Revolution. They spread their documents on the table and got down to serious discussion.

Johnson's decision on *what* should be done was understood; what he wanted now was guidance on the mode and severity of the punishment.

_____

* Without General Wheeler, who was in New York and did not arrive in Washington until 4:00 P.M., after the basic decision had been made.

Persons who have watched Lyndon Johnson on the verge of a major decision say that his calm is total; that the nervous energy that makes him a "shouter, a cusser, and a walker" drains away, and his voice drops to a low whisper. He lapses into long silences, and no one can be certain he is even listening to the talk going on around him. His eyes are unmoving (even under normal circumstances Johnson has a blink rate which newsmen compare with that of a turtle) and focused on the distance; what he is thinking about can only be conjectured.

Very rapidly the technicians ran through the possible alternatives; by 1:30 P.M. Johnson agreed that American planes should conduct the attacks, and that the targets should be installations clearly associated with the patrol boats. The JCS target list contained six recommended sites; Rusk, however, balked at the northernmost two, saying they were "getting a little close to the Chinese." Reconnaissance planes had pinpointed the normal berths of the 47 PT boats in the North Vietnamese fleet. The two northernmost bases, Rusk noted, contained only 13 of them. Hit the other 34 "with everything we can," he counseled, and let the others be. In case more raids were necessary later, "they'll still be there, and we'll have some options open to us." The northern bases were deleted.

At this hour the *Maddox* had not forwarded a complete battle report— thus Johnson made it clear that he wanted more information before the reprisal attack was launched. He wanted the raids staged before sundown, Vietnam time, so that the fliers wouldn't have to risk straying off course, and so that the punishment would have the element of immediacy. He wanted to announce the raids himself, so that the Chinese and Soviets would not mistake them for the start of a general war. But, foremost, he wanted more information. (Johnson told visiting journalists weeks later that he had acted like a "prosecuting attorney" in demanding that Rusk and McNamara give him "hard proof." There had been a second attack. Johnson couldn't understand why the destroyers had not scored more hits. "Do our Navy boys get enough target practice?" he asked the journalists. "That's ———— shooting, throwing all that lead around for hours and not hitting anything more than they did.")

Yet the machinery for retaliation had meanwhile gone into motion. Rusk hurried back to State to start aides working on the diplomatic scenario required to notify the United States' friends and enemies of the reasons for the drastic action, and to ready the resolution for submission to Congress. Johnson wanted the latter done regardless of whether the second incident was real or a false alarm. The Sunday attack in itself was sufficient reason to go to Congress; the next time one of these comes, he said, Congress might be scattered all over the country. McNamara, busy both with confirmation of the attack and preparation of the retaliation, permitted himself one terse comment when he returned to his office: "I wish the hell we had more information about what's going on out there—is the Navy's Pony Express out of order?"

No, the Pony Express was not to blame. Captain Herrick, with the *Maddox* and *Turner Joy* safely out of the Gulf, simply was finding it difficult to piece together a coherent picture of what had happened, beyond the handful of radar contacts which he saw on the radar screen early in the evening. His first post-engagement cable reflects his doubts:

> Entire action leaves many doubts except for apparent attempted ambush at beginning. Suggest thorough reconnaissance in daylight by aircraft.

At Herrick's order, division officers on both vessels began to quiz crew members, attempting to determine who saw exactly what, and when. The reports were sketchy, and Herrick's skepticism mounted as he heard them. The *Maddox's* chief gunnery officer, Lieutenant Connell, said flatly he did not think any patrol boats had come "within gun range" of the destroyer. Only one *Maddox* crewman claimed to have "seen" anything with his own eyes during the episode: José R. San Augustin, a gunner's mate second class, assigned to the signal bridge, asserted that he had seen the "outline" of a boat in the water, silhouetted by the glare from the burst of a three-inch shell. Two marines from the communications van claimed to have seen lights pass alongside the ship—however, *Maddox* officers put little credence in their story, because of their limited sea experience, and suggested that the "lights" were phosphorescence from a breaking wave.

Turner Joy personnel contributed a dab more of evidence. In addition to Barnhart, all other men on the signal and maneuvering bridge had seen a searchlight flare briefly. Four seamen had seen what they took to be an attacking boat when it came between their ship and flares dropped from one of the aircraft. During the August 2 action, North Vietnamese had fired sustained bursts from machine guns and other heavy weapons—yet Herrick, in questioning the crews of both the *Maddox* and *Turner Joy,* could not find a single man who heard or saw gunfire on August 4. [*McNamara, August 6, 1964: "The* Turner Joy *reported that during the engagement, in addition to the torpedo attack, she was fired upon by automatic weapons while being illuminated by searchlights."*]

Reports from the aircraft were confusing. Commander G. H. Edmondson, flying 750 to 1,500 feet above the destroyers, and Lieutenant J. A. Burton, his wingman, saw gun flashes; whether they were American or North Vietnamese, they did not know. Despite the rain and blackness, Edmondson thought there were "light" antiaircraft bursts at his approximate altitude. However, Swatow boats do not have antiaircraft aboard. Edmondson and Burton detected a "snaky" wake "ahead" of the *Maddox*. Yet the six other pilots of Attack Squadron 52 avowed they saw nothing but an occasional destroyer wake in the light of their flares, and the *Turner Joy* was frequently "ahead" of the *Maddox* during the night's frantic maneuvering. The eight planes made numerous passes in their 40 minutes over the area, firing rockets in the area of "targets" reported by the *Turner Joy,* but reporting no hits. [*McNamara, August 6, 1964: "By midnight local time the destroyers reported that . . . the defensive aircraft from the* Ticonderoga *were illuminating the area and attacking the enemy surface craft."*]

At 1:30 A.M. Herrick had heard enough. He sent Pacific headquarters the following evaluation:

> Review of action makes many reported contacts and torpedoes fired appear doubtful. . . . Freak weather effects and overeager sonarman may have accounted for many reports. No actual visual sightings by *Maddox*. Suggest complete evaluation before any further action.

Herrick's final sentence is a striking combination of doubt and alarm—doubt, in that he is not willing to say the attack actually occurred; alarm, in that he is well aware of Sharp's mood, as revealed in their exchanges of the last three days, and realizes "further action" well could be imminent. Despite the restraints of formal cable language addressed to a superior, Herrick is clearly telling Sharp: "Don't act too quickly on the basis of what might turn out to be a nonincident."

This particular Herrick cable was whisked to Washington almost instantaneously, and its arrival sent a discernible tremor through McNamara's immediate sector of the Pentagon. He immediately picked up a scrambler telephone, called Admiral Sharp, who had also seen the message, and told him, "We obviously don't want to carry out the retaliatory strike unless we are damned sure what happened." He added that nothing was to be done "until any doubts as to what went on are eliminated, *at least to the point of justifying retaliation.*" He directed Sharp to obtain more information from Herrick—and immediately. Then McNamara called Johnson, one of the 11 face-to-face and phone conversations they were to have that day, and reported the new uncertainty.

The quotations are as McNamara delivered them to the Senate Foreign Relations Committee in 1968. He remembered them, he said, because phone conversations within the Defense Department's operational command channel are tape-recorded (presumably to give both parties a permanent record of decisions and directives issued orally), and because he had referred to notes of his talks with the various commanders. But even with these stronger doubts before them, the JCS continued planning the retaliatory raids, and State went ahead with its political work, and the White House with Johnson's speech writing.

Sharp's sources of information during the remainder of the afternoon and evening were Admirals Moorer, Johnson, and Moore, who cascaded demanding cables upon the hapless Herrick. Sharp moved quickly. At 2:45 P.M., only 75 minutes after the cable that reflected Herrick's doubts, he was back to McNamara with a telephone report that both Herrick and Admiral Johnson were convinced that the original ambush was bona fide. As confirmatory evidence he now had the crew reports of "lights" passing the *Maddox* and *Turner Joy,* and of the "torpedoes" seen passing the *Turner Joy.* Whether Sharp qualified the strength of this evidence at all, or told of Herrick's qualms about its validity, is not known.

At 3:00 P.M. McNamara and Vance began a meeting with the Joint Chiefs of Staff to review the information available "to determine," in McNamara's words, "whether in fact an attack on the destroyers had occurred."[14] In addition to the cables they also had other information, of which the nature and exact origin remain murky. A recapitulation:

It will be recalled that the communications van on the *Maddox* had intercepted early in the evening the message ordering the North Vietnamese patrol boats to attack. Some time later, Herrick says, "We heard . . . their damage report confirm our assessment that two of the boats had been sunk." Herrick knew of these intercepts when he was sending skeptical reports of the engagement. He now accepts them as conclusive proof that he was attacked—yet he did not do so on August 5, as his cables clearly reveal. Herrick also asserts: "We had no radio contact, or heard no communications going on between the PT boats. It was suspected that on the fringes of the battle, but beyond our radar covers, were . . . patrol boats which were equipped with radar and which were vectoring the PT boats in for attacks on us." The communications van's ability to intercept North Vietnamese messages had been amply demonstrated during the preceding four days; why, then, no intercepts from the PT boats during the August 4 incident? Messages from director ships, or a headquarters on Hon Me, which were audible to the North Vietnamese would also have been audible to the *Maddox's* monitors—yet Herrick avows none were heard during the engagement. What, then, was the origin of the damage report? Further, the North Vietnamese damage report also contained a claim that two United States planes had been shot down—a total untruth. What, then, was the reliability of the entire sequence of messages?

Herrick won't go into details of the intercepts, citing grounds of communications security. But according to his cables received in Washington the afternoon and evening of August 4, his faith in their reliability increased in direct proportion to the demands of Admirals Sharp, Moorer, Johnson, and Moore for "verification" that an attack on his vessels had occurred.

McNamara considered the damage reports as "one of the major factors leading us to the conclusions that we came to," that the August 4 attacks were real.[15] But at the 1968 hearings, McNamara had this exchange with Senator Stuart Symington:

Senator SYMINGTON. Do you think you would come to these conclusions without it [the intercepts]?

Secretary McNAMARA. Yes.

Senator SYMINGTON. That is an interesting answer. It was not the deciding factor, but it justified the decision. . . . Is that correct?

Secretary McNAMARA. It did.

At 4:34 P.M. another Herrick report arrived in Washington: "Details of action present a confusing picture although certain that original ambush was bona fide." Six minutes later Sharp again phoned McNamara, repeating Herrick's report, and again referring to the "lights" and "torpedoes" supposedly seen by the crew members.

The confirmation was sufficient for the Administration to begin executing the retaliation scenario.

At 5:00 P.M. the congressional liaison staff at the White House began telephoning offices of key Senators and Representatives, telling them they were wanted at an "urgent" meeting at 6:00 P.M. Johnson read a draft of the speech announcing the retaliation, didn't like it, made some suggestions, and returned it to aide Jack Valenti for revision.

At the State Department, UN Ambassador Adlai Stevenson worked with William Bundy's staff on a presentation to be put before the Security Council on the following day, and on a telegram to Secretary-General U Thant asking that a special session be called. Rusk's office alerted ambassadors of such key allies as Great Britain and West Germany to come to the department later in the evening for highly secret policy briefings.* United States embassies were told to expect an important announcement to give to their host governments. The United States Information Service and the Voice of America prepared themselves to distribute a major—but unknown—piece of news.

Thus one phase of the crisis gradually went onto quasi-public display: the second National Security Council meeting, which was announced to the White House press; the Pentagon's two-paragraph announcement that a second attack had occurred; notice of an imminent presidential speech;

---

* Washington now makes a stock plea of "lack of time" for not consulting or informing allies of major foreign policy moves more promptly. The real reason, however, is fear of security leaks—one of the many lessons learned from the case of Kim Philby.

the congressional leadership meeting; the nation's anxious wait for the President to appear on television. From this viewpoint the incident in Tonkin Gulf was a certain truth; only the planned response was a mystery.

But for grim men elsewhere—in the White House national security staff offices, in the Pentagon's war room, in Sharp's headquarters in Hawaii, to a lesser extent on the bridge of the *Maddox*—the circumstances were exactly the opposite: The planned response was a certain truth, the incident a mystery.

Shortly after Johnson informed the congressional leaders that he intended to bomb North Vietnam because of the "unprovoked attack" on United States vessels, Admiral Sharp addressed an urgent message to Herrick:

1. Can you confirm absolutely that you were attacked?
2. Can you confirm sinking of PT boats?
3. Desire reply directly supporting evidence.

It was now past dawn in the Gulf of Tonkin. Since early on the afternoon of July 31, Captain Herrick had been under the immeasurable tension of a commander operating in waters infested with enemy craft of indeterminate and erratic intentions, with superior commanders insistent upon putting his craft into circumstances which he considered needlessly and unacceptably risky. Since midday of August 4, he had rotated between the bridge of the *Maddox,* the combat information center, and the plot room, which doubled as his office. John Herrick had not been to bed; he and all the other men on the *Maddox* and *Turner Joy* were exhausted. Now Herrick, Ogier, and other officers once again sat down to review their own memories of what had happened between 9:20 P.M. and midnight, and the testimony gathered later from other men.

The sonar reports came under especially close scrutiny, for in the absence of credible radar contacts they were the only evidence of attack, other than the questionable and fragmentary eyewitness reports. Soon after the attack ended, Ogier ordered Patrick Park to "validate" Mallow's reports of the sonar torpedo sightings. As Park remembers it, Ogier felt that since he (Park) was the only sonarman aboard who hadn't worked sonar that night, he wouldn't be "biased." Park listened to three hours of concurrent tapes— one containing the sonar pings, the other the conversation and reports in the sonar room. The tapes confirmed what Park had suspected during the engagement. "What he [Mallow] was hearing was the ship turning—noise back from the propellers and everything else. It was just too damned coincidental—you'd hear the ship turn, then get this particular reading, and Dave would yell 'Torpedo'. There were absolutely no hydrophone effects of torpedoes fired at us."[16]

Was Ogier pressing for a predetermined answer?

"He didn't want to look stupid, let's face it. There had been a hell of a lot of excitement the night before over those sonar reports, and a lot of messages sent about them. He [Ogier] didn't speak to me very often after that."

(Still later, Park spent two full days listening to the tapes, logbooks beside him, correlating Mallow's torpedo reports with changes in the *Maddox's* course. Again, confirmation. Each turn was followed immediately by the cry, "Torpedo range ———" or "Noise spoke range ——— and bearing ———." Park wrote a memorandum on his findings and gave it to Ogier, along with the tapes. He heard nothing further of it.)

Some time after 8:00 P.M., Washington time, Herrick answered Sharp's "urgent" request with a cable that revealed his continuing doubts:

> *Maddox* scored no known hits and never positively identified a boat as such . . . . Weather was overcast with limited visibility. . . . Air support not successful in locating targets. . . . There were no stars or moon resulting in almost total darkness throughout action . . . . No known damage or personnel casualties to either ship. . . . *Turner Joy* claims sinking one boat and damaging another. . . . The first boat to close *Maddox* probably fired torpedo at *Maddox* which was heard but not seen. All subsequent *Maddox* torpedo reports were doubtful in that it is supposed that sonarman was hearing ship's own propeller beat.

Herrick's message arrived in Washington at 10:59 P.M. Between then and 11:32 P.M. (the exact time has not been revealed), the Pentagon received the *Turner Joy's* response to Sharp's "urgent" request. It said Captain Barnhart had seen a "column of black smoke" rising from an area where radar indicated that a shell had hit an attacking ship, but admitted the sinking was only "highly probable" and not definite. (Anyone who claimed to have seen a column of smoke that black night was wise to use qualified language.) Previously, in reports sent during the engagement itself, the *Turner Joy* claimed to have *sunk three vessels;* now, after reflection and checks with crew members, it would say only that it had been *attacked by two vessels.*

At 10:40 P.M., 19 minutes before the receipt of Herrick's last preretaliation message, the first planes began leaving the Ticonderoga, *bound for targets in North Vietnam.*

At about 10:45 P.M. a secretary in the office of White House press secretary George Reedy finished cutting the stencil for the President's television speech and hurried it through the lobby of the West Wing, jammed with expectant newsmen, to the basement mimeograph room.

At 11:00 P.M. a State Department foreign service officer who worked for William Bundy watched the beginning of the news program and said to his wife, "What's the matter? I thought we'd have something under way by now. It's getting late—it's almost noon in Vietnam." She said, "What are you talking about?" "You'll know tomorrow, or sooner," he said, and they turned back to the announcer.

Shortly after 11:00 P.M., as the President awaited McNamara's confirmation that the *Ticonderoga* planes were airborne, Admiral Johnson, the Seventh Fleet commander, dispatched another "urgent" cable to the *Turner Joy:*

> Who were witnesses, what is witness reliability? Most important that present evidence substantiating type and number of attacking forces be gathered and disseminated.

A Seventh Fleet signal man punched Admiral Johnson's query onto tape, fed it into an encrypting machine, and within minutes it clattered onto the teleprinter in the *Turner Joy's* signal room. Barnhart began preparing an answer.

President Johnson walked the few feet from his Oval Office across a hallway and into the Fish Room, and at 11:37 P.M. he began: "My fellow Americans . . . ."

At 1:15 A.M. Barnhart's answer reached the Pentagon: "Estimate two PTs attack originally. However, must admit two factors deter. No ECM [electronic countermeasures] from PT boats. However, [PT] tactics seem to be bore-sight on wake thus accounting for lack of radar signals. No sonar indications of torpedo noises even that which passed down side. Self-noise was very high."

At the same moment, jets from the *Ticonderoga* swept over the patrol-boat base at Quang Khe and dropped the first United States bombs on North Vietnamese territory.

At 1:25 P.M. Herrick stood on the bridge of the *Maddox* and watched smoke swirl hundreds of feet into the air from the oil-storage facilities at Vinh. "We had tracked the planes overhead on radar a few minutes earlier, and realized they must be ours," he said. "But this is the first we knew of the strike."

A few weeks later, the *Maddox* and *Turner Joy* put into the United States base at Subic Bay in the Philippines, where a Defense Department investigative team headed by Jack Stempler, a personal assistant to McNamara, was to assemble a full report on the incidents. The team apparently had no interest in crew members other than those who had positive evidence of an attack. Thus Park and Stankevitz—both of whom had strong doubts—were not among the men interrogated. Stankevitz remembers one other thing about Subic Bay; there he had a chance to read copies of *Time* and

Life which featured stories on the Gulf of Tonkin incidents. He turned first to a *Life* piece headlined, "From the Files of Naval Intelligence," which a preface said was "pieced together by *Life* correspondent Bill Wise with the help of U.S. Navy Intelligence and the Department of Defense." Stankevitz (and millions of Americans) read:

> A few of them [the PT boats] amazed those aboard the *Maddox* by brazenly using searchlights to light up the destroyers—thus making ideal targets of themselves. They also peppered the ships with more 37 millimeter fire, keeping heads on the U.S. craft low but causing no real damage.[17]

Life also had a highly selective smattering of cables about the August 4 "attack." Stankevitz snorted and turned to *Time:*

> The night glowed eerily with the nightmarish glare of air-dropped flares and boats' searchlights. For 3½ hours the small boats attacked in pass after pass. Ten enemy torpedoes sizzled through the water. Each time the skippers, tracking the fish by radar [sic] maneuvered to evade them. Gunfire and gun smells and shouts stung the air. Two of the enemy boats went down. Then, at 1.30 A.M., the remaining PTs ended the fight, roared off through the black night to the north.[18]

Stankevitz snorted again, this time louder. More than four years later, he remembered the stories well. "I couldn't believe it, the way they blew that story out of proportion. It was something out of *Male Magazine,* the way they described that 'battle'. All we needed were naked women running up and down the deck. We were disgusted, because it just wasn't true. It didn't happen that way, all that [*Time*] drama and excitement."*[19]

During the next three weeks, the Defense Department conducted three separate studies of the incident. Vice Admiral Johnson reviewed the combined chronology and track charts submitted by Herrick and concluded that "Commander, Seventh Fleet, is convinced beyond any doubt that *Maddox* and *Turner Joy* were subjected to an unprovoked surface torpedo attack on the night of 4 August, 1964." Admiral Thomas H. Moorer, the Pacific Fleet commander, concurred. Beyond that one sentence, the Pentagon, claiming security, will give no further details of the Johnson-Moorer report. Lieutenant General David A. Burchinal, director of the Pentagon's Joint Staff,

---

* In a floor speech February 28, 1968, Senator Morse denounced the Pentagon's "selective leaking of confidential information," and *Life's* gullibility in accepting it. "I don't know who leaked, but I can guess why," Morse said. "The 'why' is that someone in the Pentagon decided that the American people should see some of the messages confirming that an unprovoked attack had occurred on innocent American vessels . . . . The *Life* magazine reporter was taken in. He was 'used'. The press should be warned. . . ." Wise, with *Life's* Paris bureau in late 1968, did not respond to a request from the author for a rebuttal of what Morse and Stankevitz said of his reporting.

analyzed the cable traffic and reported to McNamara: "The actuality of the attack is confirmed." Again, the Pentagon is unwilling to supply any information from the report other than its conclusion.

Burchinal's report was written on August 7—two days after the retaliatory raids; the Johnson-Moorer review on August 14, nine days later.

That McNamara was unhappy with the handling of events on August 4 became evident later that month to persons working directly under him. First, he ordered that communications equipment be installed in an anteroom of his office to permit him swift access to incoming crisis messages. A subordinate recalls his remark: "There's no reason why the Secretary of Defense should spent his time trotting down to the JCS area to read cables." Second, the Weapons Systems Evaluation Group, which reported directly to McNamara, assigned a study to the Institute for Defense Analysis, an Arlington research group, entitled, " Command and Control of the Tonkin Gulf Incident, 4–5 August, 1964." Only 40 copies were produced of the top secret report, which is reputed to be highly critical of the Pentagon's communications system, but not even the Senate Foreign Relations Committee could extricate it from the hands of Pentagon security.

The night of September 17–18, 1964, destroyers USS Morton and USS Edwards went into the Gulf of Tonkin on another DeSoto patrol. Late in the evening they frantically reported action: The Edwards was "holding radar contacts" with several enemy vessels, and the Morton was firing at them—ultimately 170 rounds of five-inch shells and 129 of three-inch shells. This "engagement" was also at night, but, unlike the blackness of August 4, it was under a half-moon, with scattered clouds and visibility of up to four miles.

On September 21–22 Rear Admiral W. G. Guest conducted a board of inquiry at Subic Bay to investigate this incident. The board received testimony that the Edwards crew saw tracer bullets, flashes of light, and shell bursts. The task group commander, Captain E. E. Holleyfield, who was aboard the Morton, confirmed that when he called for air support he said the ships had been "attacked." (Holleyfield said it was "unfortunate" that he had used this word.)

The board concluded that although the Morton and Edwards held numerous radar contacts, and had a "running battle" with them, they had not been attacked by North Vietnamese patrol craft.

Commenting on Holleyfield's communications problems during the night, the board wrote: "Response to queries from higher authorities were delayed because of inadequate communications equipment and insufficient personnel. . . . The patrol unit was unusually slow with action messages from higher authorities and was unable to handle the volume."

Holleyfield was more direct about the problem: "All the while, I was preparing answers to flash messages. Composition of a rational SITSUM [situation summary] was impossible. I refused to say we were fired on when I did not know we were, and still do not know. *I know that careless or inaccurate reports would provoke more questions as they had in the* Maddox *case.*"

INTERLUDE: Lyndon B. Johnson's Version

In his off-the-record hours with White House visitors Lyndon B. Johnson could be a President of overwhelming gregarity—skilled as a raconteur and mimic, astoundingly catholic as to whom he chose as the butt of derogatory anecdotes. As was the case with so many of his public pronouncements, Johnson's private stories tended to be a little larger with each retelling, with listeners left to decide for themselves what was hyperbole and what was accidental candor.

In early 1965, during a lengthy, critical monologue on military handling of the Vietnam War, Johnson suddenly brought up the August 4 Tonkin episode as an example "of what I have to put up with" at the Pentagon.

"For all I know, our Navy was shooting at whales out there," said the President.

Part Three

THE REVELATION

An account of the process through which the United States Senate learned of the difference between illusion and reality in the Gulf of Tonkin incidents.

Chapter Six

MR. FULBRIGHT IS AROUSED

Senator Fulbright's belief that the Johnson Administration could be trusted to tell the truth to Congress in time of crisis survived a scant year after the passage of the Gulf of Tonkin Resolution.

The disillusionment was bitter for it made Fulbright and his colleagues who had put their faith in Lyndon Johnson appear to be fools. Their attempts to assert the Senate's constitutional coequivalent role with the President in foreign affairs were brushed aside with White House insinuations about their patriotism, bravery, intelligence, even manhood. For Fulbright, the breach with Johnson was more than an end of mutual confidence between two branches of government—it was the breach of a close friendship of more than two decades, first in the House of Representatives, then in the Senate.

When he was Senate Majority Leader, Johnson had often introduced the chairman of the Senate Foreign Relations Committee as "my Secretary of State." While Kennedy was choosing his cabinet in November and December of 1960, Johnson lobbied hard to have Fulbright appointed Secretary of State—and almost succeeded, for Kennedy certainly admired Fulbright. Historian Arthur M. Schlesinger, Jr., has written: "When I talked to Kennedy on December 1, it was clear that his thoughts were turning more and more to Fulbright. He liked Fulbright—the play of his civilized mind, the bite of his language, and the direction of his thinking in foreign affairs. Moreover, as chairman of the Foreign Relations Committee, Fulbright had considerable influence on the Hill." But the Arkansan consistently voted with the Dixie bloc on civil rights, and he had made speeches critical of Israel. "Kennedy had almost decided on Fulbright, but finally, after heated arguments, the President-elect yielded and struck Fulbright's name from the list," Schlesinger writes.[1] Johnson was irked that Fulbright did not make an active campaign for the position, complaining to a committee staff member later, "I could have made him Secretary of State—

what's got into him?" And, on November 22, 1963, Fulbright was one of the men Johnson called to his office for guidance in the first tortured hours of his Presidency.

On August 26, 1964, his management of the Gulf of Tonkin Resolution fresh behind him, Fulbright stood before the Democratic National Convention in Atlantic City and seconded Johnson's nomination, praising his "sense of responsibility" in foreign affairs and citing Tonkin as evidence of the President's reliance upon "restraint which lessens rather than enhances the possibility of a major war in that area." He listened approvingly to Johnson's foreign affairs speeches, and attacked Goldwater's "irresponsibility" in speech after speech on the floor (which were reprinted for distribution by the Democratic National Committee) and in magazine articles.

On February 7, 1965, the Administration began systematic bombing of North Vietnam, with Johnson saying, "Our *continuing actions* will be those which are justified and those that are made necessary by the continuing aggression of others"—i.e., no longer would a specific incident be required to trigger a United States raid against the mainland. Thus the end of the tit-for-tat principle enunciated at the time of the Tonkin reprisals, and endorsed by the Congress. By late spring the President who campaigned asserting that "We don't want our American boys to do the fighting for Asian boys" (in a September 25 campaign speech) had begun a troop buildup in South Vietnam which totaled 181,382 men at the end of the year—and, ultimately, more than half a million. As authority, Johnson used the Tonkin Resolution, and he testily denied any fundamental shift of the United States' mission: "I would say that our policy there is the policy that was established by President Eisenhower, as I have stated since I have been President 46 times, the policy carried on by President Kennedy, and the policy we are now carrying on," he said at a February press conference. "Although the incidents have changed, in some instances the equipment has changed, in some instances the tactics, and perhaps the strategy in a decision or two has changed . . . " the policy was constant.

Fulbright listened, doubted, but remained silent. In several talks with Johnson, he counseled against involvement in a land war that would repolarize East and West. Johnson slapped his back and told him not to worry. Relying upon Johnson's assurances, Fulbright in May voted for a $700 million supplemental military appropriation for Vietnam which the President sent to the Hill with this message:

> This is not a routine appropriation. For each member of Congress who supports this request is also voting to persist in our effort to halt Communist aggression in South Vietnam. Each is saying that the Congress and the President stand united before the world in joint determination that the independence of South Vietnam shall be preserved, and that the Communist attack will not succeed.

Senator Gaylord Nelson, who nine months earlier had asked whether the Tonkin Resolution meant the dispatch of troops to Viètnam, balked. "Here was this tough Texan pointing his gun at my feet and saying 'Dance', and I was damned if I'd do it," he said.[2] Nelson joined Morse and Gruening in voting against the appropriation—thus increasing Johnson's on-the-record Senate opponents to three out of 100. (According to contemporary press accounts, both Kennedy brothers considered voting no, and thought they could carry 12 votes with them, but decided against a public clash with the President.

In June, again at Johnson's behest, Fulbright gave a major Senate defense of the Administration's war policy, opposing an "unconditional American withdrawal . . . because such action would betray our obligation to people we have promised to defend . . . weaken or destroy the credibility of American guarantees to other countries . . . and . . . encourage the view in Peking and elsewhere that guerrilla wars supported from outside are a relatively safe and inexpensive way of expanding Communist power."

But even as Fulbright gave this speech, the Senate Foreign Relations Committee staff was discovering sharp discrepancies in the Administration's explanation of why it had dispatched 21,000 Marines into the Dominican Republic that spring, the first open Latin American intervention since 1927. The revolution began April 24, 1965, when followers of former President Juan Bosch (who had been deposed in a coup in 1963) overthrew President Donald Reid Cabral. The military promptly intervened, and civil war erupted between them and the *Boschistas*. During a tedious week, the United States refused to help either Reid Cabral or the Bosch group, who claimed legality—yet on April 28, when the military junta gained power, Johnson sent in Marines at its request.

Explaining the action to the Foreign Relations Committee on April 30, Rusk said that Johnson had acted to save lives of American citizens in the Dominican Republic. He didn't mention any Communist threat. Yet two days later, in a national television address, Johnson declared, "The American nation cannot, and must not, and will not permit the establishment of another Communist government in the Western Hemisphere. Our goal, in keeping with the great principles of the American system, is to help prevent another Communist state in this Hemisphere." Many Senatorial eyebrows twitched at the change in the stated reason for the intervention. Johnson's account of violence in Santo Domingo grew progressively gorier in the retelling. On May 2 he quoted a cable from Ambassador W. Tapley Bennett: "Mr. President, if you don't send forces immediately, men and women—Americans and those of other lands—will die in the streets." The next afternoon, speaking to a union convention the cable became: "You must land troops immediately or blood will run in the streets, American blood will run in the streets." And at a June 17 press conference in his office, after an Administration list of "Communists" involved in the Bosch movement proved as inflated as an old Tammany Hall voter registration list, Johnson gave one of the extraordinary quasi-public performances of his presidency. Grabbing documents from every pocket, his big hand slamming his desk for emphasis, he declared: "In this particular instance, a fact that has been emphasized all too little, I think, [is the fact] that some 1,500 innocent people were murdered and shot, and their heads cut off. . . . " When Ambassador Bennett called Washington on April 28 to request troops, Johnson said, he "was talking to us from under a desk while bullets were going through his windows and he had a thousand American men, women, and children assembled in the hotel who were pleading with their President for help to preserve their lives."

Fulbright and Senator Eugene McCarthy, a junior committee member with an interest in Latin American affairs, decided that the wildly conflicting explanations of the intervention deserved investigation. Dr. Carl M. Marcy, the committee chief or staff, and Pat Holt, its Latin American specialist, exhaustively reviewed State Department cable traffic during the crisis; chief Administration officials directly involved—Rusk, Thomas Mann, assistant secretary for inter-American affairs, and McCone of the CIA—testified in private hearings. Mann said, among other things, that military dictators were preferable to Communist regimes in Latin America; that it was "dangerous" to bring Communists into coalition governments, through legal processes or otherwise; and that Bosch was a "poet type" susceptible to Communist direction. "If we had to," Mann declared, "we could say that this [intervention] is justified on the grounds of self-defense. This has certainly occurred to us many times."

When the hearings ended Holt wrote a speech for Fulbright, castigating Administration conduct, and the committee staff argued with the Senator's political advisers over whether it should be given. Marcy advocated its delivery as a "review and comments on developments of the last 24 months," to discuss what had happened to "turn the liberal supporters of President Kennedy into opponents of the policies of President Johnson . . . [and] the right-wing opponents of Eisenhower and Kennedy into avid supporters of the present Administration." Somewhat facetiously Marcy wrote that "perhaps it is the Russians who have changed; perhaps the Chinese; perhaps the Viet Cong; perhaps Hanoi. I suggest, however, that most of the change has come within this nation itself. We have tried to force upon the rest of the world a righteous American point of view which we maintained is the consensus that others must accept. Most of the tragedies of the world have come from such righteousness." Marcy warned that the speech would cause a break with the Administration that would "make Borah and Hiram Johnson and [Henry] Cabot Lodge, Sr., look like pikers."

Fulbright delayed the speech a month to permit the installation of a provisional government under Dr. Hector Garcia-Godoy which promised prompt free elections. Then he decided to proceed, explaining his motivation in a covering letter to Johnson 24 hours in advance. Fulbright said he didn't fault the President personally, but the "faulty advice" given him. He hoped the critical analysis "will be of long-term benefit in correcting past errors, helping to prevent their repetition in the future, and thereby advancing the broader purposes of your policy in Latin America. It is in the hope of assisting you towards these ends, and for this reason only, that I have prepared my remarks." He concluded:

> Public—and I trust, constructive—criticism is one of the services that a Senator is uniquely able to perform. There are many things that members of your Administration, for quite proper reasons, of consistency and organization, cannot say, even though it is in the longer-term interests of the Administration that they be said. A Senator, as you well know, is under no such restrictions. It is in the sincere hope of assisting your Administration in this way, and of advancing the objective of your policy in Latin America, that I offer the enclosed remarks.

The speech was scathing, both in its review of changes in United States policy in Latin America from being the supporter of reformers such as Bosch to "prisoner of reactionaries who wish to preserve the status quo," and in its analysis of the Dominican crisis. "U.S. policy . . . was characterized initially by overtimidity and subsequently by overreaction," Fulbright said. *"Throughout the whole affair, it has also been characterized by a lack of candor."* He referred specifically to Johnson's claim about those 1,500 innocent but headless corpses: "There is no evidence to support this statement . . . . A sober examination of such evidence as is available indicates that the . . . junta was guilty of at least as many atrocities as the rebels." Fulbright said that the revolution had caught the Communists by surprise, although they did attempt to seize direction of it. "The evidence does not establish that the Communists at any time actually had control of the revolution. There is little doubt that they had influence within the revolutionary movement, but the degree of that influence remains a matter of speculation." Through intervention, Fulbright charged, the United States "embarrassed before their own people the democratic reformers who have counselled trust and partnership with the United States [and] . . . lent credence to the idea that the United States is the enemy of social revolution in Latin America and that the only choice Latin Americans have is between communism and reaction."

Johnson never said a word to Fulbright about the speech—he simply struck him from the list of persons he consulted regularly, and let word out through mutual friends and journalists that he was "hurt" and "indignant."[3] Johnson also claimed (falsely) to several visitors that Fulbright had "betrayed me" because he had dined at the White House the evening before the speech and did not mention it. The speech was sent to the White

House well in advance of the dinner; Fulbright felt that if the President wanted to talk about it, fine, but he wasn't going to raise the subject at a social function.

Johnson's opinion of the speech was expressed publicly through several outlets which during this period consistently reflected his thinking. Senator Thomas J. Dodd of Connecticut harshly denounced Fulbright on the floor, saying, "It seems to me that he suffers from an indiscriminating infatuation with revolutions of all kinds, national, democratic, or Communist."* Columnist William S. White, a Johnson intimate, accused Fulbright of "turning state's evidence and assisting the prosecution of his own side." For Senate traditionalist White, even more grievous was his view that Fulbright "has also broken the unwritten rule of the game, a code which demands of those holding high committee chairmanships—and uniquely the chairman of foreign relations—a degree of self-restraint and personal responsibility not demanded of the rank and file." (My President, right or wrong?) Concluded White: "Now, in the deep institutional sense, he has destroyed his own voice. . . . He can hardly speak for . . . anything save a tiny minority of the Senate in which he sits."

Johnson's reaction—and especially his silence—hurt Fulbright deeply. In October, when the President entered the hospital for gall bladder surgery, Fulbright sent him a warm, personal letter. He consoled Johnson by saying that his wife had lost her gall bladder 30 years earlier and "never missed it a minute." He said that he "understood" Johnson didn't like the Dominican speech, but that it didn't seem he could be of help to the Administration by agreeing with every decision and opinion of the White House. Collective judgments are often in error, Fulbright wrote, and a senator deeply interested in the success of his president is duty bound, when uncertain of a policy, to raise the matter for clarification, and then to move to correct it if needed. "Subservience" won't develop new policies or perfect old ones, Fulbright said. All in all, a conciliatory note and an unabashed appeal for renewed friendship.

Some time earlier Johnson had told Fulbright that Jack Valenti was a guaranteed conduit for any letter he wanted to go directly to his desk. So Fulbright had the letter delivered by hand to Valenti the day before Johnson went into the hospital.

He never heard from Johnson.†

* Dodd attended but one of the 13 Foreign Relations Committee meetings concerning the Dominican crisis.
† Fulbright is no stranger to presidential doghouses. He broke with Harry Truman over nuclear weaponry, saying that the "atomic bomb not only blasted the Japanese into submission, but it also blasted our confidence in the [United Nations] charter." After Republican gains in the 1946 election, he said, "President Truman should appoint a Republican secretary of state and resign from office." (Since there was no vice president, the Republican would have moved up to the presidency.) Fulbright named high Truman officials in a report on the Reconstruction Finance Corporation entitled "Favoritism and Influence," which the President dismissed as asinine. Replied Fulbright: "I do not want to seem disrespectful to the President, but this statement of the President is not true."

Herbert W. Beaser, an aide to Senator Gruening, remembers attending a White House function for Senate staff members in early 1965, at which Johnson lectured them on the war. Looking straight at Beaser and another man known to be hostile to Administration policies, Johnson pulled a piece of paper from his inside coat pocket and said, "Everything I've done, the Congress of the United States has approved, and don't let anyone here forget that fact for a minute." The paper was the Gulf of Tonkin Resolution.

Senator Gore in early 1965 advocated a negotiated end to the war, a proposal then so novel that all three television networks put him on their evening newscasts. "The President was on the telephone to me the next morning and the nicest thing he got around to saying was that I looked good. Thereafter, there were several of these so-called briefings at the White House—or do they call them 'consultations'?—at which the President and the Secretary of State and the Secretary of Defense took turns in denouncing any suggestion of negotiation, treating it almost as a first cousin of sedition." To Gore's bemusement, "Only three or four months later the President made a speech in Baltimore in which he not only accepted a negotiated settlement as a goal, but advocated unconditional negotiation."

Private gloatings of the President over his "skillful" handling of Congress during the Tonkin period also began to seep into print, as did the time sequence involved in the decision to begin sustained strategic bombings of the North. Tom Wicker, then the New York Times' *White House man, wrote in a magazine article in November 1965: "He had been carrying it [the Tonkin Resolution] around in his pocket for weeks waiting for the moment."[4] And to Charles Roberts of* Newsweek, *Johnson confided that regardless of what he had been saying during the campaign, this bombing decision came in October of 1964.[5]*

Fulbright's criticisms of Johnson's actions in the Dominican Republic upset the White House for reasons more important than the break in the men's personal relationship. Foremost was the long-standing tradition that the chairman of the Senate Foreign Relations Committee not attack publicly the foreign policy of the president—and especially when he was of the same party. Here history was indeed on Johnson's side, for during most of the last four decades the Senate has given approval, rather than initiative, to foreign policy, and has permitted the president to assume unfettered responsibility for national security. The last maverick to hold the chairmanship was Senator Key Pittman of Nevada (1932–40), but his obstructionist attitude is attributable as much to alcoholism as to policy differences. Pittman kept a refrigerator in the committee room to expedite his bartending, and biographer Fred L. Israel says that "the Senator's addiction to alcohol grew progressively worse. . . . At meetings or hearings he always had a glass before him and continually sipped whiskey."[6] The committee's "vacillation and lack of leadership" during this period irked President Roosevelt; James F. Byrnes, for instance, tells of FDR's "keen disappointment"[7] at its refusal, in 1939, to repeal the embargo on arms shipments to nations at war. Once war began, however, the committee (and the rest of Congress) followed FDR unhesitatingly.

Relations between the White House and the committee continued happy after the war. President Truman involved the ranking Democratic and Republican members, Senators Tom Connally and Arthur Vandenberg, in formative sessions of the United Nations and in the Paris peace conference. "In 1946 they spent 213 days away from Washington attending international conferences," wrote Secretary of State Byrnes in his memoirs. ". . . I preferred to have their counsel rather than the aid of the technicians of the State Department . . . . Also, I wanted the Senators to know at first-hand every stage of the treaty making."[8]

Truman also involved the committee in drafting the Marshall Plan, with Vandenberg, then chairman, assigning a staff man to the task force which wrote the program. Truman credits Vandenberg with helping to steer the plan through a "Congress dedicated to tax reduction and the pruning of governmental expenditures."[9] And Vandenberg's support was instrumental in passage of the North Atlantic Treaty over vociferous objections of the Republican majority leader, Senator Robert A. Taft.

Yet Truman was capable of ignoring the Congress when it served his purposes. The morning of June 27, 1950, he called leaders to the White House and informed them, "I have ordered United States air and sea forces to give the [South] Korean government troops cover and support." The North Korean invasion was almost three days old, and Truman had been in virtual round-the-clock conferences with advisers; but until this meeting, he had told Congress nothing. As each Congressman left the Cabinet Room, he was "handed a mimeographed copy of the President's announcement which had been released to the press a few minutes earlier," writes Glenn D. Paige in his study of the Korean intervention.[10] Initially Congress accepted the affront in silence, but as the war worsened, Taft and other Republicans regularly flailed Truman for the lack of consultation.

A year later Truman again exerted presidential supremacy in foreign affairs. Testifying in support of Truman's decision to send ground troops to Europe under the NATO agreement, Secretary of State Dean Acheson declared: "Not only has the President the authority to use the armed forces in carrying out the broad foreign policy of the United States and implementing treaties, but it is equally clear that this authority may not be interfered with by the Congress in the exercise of the powers which it has under the constitution." The Senate bridled and resolved, 69-21, that no more than four divisions (the number already committed) be sent to West Europe without prior congressional approval—a dictate which Truman and succeeding presidents managed to circumvent.

During the Eisenhower years, Secretary of State John Foster Dulles regularly visited Senator Walter George for breakfast, a briefing on world affairs, and consultation on Administration plans and Senate reaction to them. Dulles' deference to the venerable Georgian enabled Ike to avoid any major foreign policy losses in Congress (and, indeed, Senate opposition, expressed privately, kept the Administration from intervening in the French-Indochinese War in 1954). Concurrently, however, Eisenhower and Dulles coaxed two blank checks from Congress that were immediate ancestors of the Tonkin Resolution: one, in 1954, giving the President broad powers to use force to protect Formosa and the Pescadores; the other giving him, in 1958, broad powers in the Middle East. Not that the Foreign Relations Committee was a rubber stamp; during hearings on the Middle East Resolution, Fulbright, then the second-ranking Democrat, lectured Dulles in language never heard even by the much-abused Rusk during his eight years as Secretary: "Not since the turn of the century have our relations with the other people of the free world been so strained—so unsatisfactory," Fulbright said. "This disastrous and remarkable collapse of our relations with our closest allies [Britain and France] has taken place under the direction of our present Secretary of State, and apparently within the relatively short space of a few months."

Yet, in summary, from the start of World War II through Fulbright's succession to the chairmanship on January 30, 1959, replacing 91-year-old Theodore Green, the committee and the Congress made no systematic attempt to stop the shift of power to the White House.

In the late fall of 1965, disappointed by Johnson's hostile reaction to his Dominican speech, Fulbright set out to arrest the erosion of congressional authority. And, in doing so, he wandered onto the path that was to lead him directly back to the Gulf of Tonkin incidents.

Fulbright began with three general postulates: (1) No longer would he have the role of private counselor to the President, capable of influencing policy in quiet conversations with the White House; (2) few persons in the country had more than a cursory knowledge of the origins and nature of the Vietnam War, and the extent of United States involvement; and (3) restiveness in the Senate over Vietnam lacked a focus, for there had never been a thorough on-the-record review of United States aims, and the likelihood of achieving them. Fulbright decided to strike at all three problems in full-blown hearings on the war, and the committee staff began preparing for them in November and December.

Concurrently, Johnson launched a highly publicized holiday season "peace offensive," halting bombing of North Vietnam while emissaries flurried from capital to capital, seeking support for a negotiated end to the war. No progress had been made by January 24, when Rusk came before the Foreign Relations Committee for his first briefing of the congressional session. Fulbright told Rusk he felt the time had come for more meaningful congressional participation in shaping war policy, and asked for assurances that Senate and House leaders would be "consulted" before the United States renewed the bombing, as he felt was on the verge of happening. He said that a renewal "would mean that we had given up any hope for the present of negotiation," and would cause "ever increasing escalation." Rusk refused. He said he would make the committee's "view known" to the President, but could promise nothing further. And he rejected Fulbright's suggestion that the National Liberation Front be invited to join peace talks.

Johnson invited Fulbright and majority leader Mansfield to the White House for a meeting that Administration spokesmen described as a "briefing"—not a "consultation"—a semantical difference which means that they were told, not asked, about the war. During the "briefing" Johnson made much of an "intelligence report" of North Vietnamese buildups during the pause, presenting it to Mansfield and Fulbright as classified information. Almost simultaneously the White House released the same information to the press. Fulbright has since said privately that he thought the entire affair was a "calculated insult." On January 27 the Senate dissidents, their ranks now swelling, gave Johnson one more chance to avoid open confrontation: Fifteen of them, led by Senator Vance Hartke of Indiana, sent the White House a letter stating: "We believe we understand in some small degree the agony you must suffer when called upon by our constitutional system to make judgments which may involve peace or war. We believe you should have our collective judgment before you when you make your decision" on a bombing resumption. Johnson replied that he was being "guided" by the Tonkin Resolution, and referred the Senators to a letter he had written to 76 dissident House Democrats some time earlier—in sum, another snub for the Senate.

Thus Fulbright's mood was testy on Friday, January 28, when the committee opened the "educational hearings" with Rusk as the lead-off witness. (As a vehicle Fulbright used an Administration request for a supplemental $415 million foreign-aid request, most of it for Vietnam.)[11] Fulbright admitted at the outset his long-standing ignorance of Vietnam "because, frankly, I did not anticipate years ago that this was a serious situation. I mean anything like it is. I thought of it primarily as another country among many to whom we were giving aid. I really never became concerned about the situation until about the time of the Bay [sic] of Tonkin." Fulbright opined that the 15 dissenting Senators who petitioned the President did so because "they are not quite clear what the purpose is, and would like an opportunity to examine the objective further before they have to vote on commitments which are irrevocable."

Rusk replied, "I am a little concerned that formal acts of the Government over a period of years in a variety of ways would appear to catch people by surprise at the moment when things began to get attention. I would hope the Senate would not ratify an alliance if it did not intend that alliance to be taken seriously." To which Fulbright responded, "We have a difference of view of what that alliance means, you see. That is what has been developed, I think."

Ultimately Rusk and Fulbright reached the question of whether Johnson was misusing the Tonkin Resolution—and for the first time the nation heard high-level allegations that he had indeed done so. Rusk's testimony is interesting as much for the answers he refused as for those he gave:

Chairman FULBRIGHT. The point is that I, along with most of the committee, did not at the time [August 1964] visualize or contemplate that this was going to take the turn that it now appears about to take. I do not know whether resuming bombing will result in escalation, but such statements as in this morning's paper by the chairman of the [Senate] Subcommittee on Preparedness* indicate that this could well be heading toward a nuclear war. I think that is a mission quite different from what I had in mind at that time.

Secretary RUSK. I think, Senator, it is entirely fair to say that the exact shape of the situation as it has developed was not known in August of 1964, and that the exact measures which might have to be taken to give effect to the policy could not then be known and completely clarified, because so much of this turns upon what the other side has been doing during this period.

But the policy of the Southeast Asia Treaty and the policy of the resolution has been long known to be the policy of the United States, as expressed both by the executive and the legislative branches.

Chairman FULBRIGHT. Wouldn't you agree though in light of that, that that should not be interpreted as an authorization or approval of an unlimited expansion of the war?

Secretary RUSK. Well, we are not in a position of an unlimited expansion of the war. The steps that have been taken have been taken over a period of time with considerable caution and restraint, while every possibility of peace was being explored. And, on these matters there has been frequent consultation with the various committees and the leadership of the Congress as the situation has developed . . . . We did not lose, contact with the Congress in August 1964. Both sides have been in

* Fulbright referred to a speech by Senator Stennis before the Mississippi State Legislature on January 27, 1966, in which Stennis said, "I would never put our boys in mortal conflict against the hordes of Red Chinese coolies without being free to use every weapon we have, when and if necessary."[12]

business, and we have been discussing this matter in great detail since then.

Chairman FULBRIGHT. Senator Mansfield certainly thinks there is a prospect . . . of what he calls an open-ended conflict which is a euphonious [sic] way to say all-out war, and Senator Stennis' statements certainly indicated that he is contemplating the possibility of that or he would not have made such a statement as he made yesterday.

Secretary RUSK. There are some dangers, of course, Mr. Chairman, in any such situation. That problem has been with us in each one of the principal crises we have been faced with since 1945.

Chairman FULBRIGHT. Well, then, the point comes down to: Don't you think we ought to understand what we are in for, and that the Congress should give its further approval to this changed situation?

Secretary RUSK. Well, that question, as to whether the Congress would wish to take special action beyond that of August or in connection with the proposal which is before the committee today, is one which is a matter for consideration between the executive and the legislative branches, and I would not have a . . . recommendation on that particular point this morning, sir.

Chairman FULBRIGHT. . . . [I]n view of that, would the approval of this very large increase in authorization [of foreign aid expenditures] be interpreted as an approval of our policy, as indicated it may be by Senator Stennis and others? . . . Is this to be taken as an approval of an unlimited expansion of the war?

Secretary RUSK. You are not being asked, Mr. Chairman, for an unlimited expansion of the war.

Chairman FULBRIGHT. I know you are not, but I am talking about the interpretation of it, to be put onto it . . . . Would you think it would be interpreted that way?

Secretary RUSK. I think the Executive and Congress must at all times move together on these matters, as they have in the past. I think these additional funds, both on the military and economic side———

Chairman FULBRIGHT. I do not think that is responsive. You do not have to answer if you do not like. You can say that is not anticipated. It is not responsive. But do you or don't you think it should be interpreted that way? You do not have to answer it, but the other is not responsive . . . .

Secretary RUSK. I will have to take it under advisement.

Chairman FULBRIGHT. That is all right if you do not wish to answer it, that is quite all right at this time. I do think before we act it ought to be answered.

Senator [Karl] MUNDT. In that connection, Mr. Secretary, do you think that we have reached a juncture in this era of uncertainty and indecisiveness where, perhaps, the Administration should send some statement down which we could approve or disapprove or amend?

Secretary RUSK. Well, as I say, that is a matter that has been under advisement. The Congress has before it two very important pieces of legislation which have to do with a very large supplement to the defense budget [$12 billion] and a very substantial increase in the aid appropriation [the $415 million request before the Foreign Relations Committee]. That is against the background and in the light of events which have developed since the August 1964 resolution was passed. I would suppose that in the course of this discussion the Congress would have a chance to discuss and to pass judgment upon the situation as we see it at the present time.

Before the hearings began, Rusk had sent Fulbright a telegram from Ambassador Henry Cabot Lodge with the suggestion that it be included in the record. Fulbright found one sentence of particular interest: "A vote for this appropriation is . . . an utterly indispensable act if one supports U.S. policy in Vietnam." He told Rusk: "That was one of the reasons why I asked that question earlier as to how a vote on this [appropriation] would be interpreted." Rusk never did answer the point.

When Rusk returned on February 18 for further testimony, his opening statement on the legality of United States participation in the war did not mention the Tonkin Resolution even by implication. Instead, he said, a "fundamental SEATO obligation . . . has from the outset guided our actions in South Vietnam." And, he noted, when the SEATO treaty was before the Senate in 1954, "all members of this distinguished committee who were then Senators voted for that treaty." Under questioning by Fulbright, he said the Tonkin Resolution was "entirely consistent" with SEATO.* "So I would hope that you would take into full account the continuity of policy, and the problem of turning aside from that policy under present conditions."

Fulbright, somewhat mournfully: "Mr. Secretary, I wish these things appeared as simple to me as they do to you. . . . I am sure it is due to my own obtuseness. . . ."

Lacking any other means of disavowing Administration policy, Morse declared, "One of the best checks we have is to say we are not going to finance it. If the President can't get the finances, then he has to change his policy."

This aroused Senator Long with what was to become the Administration's stock defense against this strategem: "I would like to ask you, do you

---

* Although Fulbright didn't delve into the legislative intent of the SEATO treaty, it might be noted that Secretary of State John Foster Dulles told the Senate Foreign Relations Committee in 1954: "We made clear at Manila [at the SEATO drafting meetings] that it was not the intention of the United States to build up a large local force including, for example, U.S. ground troops for that area, but that we rely upon the deterrent power of our mobile striking force."

intend to send those boys off over there without giving them whatever it takes for them to fight and defend themselves and to win? . . . [G]ive them whatever help it takes to see that they are not cut off and surrounded and decimated as those people were at Dien Bien Phu? . . ." (Senator Russell, in a floor comment on February 16, said that failure to "provide for [troops] there . . . would mean that all of them would perish eventually, either through sickness, from the bullets of the Viet Cong, and the North Vietnamese; in a short while they would be perfectly helpless. . . .")

Rear Admiral Arnold E. True was a recognized authority on destroyer tactics; during his active duty from 1920 to 1946 he revised the Navy's basic manual on the subject. After retirement he settled on a 1,000-acre cattle ranch in La Honda, California, and taught meteorology at San Jose State College. The Fulbright hearings stirred latent doubts about the Tonkin incidents he first felt in 1964, and soon after the sessions ended he wrote the Senator:

> *In press accounts of [the Tonkin] incident it appears that the destroyer* Maddox *on the high seas was being followed by North Vietnamese torpedo boats which also had a right to be on the high seas. These reports say the* Maddox, *suspecting an attack, 'fired a warning shot across their bows.' Next day they [the North Vietnamese boats] are reported to have made a torpedo attack.*
>
> *I commanded a destroyer, a division, and a squadron during WW II. The account sounds unrealistic: (1) A DD [destroyer] cannot fire 'across the bow' of a following ship. (2) There is no provision in international law for 'firing a warning shot' at another man-of-war on the high seas. As commander of a man-of-war I would consider any such shot as hostile and would not only be justified but required by Navy regulations to retaliate.*
>
> *It seems to me that if the accounts I read are correct, the U.S. fired the first shot in the war with N. Vietnam and then bombed the torpedo base because they retaliated, and that the resolution was passed on false premises.*
>
> *Can you tell me if this is correct?*

Replying, Fulbright said True's comments, "coming from such an experienced person . . . were of special interest." He sent along a copy of the 1964 hearings, other printed documents, and appended a postscript:

> *I have had reservations about their story, but have no way effectively to question it.*

The Fulbright hearings infuriated Johnson, for they came at the worst possible time politically. He and Rusk had concluded that North Vietnam would not accept their bargaining terms, and on January 28 (the same day the hearings began) the national security hierarchy decided that the bombings must resume. The new raids began on January 31, with the nation enthralled by the televised debate of national war strategy, and by the doubts of leading academicians and former government officials as to the efficacy of Administration policy. Johnson sat glowering before TV sets with the rest of the nation, "bluing the air with a running commentary that could *not* have gone on the air," in the words of a former adviser. Finally, with only several hours more than three days' notice, Johnson hurried to Hawaii for a meeting with Nguyen Cao Ky, Saigon's new chief of state. But the trip didn't detract from the impact of the Fulbright hearings, which, Walter Lippmann commented, "broke through the official screen and made visible the nature of the war and whence our present policy is leading us."

Nonetheless Johnson showed no outward worries about the criticisms. The White House leaked polls showing 65 percent of the citizenry supporting him, and although (at a February 26 press conference) he acknowledged the congressional opposition, he said he was "rather pleased . . . that the differences are as minimal as they are." What impact was the debate having abroad? "I think the members of the Congress are going to follow the course that they think is best for the country and I don't want to be more critical of that course unless I feel it's much more demanding." Morse met resounding failure in an attempt to have the Senate repeal the Tonkin Resolution, and the increased military and economic aid funds easily passed both houses.

For Fulbright and Johnson, however, the battle line was drawn. In an April 28 speech to the American Newspaper Publishers Association, the Senator declared: "America is showing some signs of that fatal presumption, that overextension of power and mission, which brought ruin to ancient Greece, to Napoleonic France, and to Nazi Germany." He feared that the nation was succumbing to an "arrogance of power." (Senator Goldwater suggested that Fulbright resign from the Foreign Relations Committee for giving "aid and comfort to the enemy. No American has the right or the justification to level such charges against his own country. And that goes double for doing it in a time of war.")

At a Democratic fund-raising dinner in Washington on May 12, Fulbright was sitting at the head table when Johnson made a surprise appearance. There wasn't a trace of a smile on the President's face as he said, "I'm glad to be here among so many friends—and some members of the Foreign Relations Committee." (Nervous, embarrassed laughter.) "You can say one thing about those hearings—but I don't think this is the place to say it." Johnson went on to urge all candidates present to campaign in support of his Vietnam policy. On May 19 at another fund-raiser, this time in Chicago, he didn't mention Fulbright by name—but, again, he didn't have to. "I do not think that those men who are out there fighting for us tonight think that we should enjoy the luxury of fighting each other back home. There will be Nervous Nellies* and some who become frustrated and bothered and break ranks under the strain and turn on their leaders, their own country, and their own fighting men."

Did the President want the Democratic party purged of war dissenters? Replied press secretary Bill D. Moyers, "No . . . we just want to be sure that others understand and that because we have dissent does not mean that we have been dissected."

Girls in Fulbright's office proudly donned buttons identifying themselves as "Nervous Nellies."

Had the Fulbright dissent been nothing more than scholarly ideological argument, its impact upon the Senate establishment would have been minimal. But his chief influence upon the Vietnam debate was to inspire honest inquiry—first, on the ability of the United States to fulfill militarily the 42 "commitments" made since 1945 to defend other nations against "aggression"; and, second, on the erosion of Congress' constitutional role in the making of American foreign policy. The issues put Fulbright on peculiar common ground with Senate constitutionalists and moderates who were hard-liners on the war, but who also bridled at their loss of power to the Executive. (Senator McCarthy once remarked that the "territorial imperative" governs the conduct of the Senate just as it does that of nations, or of animals in the wilderness.)

Senator Stennis' Preparedness Investigating Subcommittee, in hearings in August 1966, concerned itself mainly with whether the United States was caught in "overcommitments that would drain away our manpower and resources, and thus leave us weakened and unable to protect ourselves."[13] For two days Rusk outlined the growth of the alliance system since the end of World War II, and United States efforts to "organize a peace." Then, without preface, Stennis lectured the Secretary on the President's misuse of the Tonkin Resolution:

> I really do not think we need a legal adviser to tell us what the Tonkin Gulf Resolution means or what the Constitution means when it talks about declaring war. The Congress has just failed to comply with that requirement, and I am not raising any fuss about that now. I am a guilty party, if anyone is guilty, on the Tonkin Gulf Resolution. I am concerned about this, though, as a precedent it may set . . . . I have looked at that language [in the resolution] rather closely. But more than that, I know the debates we had on it and the discussions we had on it. It seems to me that you stand on mighty thin ice if you rely upon the

* The disrespectful nickname was first assigned to Frank B. Kellogg, Secretary of State under Calvin Coolidge, for his "Pact to Outlaw War."

Tonkin Gulf Resolution as a constitutional basis for this war. But we are not going to try to measure that. . . .

. . . I think it is a bad precedent . . . when we get into a war like this, now approaching the size of the Korean War, as far as our men are concerned, and it is a great mistake to fail to be just frank about it. . . .

Stennis' statement should have reverberated through the White House like a Klaxon horn, for here was criticism by an Establishment figure who was not only a hawk, but also a strict constitutionalist. Simple arithmetic would have shown the White House that the gradually expanding peace bloc in the Senate, were it to strike an alliance of convenience with the constitutionalists, could cut the Administration to ribbons—if not on the war directly, certainly on other foreign policy issues. Nor was the Senate Armed Services Committee (Johnson supporters to a man, in both parties) satisfied with the "continuing consultation" Rusk and McNamara (and the President) had promised at the time of Tonkin. Senator Symington complained that the Appropriations Committee, even in closed session, "cannot get an estimate of how many more men will be needed in Vietnam during the remainder of this fiscal year. No one knows. We could not get a loose estimate the other day in closed session of what probably would or might be needed in money for the remainder of this . . . fiscal year for that war."[14]

But Johnson didn't listen.

Repeatedly during the first half of 1967, Congress rebuffed the White House on specific foreign affairs issues, leaving "Capitol Hill . . . strewn with the wreckage and partial wreckage of programs dear to the heart of the Johnson Administration," in the apt phraseology of the National Committee for an Effective Congress.[15] In March the Senate killed the Pentagon's request for five fast deployment logistics ships (FDLS), so-called "floating arsenals" which would permit the fast transport of United States troops to trouble spots, and withdrew authorization for two FDLSs previously approved. In April the Senate upheld the Foreign Relations Committee's 9-0 rejection of Johnson's request to commit $1.5 billion in aid, a 30 percent increase, to Latin American nations over the next five years. The Senate refused to endorse either a Latin American Common Market or provision of United States aid through the Inter-American Development Bank, Fulbright stressing congressional control over United States aid funds. In June a broad range of Senate leaders in both parties warned the Administration against unilateral intervention in the Middle East war. In August, the Senate cut the $3.4 billion foreign aid budget by $840 million. The same month it rescinded the Pentagon's "Country X" strategem for guaranteeing loans for arms purchases by underdeveloped nations through the Export-Import Bank. This was a scheme the Defense Department was in the habit of using when it desired to help a friendly but penniless country to buy weapons. The Pentagon would arrange the loan through the Export-

Import Bank and guarantee repayment, with its own funds if necessary. The bank was not told the identity of the borrowing nation, which would appear simply as a "Country X" account. In two years, the Country X scheme accounted for $604 million in arms sales—many to nations reliant upon United States aid funds for economic survival. William Bader, a Foreign Relations Committee staff member, ferreted out the story through vigorous investigative work, and Fulbright put it into the public domain with hearings. Only a handful of Senators had been aware of the Pentagon's *sub rosa* financing—once the full account was made known, the Country X scheme was dead within weeks.

But the Senate's many frustrations with Administration foreign policy came to a head on July 6, when the State Department announced the dispatch of three cargo planes and a small group of paratroopers from the 82nd Airborne Division to the Congo, to help the government of President Joseph D. Mobutu quell an uprising by white mercenaries and Katangese gendarmes. Senator Russell, whose loyalty to Johnson was beyond question, arose in the Senate three days later and proclaimed that it was "immoral to send even one American boy into a country where we have no commitments and where we have no vital interests. . . . Vietnam started out with a not much larger force than that. It can swell and it will swell if a few of our forces are killed. We should have enough sense to keep our people out of situations like this." He attacked "our apparently irrepressible desire to rush into some of these situations" at the risk of provoking war with the Soviet Union or Communist China. Majority leader Mansfield said that he was "shocked, surprised, and dismayed" to learn of the Congo venture, and added, "From little acorns great oaks sometimes grow."

Summarizing the Senate dissent, the National Committee for an Effective Congress warned in late summer: "The confrontation is not directly over Vietnam—which is certainly the underlying cause—but over who may make fateful national decisions. More precisely, what is developing is a clash between a rising Senate and the personality of Lyndon Johnson. And when a man collides with an institution, it is not often the institution that buckles."[16]

Chapter Seven

CONGRESS IS AROUSED

The collision between man and institution came in August 1967, in hearings before the Foreign Relations Committee on Chairman Fulbright's so-called "national commitments resolution," which read as follows:

> Whereas accurate definition of the term 'national commitment' in recent years has become obscured: Now, therefore be it
>
> *Resolved,* that it is the sense of the Senate that a national commitment of the United States to a foreign power necessarily and exclusively results from affirmative action taken by the Executive and Legislative branches of the United States government through means of a treaty, convention, or other legislative instrumentality specifically intended to give effect to such a commitment.

The peculiar feature of the resolution, in a year of harsh national division over the Vietnam War, was the catholicity of its support: Although introduced by dove Fulbright, hawk Richard Russell was the first Senator to speak for it on the floor. Nor was the resolution solely an outburst of anti-Johnson rancor; as Senator George Aiken of Vermont expressed the prevailing mood: "I do not think we can excuse Congress from the situation which exists today because over the past 20 or 25 years we found it easier to tell the Executive branch to take care of that matter or this matter when it was really our responsibility. . . . I blame the Executive branch for some of its mistakes, but nevertheless Congress has to share the guilt for them because we have been too negligent and too tolerant." A secondary theme in the Senate was surprise over how far the pendulum had swung. Senator Karl Mundt of South Dakota, for instance, said he was astounded to learn during the Glassboro Summit Conference of June 1967 that Soviet Premier Kosygin "does not have the authority to commit his nation that President Johnson has . . . . Now this is kind of . . . shocking . . . when you stop to realize that Mr. Johnson was representing a popularly based government, based on the rule of the people, and Mr. Kosygin was representing a political monopoly."

Submission of the resolution marked a complete turnabout for Fulbright, who during the 1950s frequently criticized the immobility of United States foreign policy. The coincidence of the cold war and Senator Joseph McCarthy's rampages "led me to advocate greater freedom for the Executive in the conduct of the foreign policy," he said, adding defensively, "We are all susceptible to the human tendency to give undue weight to the concerns of the moment." But having seen the "frenetic mobility of the 1960s, the overheated activism and the ubiquitous developments . . . of a global mission often referred to as the 'responsibilities of power' I now see merit that I formerly did not see in occasional delay or inaction."

In the preceding six years, Fulbright noted, "The United States has taken four military actions on the basis of executive decisions made either secretly or under such alleged conditions of urgency as to preclude meaningful consultation with the Congress." In only one of these situations, the 1962 Cuban missile crisis, was the "urgency genuine," and even then, Fulbright maintains, Congress could have been drawn into the decision making "without loss of time or secrecy." In the other three instances—the Bay of Pigs, the passive intervention in Vietnam, and the Dominican Republic—it would have been very much better if action had been delayed to permit careful consultation between the Executive and the Congress. "We could as well have intervened in Cuba, the Dominican Republic, and Vietnam a few weeks later than we did and be as well off for having done so as we are now. . . ."*

That congressional authority in foreign policy has run the full circle from Executive deference to Executive dominance is all the more striking when put into historical perspective. For example, after President James Monroe declared South America to be off limits to European powers, Colombia inquired as to what exactly the United States would do in the event of extrahemispheric violation of the doctrine. Secretary of State John Quincy Adams replied that it would be a "matter for Congress to determine."

As Professor Ruhl J. Bartlett of the Fletcher School of Law and Diplomacy, a key witness at the national commitments hearings, said: "The positions of the Executive and Legislative branches of the Federal government in the area of foreign affairs have come very close to reversal since

* Actually, Fulbright *was* consulted on the Bay of Pigs, but by sheer happenstance. Pat Holt, the committee's Latin American expert, learned of the invasion plans and wrote a long opposing memorandum which Fulbright gave to President Kennedy during a Florida trip. Kennedy a few days later brought Fulbright into the meeting at which the decision was made to go ahead with the invasion. Fulbright objected. "He gave a brave, old-fashioned American speech, honorable, sensible, and strong, and he left everyone in the room, except me and perhaps the President, wholly unmoved," writes Arthur M. Schlesinger, Jr.[1] And, during the missile crisis, Fulbright and Russell argued for invasion, rather than blockade. "The President heard them out, but said he would not change his strategy," writes Pierre Salinger.[2]

1789, a change that has been gradual in some degree but with acceleration during the past half-century and breakneck speed during the past 20 years. The President virtually determines foreign policy and decides on war and peace, and the Congress has acquiesced in or ignored, or approved and encouraged this development."[3]

But the chief Administration witness, Undersecretary of State Katzenbach, viewed the strong Executive role with approval, saying, "It is difficult to imagine how it could be otherwise." Katzenbach endorsed Thomas Jefferson's statement, "The transaction of business with foreign nations is Executive altogether," adding his personal comment, "His [the President's] is the sole authority to communicate formally with foreign nations; to negotiate treaties; to command the armed forces of the United States. His is a responsibility born of the need for speed and decisiveness in an emergency. His is the responsibility for controlling and directing all the external aspects of the nation's power. To him flows all of the vast intelligence and information connected with national security."[4]

Professor Bartlett, however, rejects the notion that "decisions on national defense may need to be so immediate that no time can be allowed for the slow and possibly faltering deliberations of democratic assemblies." Declares Bartlett: "This argument has been affirmed, and repeated, and repeated, until people are mesmerized by it. The President has—and has always had—the duty to use the armed forces at his disposal to repel sudden armed attacks on the United States, and there has never been a case in the whole history of the United States where the imminence of danger to the nation was so great that decision to do more than repel attack could not be entrusted to the Congress. Others may wish to speculate on the possibility that the greatest danger to the United States is the unauthorized use of the armed forces."

On the subject of Executive monopoly of expertise in foreign affairs, Bartlett avows, "In addition to being insulting, this argument is utterly fallacious. Experts are needed in the mechanics of many things whether they are called professions or something else, but there are no experts in wisdom concerning human affairs or in determining the national interest, and there is nothing in the realm of foreign policy that cannot be understood by the average American citizen." In sum: "The arguments of immediacy, expertness, superior information, and greater wisdom are equally fallacious as bases for enlarged Presidential authority. The framers of the Constitution bequeathed to the American people a great heritage, that of a constitutional, federal, representative government, with its powers limited in scope and divided among its three separate branches, and this system was devised not because it would produce efficiency or world domination, but because it offered the greatest hope of preventing tyranny."

The national commitments hearings began with a broad discussion of the evolution of presidential powers—but inexorably came back to the Gulf of Tonkin Resolution, and the Johnson Administration's use of it.

The framers of the Constitution, as Professor Bartlett noted in his opening testimony, "clearly recognized that the President would have not only the right but the duty to use the armed forces at his disposal to 'repel' sudden attacks on the United States, and that as commander-in-chief he would direct the armed forces for any purpose specified by the Congress, but these authorities and duties did not extend to the initiation of hostilities." The power to initiate war "was not divided between the Executive and the Congress; it was vested in the Congress, and the Congress alone . . . . This is not a matter of interpretation or controversy; it is a simple fact. When Jefferson learned of the provision . . . he considered this as one of the most wise provisions for . . . it permitted the legislature 'to hold in leash the dogs of war.' "

In defense of modern Executive activism, the State Department (in a legal memorandum submitted to the Foreign Relations Committee March 8, 1966) asserts: "In 1787, the world was a far larger place, and the framers probably had in mind attacks upon the United States. In the 20th Century, the world has grown much smaller. An attack on a country far from our shores can impinge directly on the nation's security. In the SEATO Treaty, for example, it is formally declared that an armed attack against Vietnam would endanger the peace and safety of the United States. Since the Constitution was adopted there have been at least 125 instances in which the President has ordered the armed forces to take action or maintain positions abroad without obtaining prior congressional approval, starting with the 'undeclared war' with France (1798–1800) . . . . The Constitution leaves to the President the judgment to determine whether the circumstances of a particular armed attack are so urgent and the potential consequences so threatening to the security of the United States that he should act without formally consulting the Congress."

Constitutional expert Francis D. Wormuth maintains that State's history is as sloppy as is its understanding of constitutional law. "This is altogether false," he writes of the example cited.[5] President John Adams took absolutely no independent action in the "undeclared war," but followed scrupulously a series of congressional acts: suspension of commercial intercourse with France; denunciation of treaties with her; establishment of a navy and marine corps, and provision for raising of an army. Subsequent laws authorized the President to take action against France in specified situations, such as against "any . . . armed vessel which shall . . . be found hovering on the coasts of the United States, for the purpose of committing depredations on the vessels belonging to citizens thereof. . . ." Professor Bartlett considers the "undeclared war" to be the first "limited war" in United States history, and finds it "interesting not only because the President took only such action as was authorized by Congress, but also because it was a clear precedent that offensive military action short of a declared war was within the province of Congress."

Similarly, Jefferson sent a naval squadron to the Mediterranean with authority to protect American vessels against pirates, but not to engage in offensive action, even retaliation, "for in the President's view this would amount to war which the Congress had not declared," states Bartlett. Frequently during the nineteenth and early twentieth centuries, the Navy was used to suppress piracy and the slave trade (in the latter instance, by American ships), and to protect American lives and property in areas of civil disruption or in primitive regions where no government existed which could be dealt with through normal diplomatic procedures. Bartlett feels that in such cases "the President had authority to act under general laws and was not required to seek the approval of Congress in each case." Yet he doubts that "these episodes provided significant exceptions to the general rule."

President James Buchanan was the most conservative of the nineteenth-century executives in the use of war powers, and the arguments used in one of his congressional imbroglios foreshadow the language heard a century later in the Tonkin debate. Beginning in 1857, Buchanan informed Congress annually of the danger that free transit across the Isthmus of Panama might be disrupted either by American soldiers of fortune or "by wars between the independent states of Central America." He asked passage of an act authorizing the president to use force "in preventing the transit from being obstructed or closed by lawless violence, and in protecting the lives and property of American citizens travelling thereon." When British or French ships are fired upon, Buchanan lamented, their governments "can promptly employ the necessary means to enforce immediate redress for similar outrages upon their subjects. Not so the executive government of the United States. If the President orders a vessel of war to any of those ports to demand prompt redress for outrages committed, the offending parties are well aware that in case of refusal the command can do no more than remonstrate. He can resort to no hostile act . . . ."

Buchanan said in one of his messages: "Without the authority of Congress, the President cannot fire a hostile gun in any case except to repel the attacks of an enemy."

Since Congress has the right to authorize the president to recapture an American vessel which has been seized in port, Buchanan asked, "Have they no power to confer upon the President the authority in advance to furnish instant redress should such a case afterwards occur? Must they wait until the mischief has been done, and can they apply the remedy only when it is too late? . . . In the progress of a great nation many exigencies must arise imperatively requiring that Congress should authorize the Presi-

dent to act promptly on certain conditions which may or may not afterwards arise."

Senator William H. Seward of New York, the Wayne Morse of the mid-
nineteenth century, rebutted:

> It was thought, several years ago, that it was a great improvement,
> conducive to peace, essential to the permanent stability of republican
> institutions, that the Executive should be destitute of the power to make
> war, and that this last final remedy for national grievance should never
> be resorted to in any case without the deliberate consent and determina-
> tion of the nation itself. . . . The President . . . now regrets that those
> nations living under arbitrary forms of government are safer than we
> are who live under this, as we thought, improved system.
>
> But, sir, I am unable to understand the logic which brings the Presi-
> dent . . . to the conclusion that to use this application will not be a
> surrender of the war-making power. He tells us that it would not be a
> surrender of the war-making power, but that we should be making war
> ourselves. *Could anything be more strange and preposterous than the
> idea of the President of the United States making hypothetical wars,
> conditional wars, without any designation of the nation against which
> war is to be declared; or the time, or place, or manner, or circumstance
> of the duration of it, the beginning or the end, and without limiting the
> number of nations with which war may be waged?*
>
> No, sir.
>
> When we pass this bill, we do surrender the power of making war or
> preserving peace, in each of the States named, into the hands of the
> President of the United States.

Congress never granted Buchanan the desired authority. Bartlett says
that Buchanan represented "perhaps an ultraconservative view of the
Executive authority, but to a large degree it was characteristic of Presidential thinking during the 18th and 19th Century."

Theodore Roosevelt, smitten with the idea of Manifest Destiny ("It is
the Anglo-Saxon's manifest destiny to go forth as a world conqueror . . . .
This is what fate holds for the chosen people"), changed the rules. In 1903
he ordered the Navy to keep Colombian troops from landing in Panama,
then part of Colombia, to suppress a "rebellion" inspired by the United
States, and cited an obscure 1846 treaty as his authority. Teddy later sent
troops into Cuba and the Dominican Republic; when Congress threatened
to halt his freewheeling fleet movements by withholding fuel oil appropriations, Roosevelt threatened to move the ships into the Pacific and leave
them there—with dry tanks, if necessary. Congress backed down. During
the next quarter-century American soldiers and Marines were landed 30
times in Central American and Caribbean countries, and Congress did
nothing to protest the use of troops without its authority.

Woodrow Wilson courteously informed Congress of his major foreign moves, although adding *sotto voce* that its consent wasn't really required. In April 1914, for instance, he briefed leaders on deteriorating relations with the Mexican revolutionary government of General Victoriano Huerta, occasioned by the detention of several sailors and an officer in Tampico and of a mail courier in Veracruz, and by the delay of an official cable. Wilson accused Huerta of "studied contempt," and on the evening of April 20 asked Congress to approve his use of the armed forces as necessary "to obtain from General Huerta and his adherents the fullest recognition of the rights and dignity of the United States." Wilson went home to bed, and was awakened at 2:00 A.M. with word that a German ship bearing munitions was about to land in Veracruz. Without hesitation (or congressional authority) he ordered the seizure of Veracruz, an operation commenced at dawn with the loss of 19 American and several hundred Mexican lives. The United States held Veracruz for six months under military government. Congress finally passed a resolution approving a *fait accompli*.

In February 1917, Wilson similarly sought congressional approval of his decision to arm American merchant vessels for defense against German submarines. He claimed authority to do so anyway, but wanted to "feel that the authority and power of the Congress" stood behind him. The resolution authorized the President to arm the ships and "to employ such other instrumentalities" as he thought necessary. The House balked at the instrumentalities clause, and Congress adjourned. Wilson proceeded to arm the ships.

Franklin D. Roosevelt introduced the concept of what Francis Wormuth has called "war by invitation." In 1941 United States troops occupied Iceland and Greenland by invitation of the local authorities—but without congressional authority. FDR claimed the occupation was essential to hemispheric defense, although Admiral Harold R. Stark, the Chief of Naval Operations, conceded to Congress that the measures were "practically an act of war." Later in 1941 Roosevelt sent troops to Dutch Guiana by invitation of the Netherlands government-in-exile. There were no hostilities in any of the three areas, yet each was strongly susceptible to enemy attacks and Roosevelt wanted troops in them as a preventive defensive measure.

On October 8, 1941, Roosevelt ordered the Navy to fire upon any German or Italian ships west of the 26th meridian. Says Bartlett: "It seems beyond doubt that the President had placed the United States in a state of war without congressional authority, and since the President authorized naval convoy which was prohibited by the Lend-Lease Act, he not only impinged on the right of Congress to declare war, but also violated existing law." The start of total war brushed aside any questions about abuse of presidential authority.

Which brings us to the presidency of today, and the rationales offered by the Johnson and other postwar administrations for their conduct of foreign affairs. Katzenbach offered this explanation to the national commitments hearings:

> The basic objective of our foreign policy is the security of the United States and the preservation of our freedoms. How this objective is achieved obviously depends upon the kind of world in which we live and the extent to which we can bring American power and influence to bear upon it.
>
> For most of our history, we had only spasmodic foreign business. We lived in relative isolation, content to allow the European powers to maintain the balance of power on which, in fact, our national security depended.
>
> In recent years, however, there has been a revolutionary change in the political structure of the world—and of the relative importance of foreign affairs to the United States. What has been perceived by all—by presidents, by the Congress, and by the people—is that our independence and our security can no longer be assured by default. They depend in large measure on our capacity to lead in the achievement of a system of assured world peace. Within the broad horizons of such a framework—and only within such horizons—can American democracy and American society be safe.
>
> This framework, I believe, rests on three propositions. The first is that events elsewhere can have critical effects on this country; hence our security is bound up with that of other countries.
>
> The second is that we must heed more than power politics. For if we are true to our domestic ideals and are concerned for our domestic security, we cannot ignore the conditions in which people around the world must live—conditions which can and do fuel reverberating political explosions.
>
> The third is that we cannot and should not meet these first two needs alone, any more than we could or should seek unilaterally to establish a *pax Americana*. We must develop international instrumentalities to help provide collective security and to help create social progress and eliminate the flammable conditions of misery that embrace so much of the world's population.*

By Katzenbach's definition, "the voice of the United States in foreign affairs was, of necessity, the voice of the President. Consistent with that basic necessity, it also provided for the participation of Congress in a number of ways, direct and indirect." In this context, he continues: "The Constitution left to the judgment and wisdom 'of the Executive and Congress the task of working out the details of their relationship." He concedes that the formula has not been uniformly successful: Congress

---

* Katzenbach appeared as a spokesman for Rusk. After the "educational hearings" of February 1966, Rusk refused for two years to appear publicly before the Foreign Relations Committee—despite repeated requests that he do so. He reappeared before live TV cameras in January 1968 for hearings on the 1969 foreign-aid request, but the session rapidly (and predictably) turned into a war inquiry. The White House backed Rusk in his refusal to testify publicly, to Fulbright's outrage.

complained of Executive excesses in Monroe's announcement of his renowned Latin American doctrine, and in Jefferson's Louisiana Purchase; Buchanan's previously cited troubles stand as a good converse example. Katzenbach continues: "But if the constitutional formula of flexibility was not an easy one, it has surely proved to be a practical and workable one. It has always seemed to me that the genius of our Constitution rests on the recognition of its drafters that they could not provide precise resolution for all future problems, foreseen and unforeseen. And I think that the conduct of foreign affairs demonstrates the validity of this approach."

The United States relies on three basic mechanisms for what Rusk has called the "organization of a peace." First is Article 42 of the United Nations charter, which provides for agreements between the Security Council and member states by which the latter are to promise armed forces for military actions ordered by the council to maintain or restore international peace and order. Through the United Nations Participation Act, Congress in 1945 authorized the president to negotiate such an agreement with the Security Council. The act states: "The President *shall not be deemed to require the authorization of the Congress* to make available to the Security Council on its call in order to take action under Article 42 . . . the armed forces, facilities, or assistance provided therein." Hence the basis for Truman's dispatch of troops to Korea. Francis Wormuth comments: "The act does not say that the President *must* make the force available. It seems to assume that he may do so or fail to do so as he thinks best. If he chooses to do so, he need not seek the approval of Congress. This is indisputably a delegation of the power to make war."

Supplementing the UN agreements are bilateral and multilateral agreements for collective defense which the United States maintains with 42 countries. Katzenbach notes: "On each of these, the President sought and secured the advice and consent of the Senate. Let me emphasize the constitutional quality of these commitments. By their nature, they set only the boundaries within which the United States will act. They cannot and do not spell out the precise action which the United States would take in a variety of contingencies. That is left for further decision by the President and the Congress. In short, none of these incur automatic response. But they do make clear our pledge to take actions we regard as appropriate in the light of all the circumstances. . . ."

And, finally, on three occasions Congress has passed broadly worded contingency resolutions: on Formosa and the Pescadores in 1955; on the Middle East in 1957; and on Vietnam, through the Tonkin Resolution, in 1964.

Given the UN Charter and the multilateral and bilateral commitments, Katzenbach told the hearings: "The question arises as to how the Congress can and should participate in the decision to use force: (1) where there is an emergency, and (2) beyond that, in a matter such as Korea where I think there was a genuine need for speed, or in the current instance in Vietnam.

"A declaration of war would not, I think, correctly reflect the very limited objectives of the United States with respect to Vietnam. It would not correctly reflect our efforts there, what we are trying to do, the reasons why we are there, to use an outmoded phraseology, to declare war."

Fulbright interrupted, thrusting his glasses high on his forehead and staring across the 20-odd feet separating him from Katzenbach. Fulbright shows his emotions in anguished wrinkling of the face and incredulous inflection of voice.

Chairman FULBRIGHT. You think it is outmoded to declare war?

Mr. KATZENBACH. In this kind of context I think the expression of declaring a war is one that has become outmoded in the international arena.

Fulbright sank back into his chair, muttering inaudibly to Senator Gore, who was smiling and shaking his head. Senator Aiken meditatively stared at the ceiling, pencil tapping his teeth.

A committee staff member said several months later: "It's hard to look at a complex political situation and say Event A or Event B was the 'turning point'. But for all practical purposes, the hearings could have ended at that moment. Katzenbach told the Senate better than any other witness could have done what Congress amounted to in the conduct of foreign affairs—'God,' as one Senator said to me later that day, 'if the Administration thought the Constitution was outmoded, where does that leave Congress, which is a creature of the Constitution?'"

Katzenbach apparently sensed that Fulbright and other Senators were shocked by his answer, and immediately took pains to point out how Congress had been given an opportunity to "express its views," first via the SEATO treaty, then the Tonkin Resolution. But instead of digging himself a shelter, Katzenbach produced another pit into which he and the Administration promptly tumbled. Citing SEATO and the Tonkin Resolution, he said, "The combination of the two, it seems to me, fully fulfill the obligation of the Executive in a situation of this kind to participate with the Congress, to give the Congress a full and effective voice, *the functional equivalent of the constitutional obligation expressed in the provision of the Constitution with respect to declaring war.*"

Fulbright disagreed, vehemently. "They [the Administration] did not ask for a declaration of war. They do not have one yet."

Mr. KATZENBACH. That is true in the very literal sense of the word.

Chairman FULBRIGHT. It is quite true, not only literally, but in spirit. You haven't requested and you don't intend to request a declaration of war, as I understand it.

Katzenbach wouldn't retreat. ". . . [T]hat is correct, Mr. Chairman, but didn't that resolution authorize the President to use the armed forces of the United States in whatever way was necessary? Didn't it? What could a declaration of war have done that would have given the President more authority and a clearer voice of the Congress of the United States than it did?"

Now Fulbright had reached the nub of his disagreement with the White House. "The circumstances partook of an emergency, as an attack upon the United States which would fall within the procedures or the principles developed in the last century of repelling attacks temporarily as opposed to a full-fledged war like the one which we are in. . . . It has been interpreted as equivalent to a declaration of war. I think it is a very critical difference as to how we regard it.

"I had a debate on the floor with Senator Russell about whether or not this kind of resolution is now accepted as a substitute for a declaration of war. I don't think it is properly such, especially having been made under conditions of great emergency. It wasn't a deliberate decision by the Congress to wage war in that full-fledged sense against a foreign government. I think that has been one of the difficulties now, that we are not quite sure which government we are waging the war against although it seems to me it is fairly obvious."

Katzenbach rejected Fulbright's protestations that Congress was forced to act hurriedly in an "emergency situation." He said, "How much debate was there on that resolution as compared with a declaration of war when President Roosevelt sent that up? How quickly did the Congress respond?" And then he told Fulbright: "Now the language of that resolution, Mr. Chairman, is . . . as Congress knew full well, a very broad language."

Chairman FULBRIGHT. Yes.

Mr. KATZENBACH. And it was explained in the debate. You explained it, Mr. Chairman, as head of this committee.

Chairman FULBRIGHT. But I misinterpreted it.

Mr. KATZENBACH. You explained that resolution and you made it clear as it could be what the Congress was committing itself to, and that resolution provides———

Chairman FULBRIGHT. No, I didn't.

Mr. KATZENBACH. That it stays in existence until repealed by a concurrent resolution.

Chairman FULBRIGHT. I not only didn't make it clear, obviously, it wasn't clear to me. I did make statements that I thought this did not entail nor contemplate any change in the then existing policy, and, of course, there had been very great change in it. I think it is perfectly proper to examine the resolution simply because it is the latest example of the application of this problem or misapplication of the declaration of war.

But in the question of Congress setting or determining the broad question of waging of war as opposed to the repelling of an invasion or an attack, a specific attack in this case, this is where I think I went astray, and, we did, in making the language much too broad, particularly that portion to repel any aggression in the future, not just this one.

Katzenbach expanded on his concept of a declaration of war. ". . . [T]he situations surrounding declarations of war as such have changed rather dramatically since 1789, as a matter of history and as a matter of practice. You find sometimes that some provisions of the Constitution have to adjust, and there are mechanisms for their adjustment to the world around them. . . . The terms 'war' and 'declaration of war' traditionally in international law raised all kinds of consequences . . . which no longer actually exist. . . . [T]o declare war in a situation like Korea, like Vietnam, like the landing in Lebanon or any of those other situations, would be to mislead people, because of that history and that changed international development, in terms of what you meant and what you were doing.

"The declaration of war traditionally had the Congress participate in a situation that was rather total, where you were taking on a foreign nation rather totally, not for limited objectives. In the present case, the Congress did have an opportunity to participate in the decisions involved in what was in effect a major military action. At least I thought there had been the effort, embodied in these resolutions and in other ways, to give the Congress an opportunity to participate in the functional way that was contemplated by the Founding Fathers, but without the declaration of war, which I think would be misleading and which I think would be wrong in a situation where you have limited objectives."

In seeking the outer limits of the authority claimed by the Administration under the Tonkin Gulf Resolution, Gore asked: "You hold that this resolution authorized the use of U.S. forces to bomb targets in Laos?"

Mr. KATZENBACH. I think as far as—that would depend very much, Senator, on what was necessary in terms of coming to the aid of South Vietnam, but it would also depend on many of the facts and circumstances because I do not think that the Congress sought to authorize any action unless that action was justified in [repelling] an aggression.

Senator GORE. Will you please respond to the same question, but I use the word 'China' instead of 'Laos'?

Mr. KATZENBACH. I think the resolution authorized——

Senator GORE. You would give the same answer?

Mr. KATZENBACH (continuing). The necessary defensive measures in this respect.

Gore agreed with Katzenbach on the difficulties of foreseeing the future. "I doubt if any Congressman, at the time the resolution was passed, could foresee the bombing of targets within ten miles of China, or the provocation which is involved, taking into consideration the speed of supersonic planes. . . . It seems to me that the thrust of your testimony is that it is incumbent upon the Congress hereafter to consider in detail and precision the grant of authority involved in its action."

Katzenbach didn't feel this precision possible. "I think in that connection Congress has got to stay within its constitutional prerogatives and its constitutional rights in this. I do not think you can tell the President . . . for example, how his troops should be disposed, what weapons he should use or not use. I think that is the function of the commander-in-chief." Because of the difficulty in predicting contingencies, Katzenbach maintained, the resolution's phrasing, "take all necessary steps," was "fairly careful language."

Senator GORE. You have confirmed that Congress would have had great difficulty foreseeing the bombing of North Vietnam. I would have had difficulty foreseeing the commitment of ground troops, combat troops, particularly in view of the repeated statements of President Johnson in contravention of such a policy. But if the Congress would have had difficulty foreseeing the bombing of targets within ten miles of China, as I say and you now confirm, do you not think it is incumbent upon the President to seek the advice and consent of the Congress before undertaking such action?

Mr. KATZENBACH. No, I do not, Senator, I think that the fact that you have difficulty in foreseeing every contingency is not the same as saying the fact that the Congress had no difficulty whatsoever in seeing its commitment and living up to that commitment and the importance of doing so. It had no difficulty in doing that, in seeing that with clarity. And, therefore, it authorized this action.

Senator GORE. Well, I cannot bring you to the conclusion, but I come to my own, that hereafter I will be slow to vote for any grant of authority unless I know more precisely the extent of it and the purposes for which it will be used and the interpretations to which it might be put.

Katzenbach's first day of testimony was August 17. The following afternoon President Johnson held an announced-in-advance press conference (i.e., one for which he sought maximum coverage, including live television) and he was primed to answer Fulbright on the Tonkin issue. Sarah McClendon, who reports for a group of Texas newspapers, asked the question which prompted Johnson's only lengthy on-the-record exposition of the origin of the resolution, and his use of it:

Q. Mr. President, sir, the Constitution does not give you the right to carry on this war without permission from Congress. I am sure you realize that more than anybody. In view of this misunderstanding that has occurred about the Gulf of Tonkin Resolution, why don't you clear up this matter with your critics by quickly calling for a new vote on this matter?

A. Sarah, you don't always clear up your critics that easily. They will be with you before the vote. They will be with you after the vote. That is the way it is in a democratic society.

I have given a lot of thought and concern and attention to attempting to get the agreement of the Congress on the course that the government followed in its commitments abroad.

As a young Senator, I recall very vividly hearing Senator Taft speak on several occasions about President Truman's intervention in Korea. He frequently said, in substance, that while he thought what the President did was right, he did it the wrong way; that he should have consulted the Congress and he should have asked for their opinion.

Under the Constitution, the Congress has the right to declare—declare—war. It was never intended that the Congress would fight the war, direct the war, take the bombers off the ground, put them back on it, ground them. But it has the responsibility to declare the war.

Senator Taft thought that President Truman, before he committed our troops in Korea, should have asked the Congress not necessarily for a declaration, but for an opinion—for a resolution.

President Eisenhower followed that policy in several instances, asking the Congress for an opinion. He discussed it with the leaders before he submitted the resolution.

Back in May and June, 1964, before the Tonkin Gulf [incidents] we considered what we should do in order to keep the Congress informed, *to keep them in place,* and to keep them in agreement with what our action should be there in case of contingencies. There was very active debate in the government, as I remember it, back as far as May and June of that year. Then we had the Tonkin Gulf.

After the Tonkin Gulf we responded to the action with appropriate measures.

But after that, we felt that we should point out that there was likelihood there would be other instances. We could see the problem developing in that area. So we asked the leadership of the Congress to come to the White House.

We reviewed with them Senator Taft's statements about Korea, and the actions that President Eisenhower had taken, and asked their judgment about the resolution that would give us the opinion of the Congress.

We were informed that a resolution was thought desirable. So the members of the Executive and Legislative branches talked about the content of that resolution.

A resolution was drafted. That was reviewed with the leaders on, I believe, August 4, 1964.

I sent a message up to the Congress shortly afterwards and asked for consideration of a resolution. Some of the members of the Congress felt that they should amend the resolution, even after amendments had already been put into it by members, to provide that if at any time the Congress felt that the authority delegated in the resolution should be withdrawn, the Congress, without waiting for a recommendation from the President—he might differ with them —could withdraw that authority by just passing a resolution which did not require [sic] the President's veto. They could do it by themselves.

That suggestion was made to me by a prominent Senator [Richard Russell]. I readily accepted.

So the machinery is there any time the Congress desires to withdraw its views on the matter.

We stated then, and we repeat now, we did not think the resolution was necessary to do what we did and what we are doing. But we thought it was desirable. We thought if we were going to ask them to stay the whole route, and if we expected them to be there on the landing, we ought to ask them to be there on the takeoff.

I believe that every Congressman and most of the Senators knew what that resolution said. That resolution authorizes the President— and expressed the Congress' willingness to go along with the President —to do whatever was necessary to deter aggression.

We are, as I say, trying to provide a maximum deterrent with a minimum loss. We think we are well within the grounds of our constitutional authority. We think we are well within the rights of what the Congress said in its resolution.

The remedy is there if we have acted unwisely or improperly.

It is going to be tough as it gets along. The longer the fighting lasts, the more sacrifice is required in men and material; the more dissent and the more difficult it is going to be.

But I don't believe we* are acting beyond our constitutional responsibility.

Fulbright didn't rise to the bait. As he was to explain later, "As a politician and as a student of Br'er Rabbit, I must admit to a certain wariness of an opponent's suggestion as to the tactics I might use against him. I for one would gladly have tried to repeal the Tonkin Resolution had I thought the votes could be found for doing so. But I did not think the votes could be found—and I suspect the Administration shared that assessment of the situation in the Senate."

During the hearing's recess, Fulbright asked Katzenbach, by letter, to be prepared to answer a crucial question upon resumption on August 21:

"What would be the situation today regarding American involvement in

---

* Johnson used the pronoun "we" 25 times in the statement, mostly in the *ex cathedra* sense. Says Senator Case: "I have sometimes been a little annoyed by the habit presidents have of saying 'we think this' and 'we think that.' It sounds more like an affectation." The practice has also been called the "monarchic plural."

Vietnam if the Tonkin Resolution had not been passed? Would the President then be with, or without, constitutional authority to send U.S. soldiers to South Vietnam in the numbers that are there today? Would he have had authority to bomb in the North? In short, did the Gulf of Tonkin Resolution give the President authority which otherwise he constitutionally would not have had, and, if so, what?"

In a protracted prologue Katzenbach said, in effect, "That's a good question," and he admitted that there would be an "ambiguity" in his answer: "If the President did not have the constitutional authority to act as he has acted without the Tonkin Gulf Resolution, if one were to take the view that that was beyond the powers of the Presidency acting alone, then one would read the Tonkin Gulf Resolution as authorizing the actions occurring therein. If one said that the President did have that power acting alone, then one would read the Tonkin Gulf Resolution as affirming that power within the Presidency and approving of it, stating the will and the sense of the Congress with respect to it.

"So whether you say that resolution 'authorizes' or whether you don't . . . would depend upon what your point of view was of the President's authority in the first place. If you were to deny that he had the authority, then I think you would read the resolution as authorizing him to do these things. If you were to take the view that he already had the authority to do them, then you would read the resolution as an affirmation of authority, as an expression of the will and desire and the sense of Congress in that respect."

Senator McCarthy attempted to summarize Katzenbach: "The view of the Administration was that they had all of the authority they needed; that we didn't give them anything they didn't have; that we had nothing to give them. We could take it back and the Administration said it would make no difference."

"That is true in only one very limited sense," Katzenbach replied. "It is true in that I think it would be argued that the constitutional authority does exist, but to say because the constitutional authority exists that the resolution is not necessary is I think to misunderstand or at least not to see the tremendous importance that I would see in this kind of resolution."

Katzenbach said it was "extremely important that Congress and the President be as nearly as they can on the same wave length, that they agree with what is done . . . and nobody can tell you with assurance and authority, Senator, what the constitutional limits are in any number of situations. If at any time the President and the Congress are not acting together, it affects what the United States can do. So I think the President was asking for this resolution to resolve any constitutional questions that may have been raised before."

McCarthy wasn't satisfied. "I don't think the members here are really concerned about what the Tonkin Gulf Resolution did in itself, but rather the interpretation of it in terms of further policy. I think most of us knew what the purpose was, and I think the President stated it pretty clearly at his press conference last Friday.

"He said consideration was given as 'to what we should do in order to keep the Congress informed, *to keep them in place*'—I think that is the critical word. . . . As I read your statement . . . I would say what you do is prescribe a kind of four-year dictatorship in foreign policy . . . ."*

What would happen if Congress *did* withdraw the resolution, as Johnson tacitly challenged it to try to do?

Accepting the view that "he already has the constitutional authority" for conduct of the war, Katzenbach said, "the removal of the resolution would by itself not prevent him from continuing to exercise that authority." But such an action would put all parties in "an extremely difficult position," he conceded, for Congress could show its displeasure by exercising "a variety of other constitutional rights. They would not raise armies, they would not support and maintain them for this purpose . . . . So I think we would then be in a situation which I think every President and Congress over the years have responsibly sought to avoid in the conduct of international matters, the situation where they do not act together."

But the constitutional issue, "as interesting and as fascinating as it is, is not the gut issue," Katzenbach argued. "The gut issue here is whether or not the Congress supports the President in what he does and how you would then read a recision of the resolution in this regard . . . . If he doesn't have it [support] then, as a practical matter, as a realistic matter, it becomes increasingly . . . more difficult to carry out those activities."

Senator Hickenlooper, admitting confusion, asked, "Do you consider we are at war today in Vietnam?"

Mr. KATZENBACH. Will you tell me in what sense you mean the word—

Senator HICKENLOOPER. I am not defining a sense.

Mr. KATZENBACH. I would say, in popular terms, clearly we are at war there, in popular terms.

Senator HICKENLOOPER. If we are in a war, how long have we been at war there?

Mr. KATZENBACH. As far as the United States is concerned, I think we have been in what would in a popular sense be called war since such time as we sent American military units directly to engage enemy units.

Senator HICKENLOOPER. Which was really in 1961 when we sent large units in?

Mr. KATZENBACH. I would think so, Senator. It is a very difficult

---

* McCarthy has said privately that Katzenbach's testimony, and Johnson's press conference statement, were major factors in his decision to seek the Democratic presidential nomination, a quest which began in earnest two months after the hearings ended.

question because if you look at the tradition of this we probably would have committed things that would have been called acts of war before this.

Senator HICKENLOOPER. I do not want to be nitpicking on this. What I am trying to get at is this: We got into war, in the general sense of the term, by the order of the President prior to the Tonkin Bay Resolution. I am trying to lay my premise here and you can comment on it all you want to. I may be wrong, I do not know.

If that is the case, if we got into war by order of the President prior to the Tonkin Bay Resolution, why did we need the Tonkin Bay Resolution?

Mr. KATZENBACH. Senator, we did not get into war prior to the Tonkin Bay Resolution. That is the reason I interrupted you, because the North Vietnamese———

Senator HICKENLOOPER. Well, what were we in before the Tonkin Bay Resolution? I don't know.

Mr. KATZENBACH. We were involved before that in efforts to assist the government of South Vietnam to put down an insurgency movement which they had which was supported, financed, helped, directed, and so forth and so on by North Vietnamese. It was subsequent to the Tonkin Gulf Resolution that North Vietnam used regular military forces to come across the demilitarized zone and down the Ho Chi Minh Trail to engage in support of the insurgency movement there, with its own army, military forces, indeed to invade and to commit an act of aggression against South Vietnam. That came subsequent to Tonkin.

Senator HICKENLOOPER. I understand it is your contention that the President has the power, did have the power, to order these troops into Vietnam?

Mr. KATZENBACH. Yes, sir.

Senator HICKENLOOPER. Not only into South Vietnam, but the bombing of North Vietnam?

Mr. KATZENBACH. That is correct, Senator.

Senator HICKENLOOPER. Without the Tonkin Bay Resolution?

Mr. KATZENBACH. As a constitutional matter, I believe that he could have.

Senator HICKENLOOPER. That is where the confusion, of course, arises, because the only thing that the Constitution says about war as far as the President is concerned, is that he is commander-in-chief . . . [and] that the Congress has the power to declare war. It has the power to raise and support armies, but no appropriation of money to that use shall be for a longer term than two years . . . . Now, the commander-in-chief does not do those things. Under the normal acceptance of the term he runs the show after Congress had done those things.

Mr. KATZENBACH. I think it is an important point to make, Senator, because they have been doing these things through Vietnam.

Senator HICKENLOOPER. *Yes. Precedent is piling upon precedent until we finally accept it as a fact, which I am not willing to do myself.*
. . .

In connection with the thesis that the President has the right to order troops into a foreign country . . . and commit them to battle, without resolution of the Congress or without authority of the Congress, does Congress have the right to pass a proper measure, a joint resolution or something else, to bring those troops out of that country contrary to the wishes of the President?

Mr. KATZENBACH. I very much doubt that it has the power to do that. It would seem to me that that would be an invasion of the commander-in-chief———

Senator HICKENLOOPER. Do you mean to take the position that this Congress cannot order the American armies and troops out of a foreign country if it wants to?

Mr. KATZENBACH. As a constitutional matter I would not take that view. I think you raise a much closer question if it refers to support of them under the appropriations act. On that I think as a practical matter it is perfectly obvious Congress can do this.

Senator HICKENLOOPER. Do what?

Mr. KATZENBACH. Can get the troops out of Vietnam if it chooses to do it.

Senator HICKENLOOPER. I am not talking about any round-the-corner operation by withholding funds . . . . We can withhold funds from the President of the United States to pay his salary or to pay the employees that he has. Yes, we have the purse strings over here in the Congress. But I think it is a difficult doctrine for me to agree to, that the Congress cannot control the President . . . from the standpoint of the use or the withholding of the troops of this country abroad. I simply cannot go along with that doctrine.

As the hearings neared a close, Fulbright asked Senator Ervin, who appeared as an expert constitutional witness, whether the Tonkin Gulf Resolution would be affected should it develop "that there is a grave doubt that the attack . . . was unprovoked as alleged, or even that there was an attack."

Ervin didn't think so. "In determining what the resolution means, as far as I am concerned, the words of the resolution are sufficient to express its intent, and whatever happened before or whatever happened afterward, or whatever was said before, or whatever was said afterward, I do not think had any effect on it."

Fulbright found these circumstances puzzling and disturbing. "If the facts had been wholly false, if nothing whatever happened on that night in August 1964, what we did still is a binding commitment. This is a rather strange thing. In domestic law, I do not think that principle is really true. I do not know why it should be considered so here.

"We are completely at the mercy of any Executive department for the facts of this kind happening abroad. The Congress has no way of checking [the facts] immediately. In time they may . . . ."

Fulbright could have gone a step further, for in fact his committee staff at the very moment was in the process of "checking the facts"—and with intriguing results.

Chapter Eight

THE TRUTH EMERGES

The process of revelation began in the summer of 1967 when the Associated Press compiled a lengthy account of the Gulf of Tonkin incidents, based on interviews with *Maddox* and *Turner Joy* crew members. The article was the first project of a special ten-reporter investigative team that AP created in its Washington bureau in 1967 to do in-depth studies which were impossible under the normal deadline-every-minute demands of a wire service. Tonkin was chosen because it marked a turning point in the war, and because of suspicions voiced in the Senate and elsewhere about the authenticity of the Administration accounts.

Written in sparse, objective wire-service language, the article offered neither conjecture nor conclusion—it simply told the story of the August 2 and 4 episodes in the words of the participants willing to talk about them. Official cooperation was minimal. The Defense Department gave the reporters a crew list and access to men willing to be interviewed. But the Navy was supercautious. Communications between the destroyers and higher commands remained classified and unavailable. A security officer sat alongside Captain Robert Barnhart, the *Turner Joy* skipper, when he talked with an AP man at the Pentagon, nodding yes or no as to whether questions should be answered. As a starting point, the AP had only the terse account given three years earlier by Secretary McNamara to the Senate committees. But staff writers Harry F. Rosenthal and Tom Stewart wove the interviews into a chronology that, despite the limits on information, revealed several previously unpublished—and intriguing—facts about the incidents:

—The existence of the special communications van ("The Black Box" to the crew) and its rumored capability of "checking on radar and communications stations on shore."

—The *Maddox's* inability to lock its radar on surface targets on August 4, and the grave doubts about sonar reports of torpedoes in the water.

The Associated Press transmitted the article to member newspapers for use on Sunday, July 16, which by happenstance forced it to compete for space against a gush of stories on bloody racial violence in Newark, New Jersey, and elsewhere. Consequently, relatively few papers used the story, to the keen disappointment of the investigative team. The *Washington Post,* the *Washington Star,* the *New York Times,* the *Baltimore Sun*—the publications most influential in the capital—none published the story.

But the article did appear in the *Arkansas Gazette,* published in Little Rock, and regularly read by Senator Fulbright.

Several times in the preceding two years Fulbright and other Senators had poked unsuccessfully into the Tonkin incidents. Johnson's reported boast that the resolution was "ready" when the incidents occurred drew special attention, but all the committee could obtain was a statement by Assistant Secretary of State William Bundy that the early drafts were nothing more than "normal contingency planning." Fulbright and Gore had also worked on McNamara and Secretary of the Navy John McNaughton. But, as Gore complained, McNamara and McNaughton had the bullet which struck the *Maddox* on August 2. "Every time they came up here they waved that bullet around," Gore lamented. "One bullet and you went to war—Helen's face is insignificant by comparison."

In November 1966, the Foreign Relations Committee had forced publication of the 1964 resolution hearings—but only after Pentagon and State Department censors subjected the transcript to a rigorous "security review." Senator Morse protested the end product, writing to Rusk:

> In going over the transcript as approved by the Executive branch, I noted that all references were deleted to the point I raised early in the hearing concerning the raids made on North Vietnamese islands by South Vietnamese war vessels shortly before the incident between the *Maddox* and the North Vietnamese torpedo boats. By no stretch of the imagination is this security information. I can understand why the Administration wants to cover up any mention of these raids in the official records of the committee's deliberations ... but I resent the attempt to delete my comments about the subject when they were not in any way based on information from official sources.

Douglas MacArthur II, Rusk's assistant secretary for congressional relations, denied any attempt at censorship, explaining to Morse:

> We merely recommended that certain questions be deleted prior to public release. The reason for doing so was that these questions, while not classified in themselves, were questions to which classified answers were given which we feel must be deleted for security reasons. If the questions are published without the answers, it seems likely to us that this fact would give rise to public speculations as to the possible answers which might not be helpful to the national interest.

The Administration's wariness had underlined the committee's suspicion that Johnson had some Tonkin secrets locked away in a dark, inaccessible closet. Yet through mid-1967 chances of finding the closet—much less opening its door—seemed remote.

Then came a stroke of luck.

During the hearings on the national commitments resolution, Fulbright's office received an anonymous letter charging that there was mass confusion at the Pentagon on the day of the second incident, with receipt and transmission of cables delayed for hours. The writer said that, based upon the queries being sent to the Pacific from Washington, it was "obvious" the decision to attack was made in the face of contradictory reports from the field. He said that he had "lived with the problem" for three years, felt guilty about it, and wanted to "get it off my chest."

Fulbright sent the letter to William Bader, a committee staff member with experience both in naval electronic intelligence and in the State Department, with the query: "What about it?" Bader studied the letter and concluded, "This smacks of knowledge." The writer obviously knew the inner workings of the Joint Chiefs of Staff and the National Military Command Center. He discussed events which had not been publicly reported, and he presented questions "within a logical framework."

A few days later Fulbright met with Carl M. Marcy, the chief of staff, and Bader in the Foreign Relations Committee office. As he pored over a clipping of the AP article from the *Arkansas Gazette,* and the anonymous letter, occasionally reading a paragraph aloud, his curiosity and pique mounted. "————, what can we do about this?" he demanded.

Bader suggested going after the official logbooks of the *Maddox* and *Turner Joy.* Nothing is more inviolable to the Navy than a log, he said; altering or destroying one is the "most heinous crime possible." Logs are eventually sent back to Washington for storage, so off went a letter to McNamara over Fulbright's signature, requesting copies of them.

Weeks dragged by; the Navy periodically informed Fulbright that the question of whether to surrender the logs was "still under study." Fulbright's letters took on a snippy tone, and finally, in mid-November, the logs arrived. Marcy thinks the Defense Department produced the material on the assumption that the committee would find it unintelligible and drop the matter. If this theory is true, the Pentagon gravely underestimated Bader's investigative tenacity. In themselves, the logs left many questions unanswered, although through them Bader was able to reconstruct a chronology of the vessels' movements. Then he wrote a memorandum for Fulbright, specifying communications referred to in the logs that he needed, and requesting that they be obtained from the Pentagon. Here the Defense Department became tighter, and made a policy decision to supply only the cables that were specifically requested, and to volunteer no information, written or otherwise. Marcy surmises, "They were getting suspicious that we were on to something, and the higher-ups took over."

With the cables in hand, Bader could peel back another layer of secrecy. He found repeated references to something called "34-A Operations" in cables sent and received by the *Maddox,* suspected immediately that they were the South Vietnamese raids on the islands, and eventually received verification from the Pentagon.

More information, meanwhile, continued to come from the anonymous correspondent. The committee remains reticent about discussing this man's contributions; as one staff member said privately in late 1968, "He's the only person who was really hurt in this entire episode." All that is said of him is that he is a Navy commander with more than 20 years' service, and that he had an assignment in the Pentagon which enabled him to read the bulk of the cable traffic between Washington and the Pacific commanders on August 4. Several times during the fall of 1967, he phoned the committee and was referred to Bader. On orders from Marcy, Bader never asked the commander for information, only accepted that which he offered. The commander was able to direct Bader to certain key cables, identifying them by sender and addressee, and giving the exact time-block of their transmission. At the commander's request, Bader arranged for him to meet Fulbright on November 16, "cloak and dagger fashion," at a location remote from the New Senate Office Building.

Trouble came swiftly for the informant.

The day following the meeting, he told his commanding officer of the clandestine visit to Fulbright. He was immediately directed to make an appointment with a United States Naval Hospital for a psychiatric examination and did so, entering the hospital on November 20 and remaining there for about four weeks before Navy doctors released him.

A naval inspector general, investigating the hospitalization later, after Fulbright had complained to McNamara, said in a formal report to Secretary of the Navy Paul Ignatius:

> Commander [deleted]* has been on the staff of Captain [deleted] since July 1966. During the period from that time until the events at issue, he had been undergoing psychiatric care at his own expense with civilian psychiatrists and psychiatric oriented and marriage counselling organizations. Commander [deleted], during this period, considered himself to be suffering from a neurotic condition and, furthermore, was experiencing certain marital difficulties. Captain [deleted] was intimately aware of Commander [deleted]'s mental and marital problems since Commander [deleted] had related them on frequent occasions to other members of the staff who had further relayed the information to Captain [deleted]. Furthermore, Commander [deleted]'s performance of duty had deteriorated seriously.

* The Senate Foreign Relations Committee, which made the Inspector General's report available to the author, deleted the name of the Navy commander and other identifying data to avoid causing him personal embarrassment.

It was in this context that Commander [deleted] reported to Captain [deleted] on 17 November 1967 that he had made a 'secret' visit to Senator Fulbright to disclose 'sensitive military information'. Captain [deleted] considered at this point that the entire pattern of behavior of Commander [deleted], including his neurotic behavior during the preceding months, made it important that he undergo a complete psychiatric examination by the Navy. . . . Captain [deleted] took into account Commander [deleted]'s expenditure of substantial personal funds for psychiatric care, the very serious deterioration of his personal performance and finally what appeared to him to be a most unusual and irrational way of communicating to the Congress through an anonymous letter and a secret visit.

Commander [deleted] agreed with Captain [deleted] that such an examination was necessary and states that he believes that Captain [deleted] had every reason at that time to be concerned about the state of his [deleted]'s mental health. Commander [deleted] feels that he was indeed suffering from a neurotic condition at that time and that his performance of duty had seriously deteriorated as a result. In fact, Commander [deleted] states that if the positions had been reversed, he would have come to the same conclusion and made the same recommendation.

Captain [deleted] made the decision to recommend the psychiatric examination completely on his own, out of concern for [deleted]'s mental state of health and did not consult higher authority within the Navy.

A medical board of three physicians, after examining the commander, found him to be suffering from a "moderate chronic and unimproved anxiety reaction," but "determined to be fit for full duty." According to the Inspector General's report, the commander "feels that his period of hospitalization was too long and . . . that he feels that the psychiatrist in charge of his case may have been under outside pressure to find him unfit." These allegations the psychiatrist denied, saying he was "not subjected to any pressures whatsoever," the report states. It concludes:

The Inspector General finds no evidence that Captain [deleted]'s recommendation was based on anything but his best judgment of Commander [deleted]'s state of mental health at the time and that this judgment was adequately supported by the evidence available to Captain [deleted] at the time. The Inspector General further finds no evidence of any irregularities in the handling of the subsequent hospitalization and the review action now under way.

Another medical board gave the commander a second psychiatric screening, and also pronounced him fit for duty. But the Fulbright committee was to receive no more information from him.

By late December, Bader had pieced together an account of the confusion and doubts shrouding the August 4 incident, including the revelation that the Joint Chiefs of Staff were still demanding confirmation from Herrick at the very moment the raids began. This point hit the committee with bombshell impact, for Fulbright knew that he now stood on the brink of a clash with the Administration which would make the turmoil over his Dominican Republic speech a childish schoolyard quarrel by comparison.

Another factor then came into play: public disclosure of the committee's quiet inquiry, via a *New York Times* story on December 21. As a starting point the *Times* used a letter from a former naval lieutenant, John W. White, of Cheshire, Connecticut, which appeared in the *New Haven Register* on December 6. White had been assigned in August 1964 to the *USS Pine Island,* a seaplane tender which went into the Gulf of Tonkin following the August 4 incident. "I recall clearly the confusing radio messages sent at that time by the destroyers—confusing because the destroyers themselves were not certain they were being attacked," White wrote. Based on what he had heard on the ship radio, White said, North Vietnamese boats might have been in the area and engaged in harassing maneuvers, but they did not fire shells or torpedoes at the United States vessels.

White also told of a conversation with the "chief sonarman" of the *Maddox* at Long Beach Naval Shipyard six months after the incidents. He did not remember the name of this man, whom he met on a "chance encounter," but said the sonarman "told me that his evaluation of the sonarscope picture was negative, meaning that no torpedoes were fired through the water, at the ship or otherwise. And he also said he consistently reported this to the commanding officer during the attack." The *New York Times,* in quoting White's letter, said committee members were "skeptical" at the Administration's account, but also felt "considerable doubt" that they would ever obtain "sufficient evidence" to challenge it.

Fulbright is notoriously immune to pressure from the press. However, the disclosure that the committee questioned the Administration's veracity put the Senators into the position of either remaining silent, permitting public suspicions to fester, or of continuing toward hearings that would compile a public record, permitting the truth to speak for itself. In this respect, therefore, the *Times'* pessimism about finding "sufficient evidence" was premature, for Bader had enough material in his files to shatter McNamara's original story into bits. The only question facing the committee was how best to proceed.

And here Fulbright made a policy decision of his own: He would use material from informants and other unofficial sources (such as the Associated Press story) for background and guidance, but any "reconstructed account" of Tonkin would come from designated Administration spokesmen and documents. The decision served two purposes: It was a safeguard against inadvertent disclosure, by the committee, of highly sensitive communications secrets; and it insured that the Administration, not its critics, would tell the Tonkin story, obviating possible later charges that the committee had drawn information from tainted sources. Fulbright was not naive enough to think that the Pentagon had given him all existing documentation on Tonkin—yet he had enough to warrant drawing conclusions; if the Administration cared to offer rebuttal evidence, it could do so.

The *Times* story also served to alert the Administration that the Tonkin incidents were about to become another crisis for the White House and the Pentagon, and one perhaps even more critical than that of 1964. Vietnam threatened to be the key issue of the 1968 elections; were the Foreign Relations Committee to challenge the legality or circumstances, or both, of the Tonkin Gulf Resolution, the Republicans and Johnson's challengers within his own party would have months of campaign material. (And Senator McCarthy, a committee member, had already revealed that he was considering running against Johnson.) Of equal concern to the Administration was that a sizable body of war critics would unquestioningly accept any doubts raised about Tonkin, and that a new inquiry, regardless of what the committee was able to prove, would further divide a troubled nation.

Thus, in late December, Undersecretary of Defense Paul Nitze requested a private meeting with Fulbright and asked that Senator Russell, chairman of the Armed Services Committee, be permitted to attend. Nitze, accompanied by Secretary of the Navy Ignatius and a uniformed Navy intelligence captain, strongly pleaded that the Foreign Relations Committee should abandon any thought of reopening the Tonkin incident, saying it would be a "bad show" for the United States. Nitze admitted there had been some initial doubts about details of the August 4 engagement because of "reporting and communications snafus" but that all questions were resolved before Johnson ordered the air strikes. Once again he denied any complicity of the *Maddox* and *Turner Joy* in the South Vietnamese raids. Allegations to this effect, he said, would only "give one hell of a lot of credence" to Communist propaganda media. The books were closed on Tonkin, the President and his chief military and civilian advisers were convinced nothing was amiss, and a public airing of the controversy would only lessen public confidence in the President during time of war.

Nitze then produced what he hoped would be his trump card.

Pledging the two Senators to deepest secrecy, and requesting that they take no notes, Nitze showed them what he claimed were intercepts of four separate sets of North Vietnamese radio messages on the night of August 4–5, containing a total of nine transmissions to and from the patrol boats: orders for them to commence the attack; a reply that the attack was under way; a report from the commander that he had lost two vessels; and a claim that the raiders had shot down two United States aircraft. Nitze called the intercepts "conclusive evidence" that the *Maddox* and *Turner Joy* had been attacked.

Nitze apparently counted upon Russell to come to the Pentagon's defense at this point and dissuade Fulbright from proceeding any further. In the strictest sense, Russell had no business involving himself in the meeting, even by invitation, for the inquiry was a Foreign Relations Committee affair. But Russell is titular leader of Senate southerners; one word from him, in all probability, would have brought Fulbright up short.

Before coming to the meeting, however, Russell had been briefed on Bader's findings, and he agreed with Fulbright that substantive questions existed which should be resolved. I can see now that we acted too hastily back in '64, he told Fulbright. I don't know what we can accomplish by plowing this field again, but I think we owe it to the Senate—and to ourselves—to find out as much as we can.

Fulbright and Russell politely thanked Nitze for the briefing, and he returned to the Pentagon, his mission an unqualified failure.

The day after Christmas, Fulbright acquired another informant, this one anonymous and apparently well placed in the Pentagon hierarchy. (There is circumstantial evidence that this person is the same tipster who alerted Morse during the 1964 hearing.) The informant knew what Fulbright sought and how he was going after his information (facts not publicly disclosed at the time), and he offered advice:

> Getting the logs of the *Maddox* and *Turner* Joy may be of some use to you . . . but it really won't help much. What you need most is the record of events of communications passing through the National Military Command Center. Most of them have probably now been destroyed.
>
> Whatever study was made on the basis of most of these records, fresh after the event, [was] by the Weapons Systems Evaluation Group [a branch of McNamara's office] entitled 'Command and Control of the Tonkin Gulf Incident, 4–5 August 1964.' This document is Top Secret and it is very tightly held because it is based in part on the tape recordings of conversations over the phone of the President,* the Secretary of Defense, Admiral Sharp, and others during the period when the critical decisions were being made. Very probably an effort will be made to have all copies of the study destroyed when and if there is any intimation that you know of the existence of the study. The study will not disclose that the incident was a put-on job. It will disclose several embarrassing things, however.
>
> One is that the first attack . . . was very probably made because the NVN [North Vietnamese] confused the *Maddox* . . . with operations which were covering SVN hit-and-run attacks against NVN coastal areas. This was probably due simply to lack of coordination.
>
> Another point will be that the attack on the . . . following day was indeed probably imaginary.
>
> After the first report of the attack there was a report there probably had not been an attack at all. But the President was to go on the air to address the nation about the retaliatory attacks that had already been

---

* The informant erred in including the President in the recordings; the White House is outside the command communications system that is taped.

planned, and after another flurry of confusion Admiral Sharp said there had been a real attack after all.

At this point the Secretary of Defense decided to advise the President that the attack on the *Turner Joy* was real and to order the retaliatory attacks and go ahead with the speech because it was getting very late for the address . . . and moreover . . . the attack planes had been kept in a state of take-off readiness for the maximum time.

It was clearly a case of making a definite decision when operational circumstances dictated haste but the facts suggested caution.

One may wonder how much the Secretary of Defense, who is a man of honor and conscience, has worried about this since. Because later events all indicate that the second attack was at best a trick of false radar images.

I am sure that if I signed this I would lose my job, but if you proceed wisely, you should be able for the good of the country to learn the truth of all I have suggested here and much more.

The Tonkin Gulf incident . . . was not a put-up job. But it was not the inexcusable and flagrant attack upon U.S. ships that it seemed to be, and that would have justified the resolution and retaliation had there been so. It was a confused bungle which was used by the President to justify a general course of action and policy that he had been advised by the military to follow. He, like the Secretary of Defense, was a prisoner. He got from them all the critical and decisive information and misinformation and he simply put his trust in the wrong people.

The informant gave the committee the date time group of an unclassified message and suggested that Fulbright request it by name if he desired further "proof" the August 4 incident had never occurred. Fulbright did so, and the informant promptly reported to him the resultant turmoil:

You certainly have us here in DOD [Department of Defense] scurrying around trying to cover up the incident and inundate you with facts to circumvent the main point. That is, that the so-called second attack of 4 August never took place.

Before Mr. Nitze signed out the last letter to you he conferred with Mr. Bundy of State and Walt Rostow and the three of them even went so far as to confer with the President. Do you think this would have happened if there was nothing to hide? They are fully aware that this whole incident is political dynamite and aren't about to give you the facts. Why the Navy upstairs is cooperating is also curious, except for the fact it would make them look rather silly.

If you recall after Jack Stempler [Pentagon assistant general counsel] replied to your first letter, I sent you the date time group of an unclassified message which proved that the 4 August incident never happened. Yet when you sent your second letter asking for a whole list of messages as well as the interrogation of prisoners, whose interrogation proved that they knew of the first incident, but not the second, you never asked for the message which was the most important one. . . .

Why don't you ask Mr. McNamara for CTU 72.1.2 04_____Z*
and also for 04_____Z from NavCom Philippines to JCS and CNO.
Only don't just ask for a message because DOD conveniently can call it a
communication and tell you a message with that date time group doesn't
exist.

Believe me, Senator, Defense isn't going to produce self-incriminating
evidence unless you blast it out of them. The Tonkin Gulf Resolution
never should have been passed and never would have been passed if the
real facts were known. Keep after them to produce and good luck.

One of the messages cited was Admiral Moore's declaration that North
Vietnam had "thrown down the gauntlet and now considers itself at war
with the United States." The other was Herrick's report that the "entire
situation leaves many doubts except for apparent attempted ambush at
beginning"—a cable that the Pentagon had not given the committee.

Once Bader showed these messages to Fulbright, the chairman knew
what must come: he had no choice but to reopen the inquiry and to demand
from the Administration an explanation of why the United States Congress
and the American people had been so grossly misled in August 1964.

The confrontation came on February 20, 1968, in Room S-116 of the
Capitol building, across the green baize table where McNamara had faced
the Foreign Relations and Armed Services committees in August 1964.
McNamara had then appeared in the role of trusted spokesman for a
President whose reelection three months hence was a political certainty.
Now he came as adversary—the symbol of an unsuccessful war, the author
of unfulfilled optimism, an official who no longer enjoyed the confidence
of Congress and was only eight days away from the end of his seven-year,
one-month tenure as Secretary of Defense. James V. Forrestal, the first
man to hold this position, the most mentally demanding job in Washington,
had committed suicide——victim of the pressures of peace and of war;
from Congress and from the military establishment. A man doesn't "work"
or "serve" as Secretary of Defense; he "survives." And McNamara was
staggering through his last days with the bone-weariness of the long-dis-
tance runner.

Fulbright began with a solicitous remark about the health of McNamara's
wife, then hoped the Secretary would "appreciate the thought" behind two
lines from T. S. Eliot's poem, "Little Gedding":

"History may be servitude,
History may be freedom."

"Mr. Secretary, I believe all of us here share your own desire that the

* For purposes of communications security, a portion of the date time block is omitted
here, as the text of these messages is printed elsewhere in the book. The abbreviations in
the sentence were: CTU 72.1—Commander, Task Unit 72, or Herrick; NavCom Philippines
—Naval Communications Station, the Philippines; JCS—Joint Chiefs of Staff; and CNO—
Chief of Naval Operations.

United States profit from its mistakes—not repeat them," Fulbright said. "If this nation cannot learn from its past performance and acknowledge where it has been wrong or insufficient to the task, then the United States will become servile to its past—and suffer for this servitude." He stressed that the purpose of the hearing "is not to assess blame on anyone, certainly not upon you."

After a brief procedural hassle over whether McNamara's prepared statement should be given to the press (the committee opposing on the ground that it was one-sided and misleading) the Secretary dashed any thought that he had come to admit error, or to offer apology. "Even with the advantage of hindsight," he declared in his opening paragraph, "I find that the essential facts of the two attacks appear today as they did then [in August 1964] when they were fully explored with this committee and other members of Congress." And in his closing paragraph the words were as harsh and biting as any ever directed to a congressional committee by a Cabinet officer:

"As a final point, I must address the suggestion that, in some way, the government of the United States induced the incident on August 4 with the intent of providing an excuse to take the retaliatory action which we in fact took. *I can only characterize such insinuations as monstrous.* The effective repulsion of the August 2 attack, the President's warning that the United States intended to assert the right of the freedom of the seas, the destroyers' careful avoidance of North Vietnamese territorial waters" (approaching "no closer than 16 miles to the coastline"), McNamara said, are "hardly indicative of an intent to induce another attack."

McNamara paused a moment before his last line—his pale blue eyes strained behind his rimless glasses, his thinning black hair flat across his tautly fleshed head, his gaze finally settling upon Senator Fulbright:

"But beyond that," he finally continued, "I find it inconceivable that anyone even remotely familiar with our society and system of government could suspect the existence of a conspiracy which would include almost, if not all, the entire chain of military command in the Pacific, the Chairman of the Joint Chiefs of Staff, the Joint Chiefs, the Secretary of Defense, and his chief civilian assistants, the Secretary of State, and the President of the United States."

McNamara had spoken for about 20 minutes. He shoved the papers to one side and addressed Fulbright: "Mr. Chairman, that concludes my statement, and I will be very happy to try to answer any questions." And for the next six hours the United States Senate finally had the opportunity, and the beginnings of the expertise, to conduct an intelligent inquiry into the Gulf of Tonkin incidents.

The questions skip over 91 pages of testimony, the portion cleared for publication by Pentagon censors, with frequent changes of subject as Senators took their turns as interrogators. Thus for the purpose of continuity, a presentation by subject matter, rather than in chronological sequence, follows:

The Physical Evidence of Attacks

The reliability of the sonar and radar reports of the *Maddox* and *Turner Joy* was discussed earlier, as were the contradictions in eyewitness accounts (although it should be noted that the committee was not even aware of the existence of one key figure, Sonarman Patrick Park,* and had interviewed no crew members or officers). Thus there was no opportunity to cross-examine McNamara on the various eyewitness accounts that he offered as unqualified truths. Once again he cited the reports of men seeing torpedoes in the water, of the "searchlight illumination . . . by the attacking craft," and of "gunfire against the patrol"—the latter two claims, as we have seen, highly questionable.

But McNamara gave greatest emphasis to the radio intercepts, which he called "intelligence reports received from a highly classified and unimpeachable source." And he insisted on denying William Bader, the committee's investigative expert, the opportunity to study the intercept reports to determine if they were what the Pentagon claimed they were. Before giving the intercepts to the committee, McNamara insisted that all persons other than Congressmen leave the room, even after Fulbright pointed out that both Bader and Marcy had top secret security clearances. McNamara retorted that the staff "has not been cleared for certain intelligence, and we are under specific written instructions from the President, as are all Executive departments, not to furnish such intelligence to uncleared persons. . . . Clearance is above top secret for the particular information involved in this situation . . . . We are under instructions to deny it other than to members of Congress and others properly cleared."

During the off-the-record session, with no one but Senators in the room, McNamara read a letter from Lieutenant General Joseph F. Carroll, director of the Defense Intelligence Agency, emphasizing the "very serious penalties" United States intelligence could incur if the source of the intercepts were to be disclosed. He next went through the nine intercepted messages. The intercepts were not uniformly convincing: Senator Gore declared, "Another interpretation is that this was an exaggerated report by the North Vietnamese commander, just as they exaggerated the losses of our planes." He quoted McNamara's opening statement: "During this same time, intelligence sources reported that North Vietnamese vessels

---

* The Pentagon's Directorate of Defense Information omitted Park and other sonarmen from a supposedly "complete list" of *Maddox* and *Turner Joy* crew members given the author in mid-1968. I ran across his name elsewhere, and obtained his account. Several weeks later the Pentagon confirmed that he and seven other sonarmen were not on the "complete list." The incident is indicative of the enthusiasm the Pentagon has for inquiries into the Tonkin episode.

stated they had our ships under attack." Gore said, "That is a flat-footed statement that nothing you have submitted today supports. . . . Nothing you have submitted supports this unqualified statement."

During his investigation Bader had obtained a copy of an interrogation report of a North Vietnamese naval officer taken prisoner along with 18 men when several North Vietnamese torpedo boats were sunk on July 1, 1966. The officer is described as a "senior commander in the North Vietnam Navy," and his handling had several peculiar features. The question of the Gulf of Tonkin incidents did not arise until his interrogation was well under way. When the commander began talking about Tonkin the Navy intelligence officers handling him shifted all reports concerning Tonkin into a separate, sensitive communications channel, and deleted them from their final report on his interrogation.

The intelligence officers who interrogated this man, for more than 100 hours, described him in their reports as "cooperative and reliable." The man told them that he had prepared the action report following the attack on the *Maddox* on August 2. He gave full details of how the *Maddox* was attacked, by how many patrol boats, and the results of the action. He named the number of each individual North Vietnamese patrol craft involved and gave a full report on both the damage to the boats and injuries to the crew. But the naval intelligence people had this to say about the August 4 incident:

> Extensive interrogation of all potentially knowledgeable sources reveals they have no info concerning a NVN attack on U.S. ships on 4 August, 1964. They state definitely and emphatically that no PTs could have been involved. They do have knowledge of a U.S. air attack on 5 August in which at least one and possibly Swatow PGMs [North Vietnamese patrol boats] were sunk by ACFT [aircraft] in vicinity of the Gianh River . . . . Slight damage was also inflicted to ACFT on 2 PTs this date as stated Reference Alfa [referring to another of the mainland air attacks].
>
> The possibility that Swatows could have committed the 4 August attack has also been carefully explored. Here again, however, all sources disclaim any knowledge of such an attack. Based on the experience of interrogations thus far it is very possible that PT boat crews in general might not have heard of this attack since they apparently have little contact with other ship types. On the other hand, source [the North Vietnamese naval commander] obviously has traveled in higher circles and has proved himself exceptionally knowledgeable on almost every naval subject and event of interest. Yet he specifically and strongly denies that any attack took place. When pressed further on this issue he states that if such an attack did take place, it could only have been committed by Swatows.

At another point, the interrogation report quoted the prisoner as saying

Swatows were neither designed nor intended for missions against large ships.

Rebutting, McNamara claimed, "His disclaimer of PT participation is contradicted by information received by a later captive. A North Vietnamese naval officer captured in July 1967 provided the name of the commander of a PT squadron. In intelligence reports [i.e., radio intercepts] received immediately after the August 4 attack, this commander and his squadron were identified by name and number as participants." McNamara said the statement of the earlier prisoner "was not nearly as comprehensive or as illuminating" as that of the second prisoner, "which, I think, came to light only within the last few days."

McNamara's production of the second prisoner caught the committee by surprise, for nothing had been said of him earlier. On May 6 the Defense Department, in response to a Fulbright query, surrendered his interrogation report. Examination of this showed that the prisoner was not as important as McNamara had claimed.

First, he was a "senior officer in the North Vietnamese navy," as McNamara said, but he was a political cadre in the naval headquarters, not an operational commander, as was the first prisoner. According to the Pentagon's own report he "had no knowledge of navigational methods and/or naval tactics." Moreover, the officer did not say there had been an attack on August 4—all he did was to confirm that the North Vietnamese navy had an officer of the same name as one who, the Pentagon claimed to have learned through the intercepts, commanded the August 4 attack boats.

Second, despite McNamara's February 20 claim that the officer's testimony "came to light only within the past few days," and thus could not be made available to the committee staff, his name appeared in a naval interrogation report dated July 1966—some 19 months before the Secretary's appearance.

Tartly listing these discrepancies in a letter to the Defense Department on May 29, Fulbright termed the Pentagon's contention "that this second interrogation report provides comprehensive and illuminating information on the August 4 attack as totally without foundation."

The "Maddox's" Mission and the 34-Alpha Operations

It will be recalled that at the 1964 hearings McNamara had said that the *Maddox* was "engaged in a routine patrol in international waters of the Gulf of Tonkin." With the ship's mission orders in hand, Fulbright asked the Secretary if he would care to change his story. "Was the *Maddox* engaged in an electronic spy mission similar to the *Pueblo?*"

Secretary McNAMARA. I think that the equipment on the *Pueblo* was more sophisticated than that on the *Maddox;* at least, I am told that by technical experts. The *Maddox* was engaged in the same kind of patrol that we carried on in the western Pacific two or three years prior to the time she was out there, and have carried on in many areas of the western Pacific since that time.

Chairman FULBRIGHT. But was the purpose dissimilar to the *Pueblo?* It was an electronic spy mission, wasn't it?

Secretary McNAMARA. No; the purpose was not primarily electronic, and, as I say, I haven't compared, myself, item by item, the equipment on the *Pueblo* and the *Maddox;* but I am told the *Maddox* had much less sophisticated equipment and less of it, and was less capable, therefore, of electronic surveillance. Electronic surveillance was one of her missions, but was not the only mission by any means, nor was it the primary mission. . . . The primary mission was to observe North Vietnamese naval patrols and the junk fleets in that area.

Fulbright asked McNamara to explain the order to the *Maddox* "to stimulate Chicom-North Vietnamese electronic action." The Secretary said, "It means that they turn on certain kinds of equipment on board the *Maddox* which, in turn, leads the Chicoms or the North Vietnamese to turn on the radars so that we can measure the radar' frequencies, that was clearly one of the objectives."*

If the *Maddox's* chief concern was observing North Vietnamese vessels, asked Senator McCarthy, ". . . was the information that our destroyers were gathering transmitted to the South Vietnamese navy for its use?" McNamara said, "I cannot answer the question."

Senator McCARTHY. You cannot answer that? If we get information that would be helpful to the South Vietnamese navy, we would give it to them?

Secretary McNAMARA. I do not say we would not. I simply cannot answer it.

McCarthy then argued that if such information were being transmitted to the South Vietnamese, ". . . wouldn't it be the equivalent of an act of war against North Vietnam? In other words, you were not just out there gathering information for the files of the Department of Defense, were you? . . . If you picked up information one day and gave it to them, and the next day South Vietnam took military action, it becomes almost a part of the same naval operation."

McNamara wouldn't agree—but in rebutting McCarthy, he lessened considerably the credibility of his claim that the primary purpose of the DeSoto patrol was to observe coastal traffic. "I think it is extremely un-

* Four days after McNamara's testimony, the Pentagon press office released the following statement: "Naval electronic experts say that Secretary of Defense McNamara was mistaken in his belief that the U.S. destroyers, during the Gulf of Tonkin [sic], carried equipment that could turn on the radars of North Vietnam and Communist China. The ships carried only passive listening gear, such as radio receivers."

likely that we gave any information from the patrol to the South Vietnamese in the time interval such as you suggested. It is possible that over a period of weeks or months we may have. But I am certain we did not in a matter of hours or days after the collection of the information."

Consider McNamara's answer for a`moment: The "primary mission" was to observe coastal traffic—yet the information was not being given to the South Vietnamese, in a time context that would permit them to put it to effective use. Then why observe coastal traffic?

McNamara and McCarthy lost patience with each other at this juncture, with the Secretary defending the use of spy ships and planes to collect information "that would be of benefit to us in protecting our security," and the Senator complaining of the "unnecessary intrusion of American power." Their exchange gives the flavor of the subdued belligerency with which McNamara and his antagonists snapped out questions and answers throughout the day:

Secretary McNAMARA. I think American ships, when it is in our interest, should move any place in international waters——

Senator McCARTHY. Spy any place they want to, but take the consequences.

Secretary McNAMARA. I believe——

Senator McCARTHY. Get the information.

Secretary McNAMARA. If you want to change the entire legal basis——

Senator McCARTHY. I am not going to change anything.

Secretary McNAMARA (continuing). Of operations of the sea, that is your prerogative.

Senator McCARTHY. Well, there really are not any, as you know. I mean everybody claims different things.

Secretary McNAMARA. Of course, there are. Let us not say there is not a basis.

Senator McCARTHY. We do not have to go into it now.

Secretary McNAMARA. We will go into it.

Senator McCARTHY. Well, we won't.

Secretary McNAMARA. We will.

Senator McCARTHY. I would like to ask my questions. He is not answering the question I wanted to ask him . . . .

Fulbright intervened to end the quibbling, and the questions returned to course. For the record, the Pentagon later supplied a statement: "We have found no evidence that any information gained in the DeSoto patrols was used in the planning of the South Vietnamese operations."*

The point on which McNamara was most insistent—and the Senators

* The wondrously imprecise statement leaves unanswered McCarthy's question as to whether the South Vietnamese navy was making use of the information in any area other than the 34-A Operations.

most skeptical—was the relationship between the *Maddox* and the 34-A Operations. Here the starting point was McNamara's statement at the 1964 hearings: "Our Navy played absolutely no part in, was not associated with, *was not aware of,* any South Vietnamese actions, if there were any. I want to make that very clear to you. The *Maddox* was operating in international waters, was carrying out a routine patrol of the type we carry out all over the world at all times. It was not informed of, was not aware of, had no knowledge of, and so far as I know today has no knowledge of any South Vietnamese actions in connection with the two islands, as Senator Morse referred to."

By now, of course, McNamara knew the committee had read cable traffic between the Pacific command and the *Maddox* which contained frequent references to 34-A Operations—scarcely evidence that the Navy was "not aware of" the South Vietnamese ventures. Nonetheless McNamara plunged bravely forward, saying his 1964 statement "remains entirely accurate." Then he proceeded to amend it at length.

> ı can confirm today that neither the ship commanders nor the embarked task group commander [Herrick] had any knowledge of the South Vietnamese action against the two islands or of any other specific South Vietnamese operations against the North. Higher naval commands were made aware of the operations by Commander, U.S. Military Assistance Command, Vietnam, in order to avoid mutual interference or confusion between our patrols and those operations. Throughout the patrol conducted first by the *Maddox* alone and later by the *Maddox* and the *Turner Joy,* the U.S. destroyers were directed to remain in waters which would keep them from becoming operationally involved with the South Vietnamese activity . . . . The task force commander knew only that certain South Vietnamese naval operations were periodically carried on in the area. He had no detailed knowledge of their type or of where and when they would be conducted. Indeed, his lack of knowledge was such that he mistakenly identified the South Vietnamese craft returning from their operation on July 31 as Soviet P-6 class boats.

McNamara did admit to an "ambiguity" in his 1964 testimony, but reiterated, "I want to emphasize that the Navy played no part in, and was not associated with, South Vietnamese actions." (Here we mark the disappearance of the word "aware.") He continued: "Now, maybe you would say, 'Well, even that is too strong a statement,' because later in my testimony that same day I stated we had supplied the boats. Maybe that is a 'part' in it, but it is not a 'part in it' in the sense that it was of concern, and I think quite properly of concern to you at the time, and it is not a part of it in the sense that we are addressing. We didn't command the operation, we didn't associate the DeSoto patrol with it, and the particular question at issue at the time was did the DeSoto patrol commanders know of it; they did not."

Fulbright said, "Well, on that point, there is one cable which shows the following, and I quote from a cable to the *Maddox:*

> The above patrol will (a) clearly demonstrate our determination to continue these operations; (b) possibly draw NVN PGMs [North Vietnamese patrol boats] to northward away from the area of 34-A Operations. (c) eliminate DeSoto patrol interference with 34-A Operations.

It is unusual, having received that cable, that the *Maddox* did not know what 34-A was."

Secretary McNAMARA. The *Maddox* did know what 34-A was, no question about that. But *Maddox* was not associated with 34-A, was not playing a part of it, was not planning to draw forces away from it.

Senator MORSE. I thought you said they did not know anything about it.

Secretary McNAMARA. Now wait a minute. I did not say they did not know anything about it.

Senator MORSE. You said 'were not aware of'.

Secretary McNAMARA. They were not aware of the details is what I said,* of the attack, as to location, or as to time, and unless one is aware of that, you cannot properly plan a diversionary effort.

McNamara listed several actions by the Navy to keep the DeSoto patrol separate from the 34-A Operations: the authorization given Herrick on August 1 to "deviate from itinerary" if he thought the risk was too great to continue; the order on August 2 to keep the *Maddox* clear of 34-A areas; another order on August 3 moving the *Maddox* even further to the north; and the Seventh Fleet commander's decision later on the 3rd (countermanded by the Pacific commander, Admiral Sharp) to end the patrol the evening of August 4 "in order to move it away from the area and avoid any possibility of conflict with 34-A." McNamara said, "I mention this simply to tell you that the higher commands were knowledgeable about the 34-A and DeSoto and took every possible action to separate the two."

Fulbright returned to McNamara's claim that Herrick didn't know details of the 34-A Operations. If this were true, he asked, would the Secretary explain Herrick's cable of August 3, 15 hours before the second incident, stating that he had information that North Vietnam "considers patrol directly involved with 34-A Operations . . . [and] considers U.S. ships present as enemy because of these operations and [has] already indicated readiness to treat us in that category."

Secretary McNAMARA. Two points: First, we can find no basis for the commander making this statement, that the DRV considered the DeSoto patrol directly involved in 34-A Operations.

* McNamara misquotes himself, unconvincingly.

Second, Herrick himself now states he can recall no basis for coming to that conclusion.

Third, the PT boat officer that we captured and interrogated in July 1966 told his interrogators that it was clear in his mind that the DeSoto patrol was separate from 34-A Operations.

Chairman FULBRIGHT. Well, you are not saying this cable was not sent.

Secretary McNAMARA. I simply stand on what I said, Mr. Chairman. Of course, the cable was sent . . . . But I am saying it is a complete distortion of the fact to leave the record indicating that the commander of the *Maddox* task force *had any basis whatsoever for believing that North Vietnam confused 34-A and DeSoto*. He did not have that basis. He now says he did not have the basis, and a North Vietnamese captured since that time states that North Vietnam distinguished between the two operations.

John Jerome Herrick, at the time of the Tonkin incidents, was 44 years old, of sound mind, and had been an officer in the United States Navy since 1943, when he was graduated from Annapolis. The *Maddox* assignment was his fifth command position. That an officer of his experience would have concocted such a cable without reason, and dispatched it to a higher command, is incredible. It seems logical to assume that Herrick sent the cable because he felt its contents to be an accurate description of the situation he was in.

Asked in July 1968 as to why he sent the cable, Herrick replied:

"Well, when you feel that you are on the spot, and you're the primary source of intelligence, and also you feel the reason they sent you along is probably to use your head a little bit, and give an opinion, or you wouldn't be there. So, we tied in a lot of things, and probably tied in a lot of things that shouldn't have been in there. And people who had the time, knowing other intelligence and so forth, would probably have not said that."

Was it unusual for a commander to make a recommendation of this sort? Herrick replied:

"It would be normal to send back our reaction . . . . We recommended that [the patrol be terminated] but of course this was strictly our recommendation, and an evaluation."[*][2]

McNamara professed to know little about the origin and execution of the 34-A Operations. "I can't describe the exact organization although I will be happy to try to obtain the information for you," he told Fulbright. (He never supplied it.) "The operations of the South Vietnamese against

---

[*] Peculiarly, Herrick's biographical sketch in the Internal Relations Division of the Navy Office of Information[3] has an abbreviated account of the Tonkin incidents: "He was on board his flagship when it was attacked by three North Vietnamese torpedo boats on August 2, 1964, in international waters in the Gulf of Tonkin, about 28 miles off the Communist North-Viet-Nam coast. No casualties or damage was sustained by the *Maddox*." Nary a word about the disputed August 4 encounter.

the North were carried out by South Vietnamese personnel, utilizing to some degree U.S. equipment. The boats, as I think I stated before this committee in August 1964, were, I believe, wholly supplied by the United States. . . ." Actually, McNamara described a separate enterprise, Operation Market Time, in which the South Vietnamese inspected coastal junks in *South Vietnamese waters*. The 34-A Operations were an entirely different affair.

"The United States was informed of the operations to insure that they did not interfere with patrols of the kinds that we are describing now. I believe, also, some U.S. personnel may have trained, or participated in the training, of some of the South Vietnamese personnel participating in the operations. The operations, however, were under the command of the South Vietnamese and were carried out by the South Vietnamese. There were no U.S. personnel participating in it, to the best of my knowledge." Who did the training? "They were U.S. personnel, I don't know whether Navy, or Army, or some other service personnel," McNamara said.

And then McNamara hinted that he knew enough about the 34-A Operations to permit answers unqualified by such phrases as "I believe" or "to the best of my knowledge." Fulbright said the Defense Department had given the committee information that "the U.S. Navy trained South Vietnamese for interdiction missions against North Vietnam beginning in June of 1964." McNamara corrected him. "I don't believe the training started, as your question implied, in June of 1964. I think it must have started earlier than that." In fact the training did begin before June—however, approval to conduct raids on the islands did not come until June.

Although Senators didn't pursue the matter, McNamara mentioned in passing that he did not learn until "subsequent to my testimony of August 6, 1964" of the 34-A Operations of August 3–4. "It is a fact that the Navy had worked out an arrangement between the separate commands in the Pacific, the Saigon command on the one hand, and the 7th Fleet command on the other, to insure that these operations stayed out of each other's areas, and the commanders of the ships on patrol were specifically instructed to stay away from certain geographic areas in order to avoid interference or association with the 34-A Operations of the South Vietnamese." He said that "periodically, future programs for such operations were transmitted to higher headquarters above Saigon, including the Pentagon."

Why the slip on the August 3–4 raids? Various levels of Admiral Sharp's command knew the 34-A Operations were scheduled for that night—and Admiral Sharp insisted upon sending the *Maddox* and *Turner Joy* on a patrol track that called for runs straight in towards the coast, and in the immediate proximity of the two islands which had been shelled only three nights previously, even when Herrick warned of the dangers involved. And in doing so, Sharp did not inform the Secretary of Defense of the juxtaposition of the 34-A Operations and the new patrol tactic for the *Maddox* and *Turner Joy*.

Would McNamara have permitted the DeSoto patrol to continue on August 4 had he known of the second round of 34-A Operations on August 3–4? On this question the Pentagon absolutely refuses to comment.

Morse took McNamara back to the Pacific Fleet commander's order of August 4 that the DeSoto patrol continue, moving northward to "possibly draw NVN patrol boats northward away from the area of 34-A Ops," and "to eliminate DeSoto patrol interference with 34-A Ops."

"Unless there is some break in my thinking," Morse said, "that is where you lose me if it is the contention that we were not using the *Maddox* in connection in some way with the attacks. It is only my premise, and I am not reaching any final conclusion until I hear all of the record—I hope I am too good a lawyer for that—but it seems clear to me that instructions went out to the *Maddox* and to the *Joy* in relationship to 34-A, and they were being used.

"Now, if they were, does it make any difference whether they were on the high seas or not, if they were acting as a provocateur, if they were in fact cooperating with the South Vietnamese boats? You are not arguing, are you, that the North Vietnamese had no right to attack them on the high seas?"

Secretary McNAMARA. I am arguing, Senator Morse, that the reason for the change in the area border . . . from which the *Maddox* was to be restricted was designed by the U.S. commander in South Vietnam to further separate the *Maddox* from the 34-A Operations in order to assure that there was less reason for anybody, including the North Vietnamese, to associate the two.

I am arguing further that the North Vietnamese themselves have stated that they did not confuse the two.

Senator MORSE. Well, Mr. Secretary, you give us the testimony of a captured prisoner or two, which does not bespeak what the naval operators of North Vietnam not captured were thinking. After all, when you are using a prisoner as a witness, you are certainly not using the best witness.

You see, one of the things that disturbs me is that I think the cablegram itself shows that we were trying to draw those North Vietnamese boats away from the South Vietnamese boats in order to give the South Vietnamese boats greater freedom of action, and that if that is not involving our destroyers in the 34-A project, I do not know what it is.

I think we were using them as a decoy.

Secretary McNAMARA. Senator Morse, had we been using them as a decoy we would not have so substantially increased the restricted area.

This move to north of 19 degrees 10 minutes was a move of about,

I would say, 90 miles, moving the northerly boundary of the restricted area farther and farther away from the 34-A Operations.

Senator MORSE. It is a pretty good decoy if you are trying to get the North Vietnamese boats to follow them.

Secretary McNAMARA. No, because then the North Vietnamese boats *knew* that our boats had no hostile intent and played no hostile role. They *knew* that from having tracked them the previous nights, and they *knew* that from previous patrols, so there was no basis for this assertion by the author of that cable, and, by the way, he said it would possibly draw them to the north. There was no——

Senator MORSE. 'Possibly' in that context could be interpreted as 'hopefully'.

Secretary McNAMARA. In any case it was not possible and it was not a plan, and it was not the purpose of the DeSoto patrol, and *the Joint Chiefs had never considered that, and would never have approved that purpose,* nor was the patrol carried out in such a way to permit such a purpose to be achieved.

Senator MORSE. It is most unfortunate you had them anywhere near there while the South Vietnamese attacks were going on because you opened yourself, I think, to just this kind of interpretation of the messages.

Several of McNamara's assertions demand challenge. Tactically, it was an astute maneuver to restrict the *Maddox* and *Turner Joy* to 90 miles above the new 34-A Operations. The Navy knew that the North Vietnamese had both destroyers under radar and visual surveillance, and that their presence demanded the attention of North Vietnamese patrol boats. The 90 miles' separation was more than two hours' travel time for any PT boats summoned south to help beat off the new attacks. And, as noted, both the *Maddox* and *Turner Joy* spent August 3 cruising toward islands previously attacked—a gesture not intended to soothe the North Vietnamese.

One simply cannot accept McNamara's claim that the North Vietnamese "knew" on August 4 that the DeSoto patrol was completely divorced from 34-A Operations, and "knew" the destroyers' mission on the basis of previous DeSoto patrols. (Unless, unbeknownst to all of us, the *Maddox* flew a banner identifying herself as a harmless electronic surveillance ship.) Indeed, Herrick's warning cable stated exactly the opposite—and this from an officer who was on the scene in the Gulf of Tonkin, not sitting thousands of miles away in the Pentagon war room, or in Pacific Fleet headquarters in Hawaii. Nor was the endorsement of the JCS necessary to transform the *Maddox* and *Turner Joy* into decoys: this idea originated at the Pacific Command level, in the same headquarters that did not choose to alert Washington of the new 34-A Operations, activities certain to increase tension in the Gulf. At this point in McNamara's testimony, the observer is inclined to think that the time has come to dismiss the Secretary, and to summon Admiral Sharp to the stand to explain his positioning of the *Maddox* and *Turner Joy,* and his failure to notify his civilian superiors in the Pentagon of events that should have affected the crucial decisions they were trying to make.

According to McNamara's testimony, he and Admiral Sharp spoke on the telephone numerous times during the afternoon and evening of August 4. Admiral Sharp, according to McNamara, was prompt to "verify" and "confirm" that United States vessels had been subjected to "unprovoked attack"—yet not a single word was relayed to McNamara of actions which Hanoi had denounced as "provocations."

McNamara repeatedly fell back upon the geographical and chronological separation of the raids and the United States vessel in arguing that they were "not involved": that at the time of the July 30–31 operations, the *Maddox* was 130 miles distant, and was attacked 63 hours later, when she was "28 miles from the coast and steaming east"; that the *Maddox* and *Turner Joy* were 70 miles distant from the targets of the August 3–4 raids, and were 60 miles offshore, steaming east, when the August 4 incident began 22 hours later.

Morse wouldn't accept McNamara's reasoning: "I only want to say . . . that I don't think we should have been there and especially under those circumstances when the Navy and Administration knew that South Vietnamese naval vessels that we had furnished and the personnel whom we had trained were on their way in that period of time to bombard North Vietnam and its two islands. The *Maddox* and the *Turner Joy* were in the area, despite all our talk about the distances. The fact is that the North Vietnamese had no reason to believe that we were trying to keep separate the South Vietnamese operations and our patrol . . . . We don't know what conclusions they reached. I think it would be a very reasonable conclusion if they thought there was a connection.

"I happen to think there was a very clear connection.

"The very fact that you were electronically invading, so to speak, North Vietnam, while at the same time, in that same series of time, the South Vietnamese boats were going in to make their attack, puts us, I think, in the position where the North Vietnamese and the rest of the world, for that matter, would see some interrelation . . . .

"With this preparation for bombarding North Vietnam, I think that wisdom dictated that we should have had the *Maddox* and the *Turner Joy* far removed from any area, high seas or not, that would possibly justify anybody making that connection. To be on the high seas and commit an illegal act on the high seas constitutes a form of aggression, constructive or actual, that was really our position, in part, in October 1962 during our conflict with Russia over her clear act of constructive aggression against us vis-a-vis Cuba.

"So one of my bones of contention is that I don't think our hands are clean if we fall back on technical defenses of our rights on the high seas and making perfectly clear to North Vietnam we were going to enforce those rights.

"The basic question is why were we following this course of action at that time in the Gulf of Tonkin when the South Vietnamese boats were going up there to make an attack? I think all the explanation of the Secretary, all the explanation of the Administration, just ducks that problem."

The Territorial Waters Issue

The Administration's position was consistent: The *Maddox's* orders prior to August 2 were to approach not closer than eight nautical miles to the North Vietnamese mainland, nor closer than four nautical miles to her islands. After the first incident, the mainland CPA [closest point of approach] was increased to 11 miles. Statements that the *Maddox* entered "waters claimed by North Vietnamese as territorial . . . have no basis in fact," McNamara said. His case:

> At no time prior to the August 1964 Tonkin Gulf incidents did the North Vietnamese government claim a width of territorial sea in excess of three miles. The North Vietnamese government succeeded the French government which adhered to the three-mile limit. Under the rules of international law, no claim by North Vietnam in excess of three miles would be assumed unless specifically made and published. It should be noted that Cambodia, a sister successor state, publicly adopted the French three-mile rule on achieving independence. Later, it proclaimed a five-mile rule. South Vietnam claims three miles. The first statement of North Vietnam which approaches a claim in excess of three miles occurred well after the attacks on September 1, 1964, in the form of a broadcast from Radio Hanoi in which it was stated, 'The Democratic Republic of Vietnam declared that the territorial sea is 12 miles. . . .'[1]
>
> The question might be asked, however: Should we not as a practical matter have assumed a claim of 12 miles since that is the uniform position of the Communist countries? The simple answer is that Communist countries do not have such a uniform position: Cuba and Poland each adhere to the traditional three-mile limit, while Yugoslavia and Albania claim ten miles.

Actually, a claim of 12 miles would not necessarily have affected the *Maddox's* sailing orders, for as McNamara made plain: "The United States recognizes no claim of a territorial sea in excess of three miles. This consistent position of the United States was reemphasized at the close of the 1960 Convention on Law of the Sea in Geneva." Reiterating this national policy position during a discussion of the *Pueblo* case in September 1968, a State Department official elaborated: "Now, if the question is why in this case [the *Pueblo*] do you take measures to respect a 12-mile limit [claimed by North Korea] I can only say the obvious, that you would do that as a prudent and precautionary measure in the interest of not creating incidents."[4]

The question of territorial waters, and the *Maddox's* alleged violation thereof, is considerably more complex than McNamara's testimony would indicate. The CIA's radio monitoring service in the weeks immediately prior to the Tonkin incidents produced much documentary evidence that North Vietnam was in fact protesting intrusions to within less than 12 miles of her shores as violations of her territorial waters. Such intelligence was given daily to men who worked directly under McNamara, and who were involved in the decision making on August 4. Further, existent evidence points to Administration confusion during the crisis over exactly what North Vietnam did claim.

The three-mile limit on territorial waters has a long history. It was first enunciated in 1737 by a Dutch court in what is known as the Cannon Shot Rule. The rule fixed the width of territorial waters at this distance because it was the effective range of a cannon shot, and recognized the seas beyond as free to navigation by ships of all nations in time of peace.[5] Maritime states had previously claimed whatever sovereignty over the seas they had felt strong enough to enforce. Venice claimed the entire Adriatic; England all of the North Sea and large chunks of the Atlantic; Sweden and Denmark declared the Baltic a closed sea.

Nations making such claims policed the waters against piracy (thereby providing an international service), but permitted navigation by ships of all nations. Abuses by Spain and Portugal ruined the system. Bulls issued by Pope Alexander VI in 1493 "gave" the Pacific and the Gulf of Mexico to Spain, and most of the Atlantic and all of the Indian Ocean to Portugal. Britain heatedly protested Spanish claims that the expeditions of Sir Francis Drake and others violated her exclusive rights to navigation and trade, Queen Elizabeth I declaring, "The use of the sea and air is common to all." The Dutch jurist Hugo Grotius (1583–1645) in his thesis *Mare Liberum* also argued that the high seas were open for all to navigate. English naval power and Grotius' legal arguments prevailed by the end of the seventeenth century, and the principle of freedom of the seas was established. However, as a corollary, the right of coastal states to exercise sovereignty over waters adjacent to their shores was also recognized.

Herein lies the problem: By 1900, 20 of the 21 countries that had laid formal claim followed the Cannon Shot Rule. But then nations began to enter exceptions, adding "contiguous zones"* which pushed their limits further to sea, or extending their basic territorial claim to 12 miles. Several

* The contiguous zone is the band of water beyond the territorial sea in which the coastal state may exercise controls such as those over customs and sanitation.

Latin American nations asserted 200-mile limits for fishing rights; minute Guinea claims that its waters stretch 130 miles off Africa. International conferences (the most recent, in 1960) found the problem incapable of solution.

Why, then, does the United States retain the three-mile limit, both as the limit of its own territorial waters and that which it formally recognizes for other nations? Ambassador Arthur H. Dean, head of the United States delegation to the 1960 Law of the Sea Conference, told the Senate Foreign Relations Committee that year: "The primary danger to the continued ability of warships and supporting aircraft to move, unhampered, to wherever they may be needed to support American foreign policy presents itself in the great international straits of the world—the narrows which lie athwart the sea routes . . . . It is in these narrows that an undue expansion of coastal states' territorial seas could entirely wipe out existing passageways over free high seas, and, by creating national sovereignty over one segment of a vital route, subject to coastal states' interference the transit of our warships or terminate transit of our aircraft in the overlying airspace."

Some 116 major international straits could be affected by an increase beyond three miles, were not rights of free passage assured (and it might be recalled in this context that the Arabs used the 12-mile limit as a means of closing the Gulf of Aqaba to Israeli sea traffic in May 1967, one of the sparks which started the Middle East war).

In the words of Captain Geoffrey E. Carlisle, a Navy expert on the law of the sea: "Our interests are best served when we have freedom to navigate as close as possible to the coasts of other states of the world. This desire and this theoretical advantage has been the *sine qua non* of our inflexible position on the three-mile limit. But perhaps our insistence on this position has worked to our disadvantage . . . . The Soviet Union has long maintained that a state is free to set the breadth of its territorial waters to any limit up to 12 miles and has consistently claimed 12 miles for herself. . . . Communist China also claims a 12-mile territorial sea. The United States has not, from a practical standpoint, effectively challenged those claims. Contrarily, our adherence to the three-mile limit permits Russian intelligence collection trawlers to lie near our coasts and record the comings and goings of our submarines and aircraft." Bound by national policy, the Navy officially supports the three-mile limit. But Carlisle, who was director of the International Law Division of the Navy Judge Advocate General when he wrote the article cited, states that as an "enforceable breadth" it is "no longer a meaningful principle of international law."[6]

Working from its own internal messages, the Navy as late as 1963 was unsure as to the North Vietnamese territorial limit. On May 1 of that year, the director of Naval Intelligence sent this message to the naval attaché in the United States legation in Saigon:

> According best information, DRV has not publicly proclaimed limits of territorial seas or baselines and points from which measured. Absence of such proclamation possibly due fact DRV did not participate in 1958 or 1960s conferences on law of sea. In absence of a proclamation, it is *assumed* they possess the three-mile limit established [sic] by international law. *However, there is good possibility DRV will subscribe to the 12-mile limit claimed by other Communist nations if issue were raised.*

Not even the North Vietnamese claim the *Maddox* came within three miles of their coastline during the DeSoto patrol. However, its official media, *prior to the August 2 attack,* did charge violations of its "territorial waters" by ships operating less than 12 miles offshore—a clear indication that Hanoi considered its limit to be 12 miles. On July 28, 1964, Radio Hanoi, in an English-language broadcast over its international frequencies, asserted: "At 4:30 P.M. on 25 July 1965, four United States-South Vietnamese warships intruded into the *territorial waters* of the DRV at 106 degrees 43 [minutes] east longitude and 17 degrees 45 [minutes] north latitude and encircled two fishing boats belonging to inhabitants of Bao Ninh Commune in Quang Binh Province." The warships allegedly kidnapped the fishermen and their gear and fled under fire. The location cited is nine statute miles off the North Vietnamese mainland. Again, Radio Hanoi in an international broadcast on August 2 (before the attack on the *Maddox*) charged that the United States and the Saigon government "on July 30 sent warships to shell Hon Me and Hon Ngu Islands in the *DRV territorial waters.*" Hon Ngu is 2.4 miles off the coast; Hon Me, 7.2 miles. These broadcasts were available throughout the national security establishment in Washington.

The Department of Defense, in a plot of the *Maddox's* July 31–August 3 course, gave the following closest points of approach: Cap Mui Doc, 10.3 nautical miles; Cap Mui Ron, 8.2; Cap Falaise, 8.5; Hon Vat, 5.1; Hon Me, 10.2; and Cap Chao, 14.*[7]

Yet Radio Hanoi, in broadcasts before the August 4 incident, claimed that the *Maddox's* route was within its territorial limits. The morning of August 4 a spokesman for the Vietnam People's Army, quoted on Radio Hanoi, said: "In the night of July 31–August 1, the U.S. imperialists again sent a destroyer to encroach upon North Vietnam's territorial waters in Quang Binh Province. This warship had been cruising for two days, August 1 and 2, between Hon Mat Island and Hon Me Island to intimidate

---

* See map, page 229.

PROVOCATIONS BY THE U.S.S. MADDOX IN THE TERRITORIAL WATERS OF THE DEMOCRATIC REPUBLIC OF VIET NAM FROM JULY 31 TO AUGUST 2, 1964

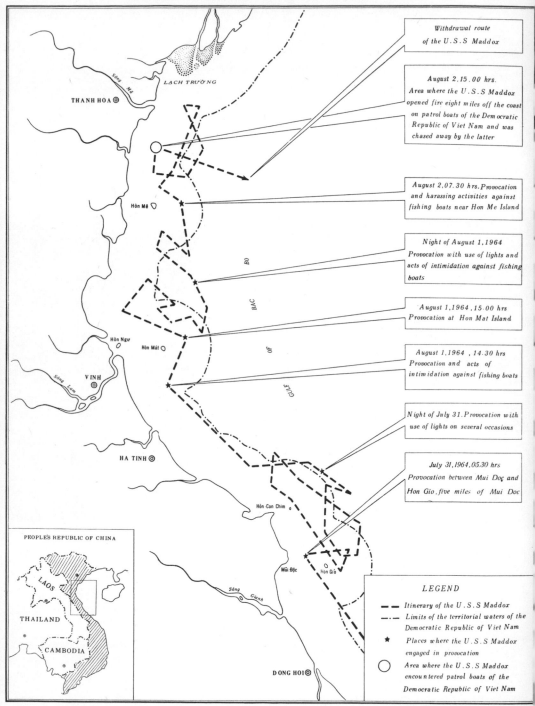

Withdrawal route of the U.S.S Maddox

August 2, 15.00 hrs. Area where the U.S.S Maddox opened fire eight miles off the coast on patrol boats of the Democratic Republic of Viet Nam and was chased away by the latter

August 2, 07.30 hrs. Provocation and harassing activities against fishing boats near Hon Me Island

Night of August 1, 1964 Provocation with use of lights and acts of intimidation against fishing boats

August 1, 1964, 15.00 hrs Provocation at Hon Mat Island

August 1, 1964, 14.30 hrs Provocation and acts of intimidation against fishing boats

Night of July 31. Provocation with use of lights on several occasions

July 31, 1964, 05.30 hrs Provocation between Mui Doc and Hon Gio, five miles of Mui Doc

LEGEND

- - - - *Itinerary of the U.S.S Maddox*
- · - · - *Limits of the territorial waters of the Democratic Republic of Viet Nam*
★ *Places where the U.S.S Maddox engaged in provocation*
◯ *Area where the U.S.S Maddox encountered patrol boats of the Democratic Republic of Viet Nam*

Source: North Vietnamese White Paper on the Tonkin Incidents Circulated September 1964 (Reproduction unedited)

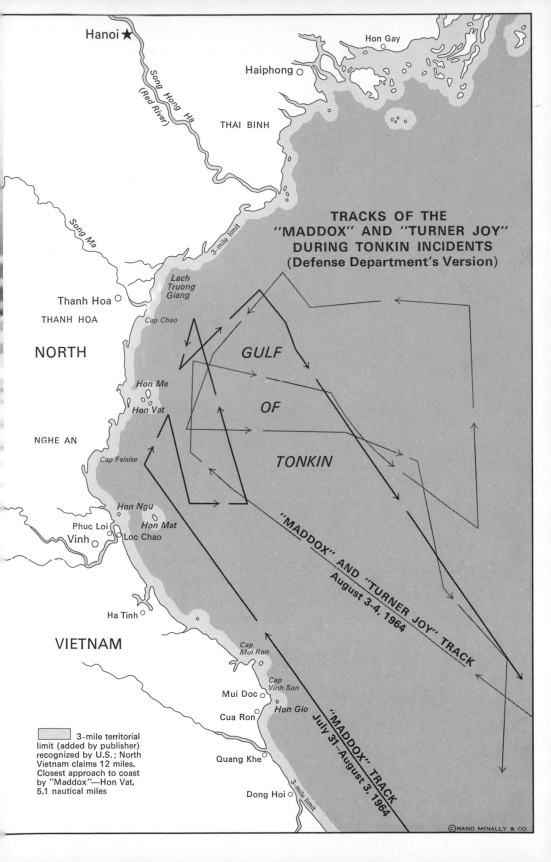

Hanoi ★

Hon Gay

Haiphong ○

THAI BINH

Song Hong Ha (Red River)

Song Ma

3-mile limit

**TRACKS OF THE
"MADDOX" AND "TURNER JOY"
DURING TONKIN INCIDENTS**
(Defense Department's Version)

Lach Truong Giang

Thanh Hoa ○

THANH HOA

Cap Chao

NORTH

GULF

Hon Me

OF

Hon Vat

NGHE AN

Cap Falaise

TONKIN

Hon Ngu

Hon Mat

Phuc Loi ○

Vinh ○   Loc Chao

"MADDOX" AND "TURNER JOY" TRACK
August 3-4, 1964

Ha Tinh ○

VIETNAM

Cap Mui Ron

Cap Vinh Son

Mui Doc ○

Hon Gio

Cua Ron ○

"MADDOX" TRACK
July 31-August 3, 1964

3-mile territorial
limit (added by publisher)
recognized by U.S.; North
Vietnam claims 12 miles.
Closest approach to coast
by "Maddox"—Hon Vat,
5.1 nautical miles

Quang Khe ○

3-mile limit

Dong Hoi ○

©RAND McNALLY & CO.

fishing boats of our people, *openly infringing upon our territorial waters.* In face of the provocations by the sea rovers, our patrol ships took action to defend our *territorial waters* and fishermen and chased the enemy ship out of our *territorial waters. . . ."*[8] The statement did not specify, in miles, what was claimed as the *Maddox's* closest point of approach. The Pentagon puts the CPA to Hon Me at 10.2 nautical miles on August 2.[9] A North Vietnamese White Paper published in September 1964 states that the August 2 episode began when the *Maddox* "opened fire eight miles off the coast . . . ."[10]

McNamara acknowledged that he was aware of the broadcasts, but disagreed with Rhode Island Senator Claiborne Pell's assertion that they "would indicate to me that they had thought 12 miles was their territorial limit." McNamara responded: "I do not think it really led us to that conclusion. We believed up to that time they thought three miles was the territorial limit because they had not stated anything beyond that." Conversely, one could conclude Washington chose not to listen to North Vietnam's warnings that a vessel which was in a certain place less than 12 miles off its shores was in its territorial waters. Formal declaration or not, the broadcasts gave Washington ample reason to tread carefully.

Contradictory statements on the limit were given by Cyrus Vance— deputy secretary to McNamara during the crisis, and a participant in the meetings at which the reprisal raids were planned—during a Voice of America broadcast on August 8, 1964, one day after the resolution passed. The interview was conducted by Richard Fryklund of the *Washington Star,* later to become a Pentagon press officer, and Jack Raymond, then the Pentagon correspondent for the *New York Times.* The Department of Defense transcript of the interview reveals the following exchange:[11]

> FRYKLUND. Is there any dispute about the Tonkin Gulf being international waters? Do, for instance, Communist China and North Vietnam claim the gulf as their territorial waters?
> Secretary VANCE. Not to my knowledge. *I think that they do claim a 12-mile limit as opposed to a three-mile limit, but there is no claim that the Gulf of Tonkin is territorial waters.*
> FRYKLUND. Does the United States recognize the 12-mile limit?
> Secretary VANCE. No, it does not. The United States recognizes three miles as the territorial limit.
> FRYKLUND. Do our naval units ever sail closer than three miles to the shore?
> Secretary VANCE. They do not.
> FRYKLUND. Are they under specific orders not to?
> Secretary VANCE. They are.

RAYMOND. Well, the real issue here is, I think, do they sail closer than 12 miles?

Secretary VANCE. They have sailed——

RAYMOND. They have.

Secretary VANCE. Sailed closer than 12 miles.

Whatever the past confusion, North Vietnam on September 1, 1964, broadcast the following over Hanoi Radio's international frequencies:

> According to Western news agency reports, the US Undersecretary of Defense [sic] Cyrus Vance declared that Washington does not recognize the limit of North Vietnam's territorial waters as 12 miles and recognizes a limit of three miles, and American ships have received a formal order not to move inside this three-mile limit.
>
> The spokesman of the DRV ministry of Foreign Affairs emphatically protests against the above-mentioned arrogant statement, and regards it as a brazen violation of the national sovereignty of the DRV.
>
> The question of defining the breadth of the territorial waters is strictly within the sovereignty of each country. The United States government has absolutely no right to decide the breadth of the territorial waters of the DRV. The DRV government declares that the question of defining the breadth of its territorial waters as 12 miles, in accordance with the juridical custom in the country, is within its sovereign rights. . . .
>
> The declaration of the . . . Undersecretary of Defense is obviously intended to justify the repeated intrusions into the DRV territorial waters by the destroyer *Maddox* and other U.S. war vessels since 31 July 1964, and to corroborate in a clumsy manner the imaginary story of a so-called attack on U.S. warships in international waters. . . .

(McNamara, incidentally, does not accept this declaration as a legal assertion of a 12-mile limit. He told the 1968 hearing, "No official documentary confirmation of the claim asserted in this broadcast is known to exist.")

One other phase of law of the sea, that of the right of "hot pursuit," is involved in the Tonkin incidents. If the North Vietnamese statement of facts is accepted as correct (that is, her boats attacked a U.S. vessel on August 2 which was engaged in raids on the islands, and chased it into international waters), then the United States position is legally flimsy. Conversely, if the American version is the accurate one (that is, her boats had no connection with the raids and remained in international waters) then North Vietnam is the aggressor. Aaron L. Shalowitz, longtime sea-law expert for the Coast and Geodetic Survey of the United States Department of Commerce, wrote in 1963: "Hot pursuit is the right which a coastal state has to pursue a foreign vessel on the high seas that has committed an offense in territorial waters. The limitations on this right are that the pursuit must follow immediately upon the escape of the vessel and must be continuous. Hence, normally, hot pursuit cannot originate if the offending vessel is first spotted in the contiguous zone, since that is part of the high seas. But the Convention on the High Seas ... permits such pursuit if there has been a violation of the rights of the coastal state for the protection of which the contiguous zone was established."[12] According to Shalowitz, the right of hot pursuit begins when a state has "good reason to believe that the ship has violated the laws and regulations of that state .... It may be undertaken if the suspected vessel or one of its boats is within the internal waters,* the territorial sea, or the contiguous zone of the pursuing state, but in the last case only if there has been a violation of the rights for the protection of which the zone was established. Hot pursuit may be continued outside the territorial sea or contiguous waters if it is uninterrupted, and if a visual or auditory signal to stop is given and is ignored by the fleeing vessel."

Verification of the Incidents Before Retaliation

Knowing that the Senators held military cables which reflected doubts that the second incident had happened as reported, McNamara tried in his opening statement to soften the blows waiting for him. He claimed he had noted during his 1964 testimony that "sonar and radar readings may be subject to interpretation and argument because of sea and atmospheric conditions." If he in fact did so, not a word of it is contained in the censored version of the hearings which the Pentagon allowed to be published in 1966. Further, committee staff members who attended the 1964 hearings say that if McNamara did touch upon these points, the references were so slighting, so oblique, they no longer remember them.

But it is apparent from the 1968 testimony that McNamara chose to put into the record, as early and as strongly as possible, the Pentagon's version of the origin of the doubts, and its claimed resolution of them before the reprisal raids. From 9:20 A.M. on August 4 (Washington time) through early afternoon, McNamara said that flash-message reports, "some ambiguous and some conflicting," poured into the Pentagon. In meetings with civilian and uniformed advisers, "the apparent ambiguities and contradictions in the reports were examined and reconciled to our satisfaction." McNamara's greatest hurdle was the Herrick cable casting doubt on the entire August 4 episode save for the initial attempted ambush, and suggesting "complete evaluation before any further action." He approached it casually:

> For example, I saw a message from the onscene task group commander which expressed doubts as to the validity of many of the sonar reports.†

* Internal waters consist of water areas in bays and mouths of rivers and estuaries.
† The Herrick cable cast doubt not only on the sonar reports, but also on the entire incident.

I discussed this message by telephone with the commander-in-chief, Pacific, and informed him that, although we would continue with the preparations, the reprisal strike would not be executed until we were absolutely positive of the attack. He of course agreed and in a later telephone call informed me that he was satisfied from all the reports he had on hand, that an attack on our ships had taken place.

The various phone and cable messages between the Pentagon, Hawaii, and the destroyers were recounted at length in Chapter Five. McNamara also cited the crew and radar reports, as well as the radio intercepts, as proof positive of the August 4 incident. Nonetheless, he indirectly admitted that he was not satisfied. Asked by Fulbright why he "convened a formal inquiry into that incident," McNamara said:

"I think that I first sent out certain representatives of my own [Jack Stempler, then assistant general counsel of the Pentagon, and Alvin Friedman, Deputy Assistant Secretary of Defense for Far Eastern Affairs] on an informal basis to check—to see whether there was sufficient basis for questioning whether the incident took place and then later asked the Navy to set up an investigating group."

By the time the Stempler-Friedman inquiry and others got under way, of course, days had passed, and the reprisal attacks had been conducted. If sufficient doubt existed to warrant the extraordinary investigations, why the hurry on the bombing of North Vietnam?

The Administration's only on-the-record explanation was given by Secretary Rusk on August 5, 1964, in an interview with Elie Abel of NBC TV. Abel asked the Secretary why the United States responded "as swiftly and abruptly as we did without taking time even to notify our allies?" Rusk's answer: "Well, in the first place, we had some ships in the Gulf of Tonkin who were under attack, and they were dodging torpedoes [sic]. Here is a vast expanse of international waters, in which we had a perfect right to be. . . . We had to strike immediately because we didn't expect to ask those ships to run a continuing gauntlet of torpedoes on their way back to the Gulf of Tonkin when this mission was completed, nor were we prepared to have them denied international waters. . . . Further than that, if under these attacks, there had not been an immediate and appropriate response, then Hanoi and those who might be standing behind Hanoi in this might well have come to a very formidable mistaken judgment about what is possible in the Southeast Asian situation."[13]

Rusk seems to be confused about the danger. The August 4 engagement broke off shortly after midnight, and an hour later the *Maddox* and *Turner Joy* were snuggled into the United States fleet on Yankee Station, far out of range of the North Vietnamese patrol boats and safe under the protective umbrella of the *Ticonderoga*. No one within the Administration has ever claimed that to have delayed the bombings by 24 or 48 hours, to permit further verification, would have emboldened the North Vietnamese to storm out of the Gulf of Tonkin in pursuit of the Seventh Fleet. But Washington chose to do its verification *ex post facto*.

Another study of the incidents—made by John Ponturo, a defense research specialist for the Institute for Defense Analysis—McNamara flatly refused to discuss. The institute is a private think-tank which works almost exclusively for the Pentagon (retired General Maxwell Taylor is the director). Ponturo labored for weeks in 1964 on a study entitled, "Command and Control of the Tonkin Gulf Incident, 4–5 August 1964." His chief conclusions were that there were significant delays in receiving messages from the *Maddox* and *Turner Joy* throughout August 4, and that doubts as to what happened during the engagement progressively increased when Herrick sent in supplemental battle reports, as compared to his sketchy flash reports on events he did not have time to evaluate or put into perspective. The report hints that the cables from Washington and the Pacific commanders "pressured" Herrick into giving information to "support" his flash report of an attack, rather than writing a balanced account; and that the Pentagon was "highly selective" in picking the "positive" segments out of his cables and downgrading or ignoring the "negative."

McNamara said he had never even heard of Ponturo's study until the Foreign Relations Committee asked for it in January 1968. "I glanced through it. It raises lots of questions, because its classification is not high enough to indicate that it covers all of the intelligence information which contributed significantly to our conclusion that an attack took place, and, two, I know that the author of it did not discuss with me, and I am told he did not discuss with General Wheeler, events, which took place during the day, and there are certain events . . . that only General Wheeler, or I, or the President, or one or two others whom the author did not contact, had knowledge of."

General Wheeler described the Ponturo paper as a "critical incident report" designed to improve procedures and operations of the Joint Chiefs of Staff. However, he contended it had not been reviewed nor cross-checked by the Joint Chiefs, and that in scanning it "I find errors of fact and I believe omissions that would be pertinent to any definitive study of the operation." Wheeler conceded he had read only "maybe half a dozen pages" of what McNamara called a "very thick document"; on that basis, he maintained, "Any comment I make [on it] would be incomplete and misleading."

Fulbright persisted in his quest for the IDA study, and was refused flatly and finally by the Pentagon on April 4, 1968, through a letter signed by

Assistant Secretary of Defense Paul Warnke. General Wheeler, Warnke wrote, "confirms the fact that this was an internal study and one of a series directed to the mechanics of the national military command system. It was not intended to be, nor does it constitute, a comprehensive evaluation of the incidents themselves. It was not prepared for review by the Chairman of the Joint Chiefs of Staff. As you have previously been informed, the author of the study did not have access to sources of information that would be essential to an over-all evaluation of the incidents. In light of the foregoing, the study is not considered appropriate for dissemination outside the Department."

Thus does the Pentagon bury the critical commentary of outsiders.

Tonkin and United States Troop and Plane Buildups in South Vietnam

In late July 1964 the Johnson Administration confused many persons—many of them in the government—when it leaked its intention of increasing the 16,000-troop contingent in South Vietnam by 5,000 more men. Pentagon officials released the figures on a background (i.e., not-for-attribution) basis, then refused to confirm them for the record. Congress emitted some worried murmurs, for in previous months the Administration had not sought to conceal increases in troops levels—indeed, Johnson had announced several of them from the White House. At a press conference in the last week of July, Rusk sought to minimize the 30 percent buildup, saying, "I don't myself believe that there is much magic in these theoretical numbers about strength tables." He termed it "perfectly normal" that the announcement came from Saigon—although this had never been done before.[14] The Tonkin incidents the next week, and Congress' concern with the resolution, overshadowed the troop reinforcements, and they were never questioned again.

When the Tonkin inquiry reopened in 1968, Senators were suspicious about two phases of the buildup: (a) whether the Administration magnified Tonkin out of proportion for the purpose, among others, of quieting criticisms of the increased troop levels; and (b) whether the Tonkin incidents were a pretext for the dispatch of planes to Vietnam and Thailand bases so that they would be in position to begin bombing the North when Johnson decided to do so.

The hearing produced no conclusive evidence on either point, with Wheeler denying that he knew of any orders alerting the planes for movement prior to August 4, 1964, or of any plans for "an intensification of the U.S. involvement" in the war.

Later, the Pentagon supplied Fulbright with the following breakdown of aircraft movements to South Vietnam and Thailand immediately after the Tonkin incidents:

Type of Aircraft	Number	From	To
		August 4, 1964*	
KB-50	4	Yokota Air Base, Japan	Takhli Air Base, Thailand
B-57	36	Clark Air Base, Philippine Islands	Bien Hoa Air Base, South Vietnam
F-100	4	Clark Air Base, Philippine Islands	Takhli Air Base, Thailand
RF-101	2	Misawa Air Base, Japan	Tan Son Nhut Airfield, South Vietnam
F-102	6	Clark Air Base, Philippine Islands	Da Nang Airport, South Vietnam
F-102	6	Clark Air Base, Philippine Islands	Tan Son Nhut Airfield, South Vietnam
F-105	17	Yokota Air Base, Japan	Korat Air Base, Thailand
		August 7, 1964*	
C-123	16	United States	Tan Son Nhut Airfield, South Vietnam
		September 7, 1964*	
RB-57E	2	United States	Tan Son Nhut Airfield, South Vietnam

* Date authorized by the Secretary of Defense

In sum, 93 warplanes were moved to South Vietnam and Thailand within a month after the Tonkin incidents—and were ready for action the following February when Johnson decided to commence sustained strategic bombing of North Vietnam.

The hearing was nearing an end when Senator Morse read McNamara one of the anonymous letters which had helped the committee tread its way through Pentagon secrecy and begin to find the truth about the Tonkin incidents. For almost seven hours McNamara had been on the offensive, with the Senators methodically pointing out the contradictions in his testimony. Not once did McNamara even begin to concede that the Administration had blurred certain of the details in 1964. Morse's reading of the letter brought an outburst of pained indignation from the Secretary:

"For seven years I have tried not to hide the actions of the Department [of Defense]. We have disclosed more to our nation and to our enemies, for that matter, about the national security of this country and the factors that we take account of in protecting it than has ever been disclosed before. I believe in disclosure, and I believe that the truth will support itself, and I am perfectly prepared to have the anonymous accuser or anyone else come in and examine the raw material available in the Department which bears on this."

One can only sigh in weariness, and bemoan the immensity of the gulf between statements of policy by the Pentagon and the Johnson Administration, and the execution of that policy. Which, in essence, is really what the Gulf of Tonkin is all about: illusion and reality.

EPILOGUE

Thus the record of the Gulf of Tonkin affair, which emerges as a multi-level deception: a deception of the Congress and the American people by the Johnson Administration, in its failure to be explicit about the true mission of the *USS Maddox,* her preattack troubles, and the doubts about the August 4 incident; a deception of the Johnson Administration by the military, in the Pacific Command's failure to apprise Secretary McNamara of the August 3–4 South Vietnamese raids, among other things; and a deception of the Johnson Administration by itself, in its overeager acceptance of unconfirmed field reports as justification for a grave act of war.

—The Johnson Administration claimed that the *Maddox* was on "routine patrol in international waters." The fact, as revealed through the Pentagon's own documents, is that the *Maddox* was conducting electronic espionage, and that Pentagon officials themselves were confused as to what territorial limit North Vietnam would claim if the question arose (as evidenced by the cable from the director of Naval Intelligence to Saigon, dated May 1, 1963).

—The Johnson Administration claimed that the *Maddox* and the Navy were "not aware" of the South Vietnamese Operation Plan 34-Alpha raids, an assertion repeatedly belied by the many references to Op 34-A in Navy cable traffic.

—The Johnson Administration claimed that "it was clear" (the words are McNamara's) to the North Vietnamese that the *Maddox* patrol was separate from Op 34-A raids. Yet Herrick, in a cable on August 3, said that the DRV "considers patrol directly involved in 34-A Operations . . . [and] considers U.S. ships present as enemies because of these operations

. . . ." Herrick's conclusion was based on intercepts of North Vietnamese military radio communications.

—The Johnson Administration claimed that the Navy did everything possible to keep the *Maddox* separated from the Op 34-A raids. Yet on August 2, several hours after the first incident, Admiral Thomas H. Moorer, the Pacific Fleet commander, ordered the *Maddox* and *Turner Joy* to make direct runs at the North Vietnamese coast during daylight hours, coming to within four nautical miles of islands shelled by the South Vietnamese two days previously.

—The Johnson Administration claimed that the first shots of the August 2 incident were "warning shots" by the *Maddox* when the North Vietnamese patrol boats approached within 10,000 yards (5.8 miles). Yet the *Maddox* log does not describe the first volley as "warning shots," and the Defense Department told the Foreign Relations Committee, in a statement submitted for insertion into the record of the February 1968 hearings: "There is a difference of opinion as to the use of warning shots between combatants. Obviously, a commanding officer would only have recourse to such shots under very special and compelling circumstances."

—The Johnson Administration claimed, via McNamara's testimony of August 6, 1964, that when the *Maddox* was attacked she was "about 30 miles from the coast." According to Herrick, the attack began when the *Maddox* was about 16 miles from a North Vietnamese island, and she had been much closer to the mainland earlier in the day. McNamara also asserted that the second incident began when the *Maddox* and *Turner Joy* were "approximately 65 miles from the nearest land." They, too, had been within eyeshot of the coast during daylight hours.

—The Johnson Administration claimed that it had "incontrovertible evidence" that the August 4 attack had occurred before Johnson approved the retaliatory raids. Yet even as bombers flew over North Vietnam, the Pentagon "urgently" pleaded with Pacific commanders for substantiating evidence.

—The Johnson Administration claimed that various "eyewitness" testimony proves the August 4 incident was real—McNamara telling the February 1968 hearing, for instance, that "searchlight illumination had been utilized by the attacking craft and that gunfire against the [United States] patrol had been observed." Yet the *Turner Joy* skipper, Captain Barnhart, says no searchlight ever touched his ships, although he saw one flicker as an apparent recall signal. McNamara did not produce the name of a single man on either ship who reported seeing or hearing enemy gunfire. Herrick says he received no reports of gunfire on August 4. He and other men aboard the *Maddox* debunk the sonar reports of "torpedoes," and also the eyewitness accounts of persons who claimed to have seen them in the water.

Indeed, Herrick told Washington in one of his first postattack cables that the sonar "sightings" came from an "overeager sonarman."

—The Johnson Administration claimed that an exhaustive postattack review, which included interviews with *Maddox* and *Turner Joy* crewmen, established beyond a doubt that the August 4 attack occurred as described in 1964. Yet the Pentagon interrogators did not take statements from such skeptics as Sonarman Patrick N. Park and Radarman James Stankevitz, both of the *Maddox*. And, despite the passage of more than four years, the Pentagon, on grounds of security, refuses to make public the statements it did take from crewmen, preferring to rely upon the highly selective quotations which McNamara gave the Foreign Relations Committee in 1968. ("I believe in disclosure," McNamara testified, "and I believe that the truth will support itself, and *I am perfectly prepared to have ... anybody ... come in and examine the raw material available in the Department ....*")

—The Johnson Administration claimed that it did not misuse the Tonkin Gulf Resolution, and that Congress was well aware of the potential consequences of its passage. Further, the Administration claimed that approval of the resolution was the "functional equivalent" of a declaration of war, and thus satisfied the constitutional requirements. But as the Senate Foreign Relations Committee remarked in its 1967 report on the National Commitments Resolution, ".... [T]he Senate responded to the Administration's contention that the effect of the [Tonkin Gulf] resolution would be lost if it were not enacted quickly. The desired effect was a resounding expression of national unity and support for the President at a moment when it was felt that the country had been attacked. In order, therefore, to avoid the delay that would arise from a careful analysis of the language of the resolution and the further delay that would arise if the resolution had to go to a Senate-House conference to reconcile differing versions, the Foreign Relations Committee and the entire Senate speedily approved the resolution in the language in which it had already been adopted by the House of Representatives. *The prevailing attitude was not so much that Congress was granting or acknowledging the executive's authority to take certain actions but that it was expressing unity and support for the President in a moment of national crisis, and, therefore, that the exact words in which it expressed those sentiments were not of primary importance....*" The committee admitted a "discrepancy between the language of the resolution and the intent of the Congress," saying, "Although the language of the resolution lends itself to the interpretation that Congress was consenting in advance to a full-scale war in Asia should the President think it necessary, that was not the expectation of Congress at the time. In adopting the resolution Congress was closer to believing that it was helping to prevent a large-scale war by taking a firm stand than that it was laying the legal basis for the conduct of such a war. . . . In adopting a resolution with such sweeping language, however, Congress committed the error of making a personal judgment as to how President Johnson would implement the resolution when it had a responsibility to make an institutional judgment, first, as to what any President would do with so great an acknowledgment of power, and, second, as to whether, under the Constitution, Congress had the right to grant or concede the authority in question."

The discrepancies go on and on. The Johnson Administration claimed that the radio intercepts were "conclusive proof" of the attacks; yet even after their receipt and evaluation, the Pentagon continued to pressure Herrick and other Pacific commanders for confirmatory evidence. The Administration claimed that "Our Navy played absolutely no part in, was not associated with . . ." the Op 34-A raids. Yet the Navy furnished the boats used in the raids, the CIA assisted in the target selection, and a Navy officer directed training of the crews.

Enough. The record speaks for itself. What one hears throughout it is a medley of misrepresentations, contradictions, and half-truths.

For the Johnson Administration, the reopened Tonkin inquiry was an event which contributed heavily to the President's dramatic decisions to halt the bombing of most of North Vietnam and not to seek reelection. Unpopularity with the American people Johnson dismissed as the inescapable fate of a wartime President, and he found comfort in public recitations of the abuse suffered by Lincoln. But unpopularity with the Senate was another matter, for Johnson considered himself one of its very own, and to be spurned at one's own fireside is something which no politician (or man) can survive. Throughout the hearings, only one Senator was friendly towards McNamara and the Administration position—Frank Lausche of Ohio, whose questions were often so erratic as to be incomprehensible, and who left early without offering any substantive defense of the White House.

Tonkin alone would not have been politically fatal to Johnson, but the timing of the exposure of Administration deceit and duplicity made it a *coup de grace* for a President reeling under other blows. In late January of 1968 the Viet Cong had shocked the world with the savage Tet offensive. General Earle G. Wheeler, then chairman of the Joint Chiefs of Staff, hurried to South Vietnam to assess damages and brought home a request by General William C. Westmoreland, then United States commander, for 206,000 troops to reinforce the half-million Americans already there. Word of the request spread quickly through Washington—leaked by Pentagon and State Department officials, some of whom opposed the war and others who supported it. The hard-liners wanted to pressure Johnson into "giving Westy what he needs," while the horrified dissidents sought to stir opposition to further commitments of American men to the open-ended conflict. The Administration discussed the request with ranking members of the Armed Services Committee—but not with Foreign Relations, which Johnson by now considered his avowed enemy.

The censored transcript of the Tonkin hearings was released February 24, 1968, for publication in Sunday newspapers the following day. Fulbright gave Senators ten days to read McNamara's defense of the Tonkin resolution, and the circumstances of its passage. Then, on March 7, Fulbright began an extraordinary Senate debate on the war with the flat declaration that the resolution, "like any contract based on misrepresentation, in my opinion is null and void . . . . The resolution has effectively been repealed because it was based on false representations. . . . I do not think we could consider that any more valid than we would any other contract based on false representations."

For more than three hours Fulbright, Mike Mansfield, and other Senators warned the White House: "Enough!"—demanding (in Mansfield's phrase) that "We face the realities of the last four years, see where we are, and try to look ahead." Senator Robert F. Kennedy, in one of the last floor speeches of his life, asked, "Are we like the God of the Old Testament that we can decide, in Washington, D.C., what cities, what towns, what hamlets in Vietnam are going to be destroyed? . . . Do we have that authority to kill tens and tens of thousands of people because we say we have a commitment to the South Vietnamese people? . . . If we are going to continue what we have been doing, when we are told we were just a little way from victory before, and sent 100,000 men or 200,000 men more there, the Senate should be consulted and its approval should be received."

For President Johnson, thumbing through the marked *Congressional Record* the next morning as part of his daily breakfast reading fare, the stunning feature of the debate was not the outrage of Fulbright, Mansfield, Kennedy, and others—but that not a single member of his party's Senate establishment raised a voice in his defense. Senator John Stennis, spokesman for the pro-Administration militants, made a perfunctory attempt to stifle the debate on parliamentary grounds—but fled when Fulbright sarcastically invited him to join the discussion, not end it. But where were the President's friends who had supported him each time in past years when he had asked for more men and more money for the war? Where was Richard Russell, chairman of the Armed Services Committee and creator of Johnson as majority leader? Stuart Symington? Henry Jackson? Sam Ervin?

Silence—the sort of silence that was, to Johnson, far more eloquent and audible than any floor speech. And he had expected it, for Senator Russell had warned him, in a long private talk several days earlier, of the mood of the Senate.

Johnson had invited Russell to the White House to talk about Westmoreland's request for 206,000 more men, and asked for his opinion. You'll never get them, Russell told the President. The time has come for you to start looking for a way out of this war. Unless you're ready for an all-out war—and by that I mean bombing of everything in the North, and maybe even an invasion—no more men. We can't go on this way, and we won't go on this way. Russell said he would not speak out against the President if Congress were asked for a supplemental appropriation to finance a new troop buildup, but neither would he work for it. Russell also warned that he expected Fulbright to press for debate on revision of the Gulf of Tonkin Resolution if Johnson requested more troops.

The many factors that contributed to Johnson's dramatic announcement of March 31, 1968—that he would not seek reelection, and that he was ordering a partial halt to the bombing as a means of starting peace talks—are too involved for discussion here. But the Tonkin affair ranks high among them because it marked the total alienation of the Senate and the loss of a power base which had sustained Johnson earlier in the war. Man had clashed with institution—and the institution had not yielded.

Soon after the Tonkin hearings ended, but before Johnson's March 31 speech, Fulbright promised in a floor speech, "I can assure Senators that the committee intends to press the Department of Defense for the information we have thus far not received" on the Tonkin incidents. Foremost among the desired items was the command and staff study by the Institute for Defense Analysis. During the hearings Fulbright ascertained from McNamara that the department would not object if the committee called John Ponturo, the civilian author of the IDA study, Herrick, and possibly other crew members and Pentagon officials to testify. Fulbright also asked about a "very responsible scientist who was well informed about and working in defense intelligence, by the name of Fubini." McNamara said, "I have no objection to his being called," even though Fubini had left the government and "I don't think he was working in defense intelligence." Eugene G. Fubini, as assistant secretary of defense for research and engineering from June 1963 through June 1965, was Pentagon overseer of the National Security Agency, the intelligence agency responsible for defense and interception of civilian and military communications.

But after March 31 Fulbright pursued Tonkin no further. He sent a perfunctory letter to the Pentagon inquiring about the "status" of the IDA report, and accepted without protest a curt rejection of his request. Nothing further was heard of his implied intention of calling witnesses, other than McNamara.

On December 16, 1968, the committee released a 14-page supplement[1] to the hearing transcript, consisting of letters exchanged between Fulbright and the Pentagon on three matters: the territorial waters issue; interrogation reports on North Vietnamese prisoners of war; and deployment of air units to South Vietnam and Thailand following August 1964. In a foreword, Fulbright wrote, "While several participants in the Tonkin incidents —or individuals in some way associated with the incidents—have voluntarily offered information, it was decided early during our reexamination of this incident to limit published material to that related directly to official documents or communications. I might add, however, that nothing of an unofficial nature which has come to the committee's attention would, in my opinion, alter in any significant way conclusions which might be reached by a careful examination of the printed record." And, almost apologetically, Fulbright continued, "These documents are not offered with the view to revive the controversy over the incidents in the Gulf of Tonkin but to complete, *to the best of the committee's ability,* the public record."

So there the matter rests—with a court that will not render a verdict, nor call all of the relevant witnesses, nor demand the surrender of all available and relevant documentary evidence. Fulbright has offered several explanations for his abrupt termination of the inquiry: From March 31 through the end of the Johnson Administration he did not wish to do anything to disturb the Vietnam peace talks, and he did not want to engage the Pentagon in a public, messy brawl at the start of the Nixon presidency. He felt that the record compiled by the committee was sufficient to establish that the Johnson Administration acted hastily, rashly, unwisely, and deceptively in August 1964. Were he to start calling "all witnesses," the hearings could drag on for months, for the committee would be obligated to hear any crew members willing to offer eyewitness accounts of the incidents, as well as the skeptics. Fulbright felt that he had made a good enough case through McNamara's direct testimony and cross-examination, and that the matter should be put to rest.

"What a sham!" thunders journalist I. F. Stone.[2] I agree, for important questions remain about Tonkin that demand answers, and the persons who can answer are available only to an official inquiry. Were Tonkin simply another of the many sleight-of-hand tricks of the Johnson years, we could forget the episode. But Tonkin is something far more serious, for McNamara's testimony raises grave questions about the conduct of certain naval officers involved in the crisis. These officers are Admirals Sharp, Moorer, Johnson, and Moore, the men directly responsible for the

Maddox mission in August 1964, and directly responsible for relaying to Washington the information, analyses, and conclusions that formed the basis for the retaliatory raids on North Vietnam.

Questions evoked by McNamara's testimony are:

—What was the rationale for continuing the *Maddox's* mission after the belligerence of the North Vietnamese on August 1 and 2, and the charges by North Vietnam that the *Maddox*—although more than three miles off-shore—had "violated" its territorial waters? These charges were a clear and unmistakable signal that the *Maddox* was due for trouble if she continued the mission. Was the *Maddox* patrolling, "showing the flag," or attempting to provoke an incident? And did the Navy and the intelligence agencies which planned her mission think the value of the information she might collect outweighed the risks inherent in continuing the patrol?

—Which level of government was informed of the various North Vietnamese threats against the *Maddox,* and of Herrick's warnings about the consequences of following his assigned patrol route? Did the Navy commanders in the Pacific advise Washington of these threats? If so, who in Washington authorized the patrol to proceed? During research for this book I was told—but could not confirm from anyone with firsthand knowledge—that the White House national security staff did not hear of the August 1–2 threats until the North Vietnamese had fired on the *Maddox* on August 2. Had Johnson ordered the patrol terminated *after* the first incident, of course, the North Vietnamese could have gloated about the "paper tiger." Had Johnson ordered the patrol terminated *before* the first incident, the crisis could have been avoided.

—Why did Admiral Moorer order the *Maddox* and *Turner Joy* to make runs at the North Vietnamese coast on August 3 and 4, a procedure roughly comparable, in wisdom and danger, to poking a hornet's nest with a stick? Did Moorer obtain Washington's approval for this activity?

—Why didn't the Pacific command bother to tell Washington that the South Vietnamese conducted a second series of Op 34-A raids the night of August 3–4? What conceivable reason could the Pacific command have for not forwarding this crucial intelligence to Secretary McNamara? By McNamara's own testimony, he spoke with Admiral Sharp by telephone numerous times during the afternoon and evening of August 4.

—Why did Admiral Sharp, from his headquarters in Hawaii, think that he was able to confirm to McNamara "he was satisfied" that the August 4 attack had occurred, when Herrick, the commander on the scene, could not do so? Sharp's primary source of information was Herrick, but other officers separated them in the chain of command. What happened to the doubts expressed in Herrick's reports as they went through that chain to Sharp and to Washington? Did Sharp give McNamara an objective evaluation of the situation—or a report he felt Washington wanted to hear?

These are questions that the responsible officers should be required to answer, under oath, in an official, *nonmilitary* forum. I do not claim to be the originator of this proposal. Senator Morse, in a floor speech on February 28, 1968, declared: "The time has come for a thorough study by objective civilians of the operations of the military establishment in the United States—the military establishment of which we were warned by General Eisenhower as he left the Presidency. We need the equivalent of a British Royal Commission. I do not believe the President of the United States has today the means to know the truth of Tonkin . . . . I do not say this because there are evil men who would keep the truth from the President. I say it because men with vested interests act to protect those interests. Mistakes perpetuate themselves." And from the military establishment itself, via retired General David M. Shoup, commandant of the Marine Corps for four years before his retirement in December 1963, comes the disturbing declaration: "If the Johnson Administration suffered from lack of credibility in its reporting of the war, the truth would reveal that much of the hocus-pocus stemmed from schemers in the military service, both at home and abroad."[3]

And the mistakes seen in Tonkin recur all too frequently. The plight of the *Maddox* has revealed convincingly the danger of sending spy ships into areas of international tension—so the United States proceeded to lose 34 men of the *Liberty* in 1967, and the *Pueblo* and its entire crew in 1968. The question of territorial waters was inextricably interwoven with the Tonkin incidents—so the United States found itself in a mini-crisis with Peru in February 1969 over seizure of United States fishing boats inside that country's claimed 200-mile limit, and the Navy resists any change in the recognized bounds of coastal waters, because the admirals insist that any limit greater than three miles would restrict fleet movements. The *Maddox* had trouble communicating swiftly with higher commands on August 2 and 4—so in 1967, as we have seen, the critical messages for the *Liberty,* in the Middle East, went to the Philippines, to Fort Meade, Maryland, to Asmara, Ethiopia, and to Morocco, but never to the *Liberty*.

But these are mechanical, procedural problems. Vastly more important are the lingering, unresolved questions of national commitments, and of the war-making authority. Here is an example of how the United States can be drawn into a "commitment" without the approval (or even the knowledge) of the President, much less the Senate:

In late 1968 General Wheeler, the JCS chairman, detailed Major General David A. Burchinal* to handle the military phase of negotiations of a new lease on two air bases and a submarine facility that the United States occupies in Spain. As their price, the Spaniards wanted far more weapons

* In December 1968 Burchinal was deputy to the NATO commander. Earlier, during the Tonkin incidents, as director of the Joint Staff of the Joint Chiefs of Staff, he made a postattack study of the event for General Wheeler.

than the State Department felt they needed ($700 million versus $140 million). The Pentagon, not nearly so budget-conscious as State, did not object to the higher figure. Burchinal's task was to assess the actual external threats faced by Spain, and to persuade her government to accept only the arms necessary to fulfill a defensive mission. The greater the threat to Spain, of course, the greater the amount of arms she would need. After several days of talks, Burchinal signed a "joint minute" with the Spaniards agreeing that they faced a serious "threat from North Africa." Later he expanded the minute to say that the United States was obligated to defend Western Europe "of which Spain is an integral part." Both the State Department and the Senate exploded when they learned what Burchinal had signed, for in diplomacy a "joint minute" is equivalent to a set of stipulated facts in a court. Senator Mike Mansfield asserted that the document "does raise questions about the possibility of an involvement . . . in Africa . . . if it is put into effect as it has been enunciated." And State Department officials pointed out that Burchinal had, apparently unwittingly, offered to extend the NATO guarantee to include Spain—something which is grossly illegal without Senate ratification.[4]

Burchinal was called home for a lecture by Secretary of Defense Melvin R. Laird and Secretary of State William P. Rogers in February 1969, and the Spaniards were tactfully advised he had spoken without authorization. Yet the episode is a frightening reminder of the haphazard manner in which foreign policy can be conducted. What is the solution? Under the existing system, treaties are negotiated, then presented to the Senate to accept or reject, *in toto,* without revision. The Senate would have more meaningful participation in the national commitments process were a member or staff man from the Foreign Relations Committee to be invited to attend negotiations, even if in a silent, *ex officio* role. His attendance would insure, at the minimum, that the Senate was aware of the prospective contents of a treaty before it was presented for ratification, and would also give the Administration an early warning on features that might stir Senate opposition.

Fulbright's national commitments resolution formalizes current Senate sentiment against "blank-check" requests which a President can cash at an unknown future date for unspecified amounts (as Johnson did with the Gulf of Tonkin Resolution). Yet it does not strike to the core of the Tonkin episode, for Congress continues to lack the ability to verify independently information given to it by an Administration during a time of crisis. Professor Ruhl Bartlett, of the Fletcher School, has said, "Nothing is more destructive of democratic institutions than the concealment of information essential to them. The idea that the President should be allowed to determine foreign policy because he has access to better or more complete information than the Congress is an idea that the Congress can accept only at its peril."[5]

Hence another proposal: Detail "congressional representatives" to the White House, the National Security Council, and the State and Defense departments to keep a continuing, daily watch on national security matters. The present liaison system between the Armed Services and Foreign Relations committees and the departments responsible for national security is far too casual and informal to be of value in a crisis; put congressional people into these agencies on a full-time basis, and Congress would have independent sources of information. The Senate's experience with McNamara during Tonkin adequately demonstrated the futility of relying upon Executive officials for candid accounts of events. Similarly, consultation during planning of the Bay of Pigs invasion came after the decisions had already been made, and Senators had little inside information upon which to appraise the project when the White House finally asked their opinion. The Tonkin Gulf Resolution most probably would have passed even if a "congressional representative" with the intelligence background of William Bader of the Foreign Relations Committee had sat in the Pentagon war room reading Herrick's cables the afternoon of August 4. But the presence of such a man, and the knowledge he could have relayed to the Senate, would have insured that the resolution would have been considered on the basis of reality, not on the illusion that was presented by the Johnson Administration.

A President who accepts responsibility for ordering the waging of war— as Johnson did on August 4, 1964—and then asks the approval of a coequal branch of government—as Johnson did through the Tonkin Resolution— should not protest if the other branch demands full and immediate access to the information upon which he acted.

The United States Senate was denied that full and complete access to such information in August 1964 and we now know the price: demoralizing national discontent during a time of war, and a loss of public faith in the institution of the presidency.

Near midnight, Tuesday, August 4, 1964. The world of Patrick N. Park, United States Navy, consists of a round, greenish-hued radar screen . . . . The bridge gives Park a range reading from the main radar room: "The firmest target we've had all night," the voice tells him. Park hastily directs the gun-control radar toward the area of the contact.

"It was a damned big one, right on us, no doubt about that," he says. "About 1,500 yards off the side, a nice, fat blip." Park asks for the "firing key"—that is, for control of the triggering device on the five-inch gun mounts, and for permission to fire. "Open fire," is the response. . . .

"*I had six five-inch guns right at the* Turner Joy, *1,500 yards away,*" *says Park.* "*If I had fired, it would have blown it clean out of the water.*"

What if Seaman Park *had* fired? The possible consequences are too frightening to contemplate. But one thing is evident: Truth would have been the first casualty.

Part Four

APPENDIX

CHRONOLOGY OF EVENTS IN GULF OF TONKIN INCIDENTS

All distances are stated in nautical miles. Events in Washington are shown in italics. Local Gulf of Tonkin time has been converted to Eastern Daylight Time by the subtraction of 12 hours: that is, 4:00 A.M., August 5, in the Gulf of Tonkin is 4:00 P.M., August 4, in Washington. The notation "DOD" denotes items taken from an official Department of Defense chronology issued August 5, 1964, in the name of Defense Secretary Robert S. McNamara. The other items are drawn from the Senate Foreign Relations Committee hearing of February 20, 1968, interviews with crew members, and other research by the author. For purposes of communications security, times have been deleted or stated approximately for certain of the events.

July 30

Approximately
2:00 P.M.
(2:00 A.M. EDT)

South Vietnamese patrol boats leave Da Nang for Operation 34-A attack on Hon Me and Hon Ngu.

July 31

12:21 A.M.
(12:21 P.M. July 30
EDT)

Attack commenced on Hon Me.

12:20–12:30 A.M.
(12:20–12:30 P.M.
July 30 EDT)

Attack commenced on Hon Ngu.

1:00 A.M.
(1:00 P.M. July 30 EDT)

Both attacks terminated

Approximately 10:00 A.M.
(Approximately 10:00
P.M. July 30 EDT)

USS Maddox, refueling on Yankee Station, sights 34-A boats, first reports them as Soviet P-6 craft, later learns they are South Vietnamese. *Maddox* begins patrol.

August 1

5:00 P.M.
(5:00 A.M. EDT)

Maddox arrives in vicinity of Check Point Charlie, nine miles off Cap Falaise.

Approximately
7:00 P.M.
(7:00 A.M. EDT)

Maddox seven miles off North Vietnamese coast, 13 miles south of Hon Ngu, steaming north toward Hon Me.

8:30 P.M.
(8:30 A.M. EDT)

Maddox comes within four to six miles of Hon Me and turns south toward Charlie.

August 2

2:00 A.M.
(2:00 P.M. August 1 EDT)

Maddox 12 miles due east of Point Delta, detects radar contact north of Hon Me, turns southeast away from island.

3:45 A.M.
(3:45 P.M. August 1 EDT)

Maddox reports that "intelligence information" (radio intercept) indicates "possible hostile action from North Vietnam" in vicinity of Charlie.

6:45 A.M.
(6:45 P.M. August 1 EDT)

Maddox, now several miles southeast of Charlie, says information on hostile intent now "positive," believes continuation of patrol is "unacceptable risk," puts to sea. Admiral Roy L. Johnson, Seventh Fleet commander, orders *Maddox* to resume patrol.

9:00 A.M.
(9:00 P.M. August 1 EDT)

Maddox proceeds to Point Delta, 11 miles east of coast off Lach Chao River, arriving at 9:45 A.M. Turns south for point four miles seaward of Hon Me.

10:00 A.M. (DOD)
(10:00 P.M. August 1 EDT)

"*Maddox* reported observing an estimated 75 junks near her assigned patrol area . . . . She reported changing her course in order to avoid the junk concentration."

11:00 A.M.
(11:00 P.M. August 1 EDT)

Maddox sights and tracks by radar three patrol craft apparently heading toward Hon Me. *Maddox,* its position at time 11 miles from Hon Me, turns away from island and heads for Point Delta.

12:30 P.M. (DOD)
(12:30 A.M. August 2 EDT)

"*Maddox* reported that three torpedo boats were on a southerly course heading toward the ship at extreme range (over ten miles). The *Maddox* at this point was about 30 miles from the coast."

2:40 P.M. (DOD)
(2:40 A.M. EDT)

"*Maddox* reported she was being approached by the high speed (estimated 45 to 50 knots) craft whose apparent intention was to conduct a torpedo attack and that she intended to open fire in self-defense if necessary."

3:08 P.M. (3:08 A.M. EDT)	*Maddox* fired three "warning shots" at PT boats that had closed to 9,800 yards.
3:08 P.M. (DOD) (3:08 A.M. EDT)	"*Maddox* reported she was being attacked by the three PT craft. She opened fire with her five-inch battery after three warning shots failed to slow down the attackers."
3:08 P.M. (DOD) (3:08 A.M. EDT)	"The PTs continued their closing maneuvers and two of the PTs closed to 5,000 yards, each firing one torpedo. The *Maddox* changed course in an evasive move and the two torpedoes passed close aboard on the starboard side (100 to 200 yards). *USS Ticonderoga* ... advised she was sending four already airborne F-8E's (Crusaders) with rockets and 20-mm. ammunition to provide air cover for *Maddox*."
3:21 P.M. (DOD) (3:21 A.M. EDT)	"The third PT moved up to the beam of the *Maddox* and received a direct hit by a five-inch round, and at the same time dropped a torpedo into the water which was not seen to run. Machine gun fire from the PTs was directed at the *Maddox*. However, there was no damage or injury to personnel. The *Maddox* continued in a southerly direction to join with the *C. Turner Joy* ... as *Ticonderoga* aircraft commenced attacking the PTs. Zuni rocket runs and 20-mm. strafing attacks were directed against two of the PTs and they were damaged. The third PT remained dead in the water after the direct hit by the *Maddox*."
3:29 P.M. (3:29 A.M. EDT)	Engagement ends. Aircraft escort *Maddox* toward South Vietnamese waters.
Early evening (Early morning EDT)	Admiral Moorer, Pacific Fleet commander, orders new patrol, with *Turner Joy* joining *Maddox*. New route calls for them to steam toward shore during day, retire to sea at night.
Late evening (Late morning EDT)	Herrick advises *Maddox* and *Turner Joy* North Vietnam has "thrown down the gauntlet" and they will be "treated as belligerents from first detection and must consider themselves as such."

August 3

Destroyers proceed north up coast from 17th Parallel, turning in mid-afternoon to pass 9.2 miles off the islands of Hon Vat and Hon Me; turn east to sea at dusk.

4:00 P.M. (4:00 A.M. EDT)	South Vietnamese 34-A boats leave Da Nang and proceed up coast, approximating earlier course of *Turner Joy* and *Maddox*.
Evening (Morning EDT)	Herrick recommends termination of patrol.
Evening (Morning EDT)	Admiral Sharp, Pacific forces commander, refuses. Directs destroyers, on August 4, to remain north of 19 degrees, 10 minutes north between Charlie and Delta to avoid interference with 34-A Operations and "possibly draw North Vietnamese PGMs to northward away from area of 34-A Ops."

August 4

12:30 A.M. (12:30 P.M. August 3 EDT)	Operation 34-A boats commence attacks on radar station on Cap Vinh Son and security post off Cua Ron, both in North Vietnam. Attacks end around 1:00 A.M. (1:00 P.M. August 3 EDT).
Approximately 2:00 A.M. (2:00 P.M. August 3 EDT)	Herrick reports that "intelligence information" (radio intercepts) indicates that North Vietnam considers his patrol to be a part of 34-A Operations. Asks constant air cover for protection.
Approximately 4:00 A.M. (4:00 P.M. August 3 EDT)	Request for continuing air cover refused, but Herrick is told aircraft are ready for "launch and support on short notice."
	Maddox and *Turner Joy* spend daylight hours cruising along North Vietnam coast; pass Hon Me at 13 miles' distance around dawn.
Early afternoon (Early morning EDT)	*Maddox* reports "material deficiency" in its sonar; later says repairs made.
2:30 P.M. (2:30 A.M. EDT)	*Maddox* makes radar contact 15 miles to west.
Late afternoon (DOD) (Early morning EDT)	"The *Maddox* reported radar contact with unidentified surface vessels who were paralleling its track and the track of the *Turner Joy*." (The contact was intermittent, and was not held by the *Turner Joy*, according to Herrick's cables.)
7:40 P.M. (DOD) (7:40 A.M. EDT)	"The *Maddox* reported that from actions being taken by the unidentified vessels, an attack by them appeared imminent. The *Maddox* was heading southeast near the center of the Gulf of Tonkin in international waters approximately 65 miles from nearest land."

(Deleted)	*Maddox* detects contact at 36.4 miles; speed 33 knots. Contact not held by *Turner Joy*. Considered threat by *Maddox;* maximum boiler power ordered by both destroyers.
(Deleted)	*Maddox* holds surface contact at 37 miles; within five minutes two more contacts at same locale.
(Deleted)	Herrick evaluates situation as a "trap."
(Deleted)	*Turner Joy* still has no contacts.
(Deleted)	*Maddox* reports three radar contacts merging into one at range of 32 miles.
Approximately 8:15 P.M. (8:15 A.M. EDT)	*Maddox,* now 60 miles from coast, says it has "received information" (another radio intercept) that attack is imminent; proceeds south at full speed.
8:36 P.M. (DOD) (8:36 A.M. EDT)	"The *Maddox* established new radar contact with two unidentified surface vessels and three unidentified aircraft. At this time, U.S. fighter aircraft were launched from the *USS Ticonderoga* ... to provide protection against possible attack from the unidentified vessels. . . ."
9:08 P.M. (DOD) (9:08 A.M. EDT)	"The *Maddox* reported that the unidentified aircraft had disappeared from its radar screen and that the surface vessels were remaining at a distance. The U.S. aircraft ... commenced defensive patrol over the *Maddox* and *Turner Joy*."
9:30 P.M. (DOD) (9:30 A.M. EDT)	"Additional vessels were observed on the *Maddox* radar, and these vessels began to close rapidly on the destroyer patrol at speeds in excess of 40 knots. The attacking craft continued to close rapidly from the west and south and the *Maddox* reported that their intentions were evaluated as hostile."
(Deleted)	*Maddox* ordered aircraft to investigate unknown target (designated "U") at 13 miles, speed 30 knots. Results negative.
(Deleted)	*Maddox* opened fire in area of another contact designated "V." *Turner Joy* fires on contact "V-1" to the right of "V."
(Deleted)	*Maddox* loses contact with "V." At same time *Maddox* sonar reports torpedo. Warning is transmitted to *Turner Joy*.

9:52 P.M. (DOD) (9:52 A.M. EDT)	"The destroyers reported they were under continuous torpedo attack and were engaged in defensive counter fire."
(Deleted)	*Turner Joy* changes course to evade torpedo reported by *Maddox*. *Turner Joy* reports sighting wake. According to reporting cable: "At no time did *Turner Joy* sonar detect torpedo noises."
9:30 P.M. to midnight (9:30 A.M. to noon EDT)	Stankevitz, in combat information center, states he had no meaningful radar contacts after initial approach of unidentified vessels.
(Deleted)	Aircraft arrive from *Ticonderoga;* at request of *Turner Joy*, begin strafing general area; *Turner Joy* continues firing. *Maddox* radar unable to pick up any target contacts.
(Deleted)	*Maddox* sonar reports another torpedo, warning passed to *Turner Joy*.
10:15 P.M. (DOD) (10:15 A.M. EDT)	"The destroyers reported that they had avoided torpedoes and had sunk one of the attacking craft."
10:42 P.M. (DOD) (10:42 A.M. EDT)	"The destroyers reported that they had evaded additional torpedoes and had sunk another of the attacking craft. Other protective aircraft had arrived overhead, but weather and darkness were hampering their capabilities."
10:52 P.M. (DOD) (10:52 A.M. EDT)	"The *Maddox* reported that the destroyers were again under attack."
11:15 P.M. (11:15 A.M. EDT)	*Turner Joy* reports that five torpedoes have been fired, and that she is planning to ram one of the North Vietnamese boats.
Approximately midnight (Approximately noon EDT)	*Turner Joy* reports: "We think a PT boat sunk one of its own boats."
Noon EDT (*Midnight Tonkin time*)	*President Johnson convenes National Security Council, then lunches with McNamara, Rusk, McCone, and McGeorge Bundy. Johnson orders drafting of target list for retaliatory raids.*
Midnight (DOD) (Noon August 4 EDT)	"The patrol reported that, even though torpedoes had been fired at them, they had suffered no hits nor casualties and that the defensive aircraft ... were illuminating the area and attacking the enemy surface craft."

August 5

Approximately 12:10 A.M. (Approximately 12:10 P.M. August 4 EDT)	*Maddox* reports that seven torpedoes already fired, two more "now" in the water.
Approximately 12:25 A.M. (12:25 P.M. August 4 EDT)	*Maddox* reports that she and *Turner Joy* counted 22 torpedoes fired.
12:32 A.M. (DOD) (12:32 P.M. August 4 EDT)	"The patrol reported that at least two enemy craft had been sunk and that low ceilings continued to hamper the aircraft operations."
Approximately 12:35 A.M. (12:35 P.M. August 4 EDT)	Captain Barnhart, on *Turner Joy* bridge, sees flicker of searchlight. Neither he nor Herrick have heard gunfire nor reports of gunfire, other than their own, during night.
12:54 A.M. (DOD) (12:54 P.M. August 4 EDT)	"The *Turner Joy* reported that during the engagement, in addition to the torpedo attacks, she was fired upon by automatic weapons while being illuminated by searchlights."
1:25 A.M. (1:25 P.M. August 4 EDT)	Herrick reports the *Turner Joy* claims to have "positively" sunk three vessels, but adds, "entire action leaves many doubts except for apparent attempted ambush at beginning. Suggest thorough reconnaissance in daylight by aircraft." States "freak weather conditions and over-eager sonarman" may have accounted for supposed torpedo sightings, and "suggest complete evaluation before any further action."
1:30 A.M. (DOD) (1:30 P.M. August 4 EDT)	"The destroyers reported that the attacking craft had apparently broken off the engagement."
3:00 P.M. August 4 (EDT) (*3:00 A.M. August 5 Tonkin time*)	*McNamara begins meeting with Joint Chiefs and Deputy Secretary Cyrus Vance to review data and plan raids.*
4:34 P.M. August 4 (EDT) (*4:34 A.M. August 5 Tonkin time*)	*Pentagon receives Herrick report that "details of action present a confusing picture although certain that original ambush was bona fide."*
4:40 P.M. August 4 (EDT)	*Admiral Sharp, Pacific commander, discusses Herrick report with McNamara by phone from*

(4:40 A.M. August 5 Tonkin time)	Hawaii, cites Turner Joy "identification" of cockpit lights on attacking boats and torpedo wakes as evidence attacks occurred. McNamara tells him to be "damned sure that the attack had taken place."
Approximately 5:00 P.M. EDT (5:00 A.M. August 5 Tonkin time)	Sharp asks Maddox to confirm "absolutely" that ships were attacked; directs that answer go to Ticonderoga to insure prompt forwarding to his headquarters.
5:00 P.M. EDT (5:00 A.M. August 5 Tonkin time)	Congressional leaders told to come to White House at 6:00 P.M. for meeting with Johnson.
5:23 P.M. EDT (5:23 A.M. August 5 Tonkin time)	McNamara again receives telephone report from Sharp he is sure attack occurred; cites radio intercept intelligence.
Approximately 5:25 A.M. (5:25 P.M. August 4 EDT)	Turner Joy ordered to "locate debris to substantiate" its claim of sinkings.
5:47 P.M. EDT (5:47 A.M. August 5 Tonkin time)	Johnson orders McNamara to make one final check with Sharp.
6:00 P.M. EDT (6:00 A.M. August 5 Tonkin time)	Johnson opens National Security Council meeting with announcement he has ordered retaliatory bombings.
6:00 P.M. EDT (6:00 A.M. August 5 Tonkin time)	Pentagon issues announcement of second incident.
6:07 P.M. EDT (6:07 A.M. August 5 Tonkin time)	McNamara issues attack order to Sharp over phone.
6:10 A.M. (6:10 P.M. August 4 EDT)	Rear Admiral Moore, Task Force 77 commander, receives order to be prepared to strike, but to hold for final order.
6:15 P.M. August 4 (EDT) (6:15 A.M. August 5 Tonkin time)	Johnson tells congressional leaders strike has been ordered.
8:00 A.M. (8:00 P.M. August 4 EDT)	Turner Joy, replying to demand for confirmatory evidence, says that crew members saw torpedoes and that a target burned when hit; Barnhart

among men who saw black smoke. Cable admits sinkings only "highly probable," not "definite."

8:00 A.M.
(8:00 P.M. August 4 EDT)

Moore receives go-ahead to bomb North Vietnam.

9:00 A.M.
(9:00 P.M. August 4 EDT)

At Washington's order, Hawaii sends *Turner Joy* an "urgent" message to amplify its battle reports: "Who are witnesses? What is witness reliability? Most important that positive evidence substantiating type and number of attacking forces be gathered and disseminated."

10:40 A.M.
(10:40 P.M. August 4 EDT)

First planes leave *Ticonderoga* and *Constellation,* bound for North Vietnam.

10:59 P.M. EDT
(*10:59 A.M. August 5 Tonkin time*)

Herrick report finally reaches McNamara's Pentagon command post. States that air support did not locate any targets; that Maddox *scored no known hits, and never positively identified a boat. Notes that "probable" torpedo was detected on sonar: "The first boat to close* Maddox *probably fired torpedo at* Maddox *which heard but not seen. All subsequent* Maddox *torpedo reports are doubtful in that it is suspected that sonarman was hearing ship's own propeller beat."*

11:37 P.M. EDT
(*11:37 A.M. August 5 Tonkin time*)

President Johnson tells nation over television that "air action is now in execution" against North Vietnam.

1:15 P.M.
(1:15 A.M. August 5 EDT)

Jets from *Ticonderoga* drop first bombs of war on North Vietnam, hitting patrol-boat base and support facilities at Quang Khe.

1:15 P.M.
(1:15 A.M. August 5 EDT)

Turner Joy responds to "urgent" message for confirmation; says officers of "good reliability" saw torpedo wake. "Estimate two PTs attacked; however, must admit two factors deter—no ECM [electronic activity] from PT boats. No sonar indication of torpedo noises."

1:25 P.M.
(1:25 A.M. August 5 EDT)

From the bridge of *Maddox,* Herrick sees smoke rise from jet strikes on oil storage facilities at Vinh, realizes for first time scope of United States retaliation.

CHRONOLOGY OF UNITED STATES
SENATE INVOLVEMENT
IN GULF OF TONKIN INCIDENTS

1964

August 3   Secretaries Rusk and McNamara brief Armed Services and Foreign Relations committees on first incident in off-the-record session, tell them attack was "unprovoked and in international waters"; deny any United States involvement in South Vietnamese raids on North Vietnamese islands.

August 4   Leaders are called to White House in early evening to hear Johnson announce plans for retaliatory raids and ask passage of joint resolution approving his action and also his "determination . . . to take all necessary measures to repeal any armed attack . . . and to prevent further aggression."

August 5   Resolution introduced and referred to Armed Services and Foreign Relations committees for joint hearing. Informant warns Senator Morse that *Maddox* was connected with South Vietnamese raids, and that doubt exists as to whether second attack actually took place. Suggests that he obtain ship's logs.

August 6   Combined committees hear Rusk and McNamara for one hour and 40 minutes, again hear denials on South Vietnamese raids and on violations of North Vietnamese waters. Only unfriendly questions come from Morse, who also casts only negative vote. Resolution reported to floor, where Morse, during four-hour debate, charges *Maddox* with complicity in raids, and with operating provocatively close to North Vietnam shore. Senator Fulbright, floor manager of resolution for Administration, denies Morse charge; also says resolution means no change in basic United States mission in South Vietnam.

August 7   Fulbright dissuades Senator Nelson from submitting amendment requiring congressional approval before dispatch of land army to South Vietnam, saying he doesn't contemplate this will happen under resolution, even though wording permits President to do whatever he wishes. After two and a half hours of debate, resolution passes 88 to 2, Morse and Senator Gruening casting only dissenting votes. House vote is 416–0.

1965

September— December
Breach between Johnson and Fulbright begins with Senator's critical speech on intervention in Dominican Republic; widens rest of year as several Senators denounce sustained strategic bombing of North Vietnam.

1966

January
In "educational hearings" on Vietnam War, Fulbright avows he and most of members of Foreign Relations Committee did not, in August 1964, "visualize or contemplate" that Johnson would make such broad use of Tonkin Resolution; asks that Administration consult Congress before expanding war further; is rebuffed by Secretary Rusk.

May
Assistant Secretary of State William Bundy, in secret testimony before Foreign Relations Committee, says he wrote draft paper similar to Tonkin resolution in May or June 1964, several months before incidents, as part of "normal contingency planning."

May
Retired Rear Admiral Arnold E. True writes Fulbright that naval law does not recognize "warning shots" which Administration said *Maddox* fired as first volley of August 2, 1964 incident; Fulbright responds he has "reservations about their story . . . but no way effectively to question it."

August
Senator Stennis, at hearings of Senate Preparedness Subcommittee, tells Rusk the Administration "stands on mighty thin ice" in relying upon Tonkin resolution as legal justification for war; says that when nation goes to war, "it is a great mistake to fail to be just frank about it. . . ."

1967

Spring
Senate rebuffs Johnson on long list of foreign policy measures: cutting foreign-aid bill; refusing money for fast-deployment logistics ships; rejecting long-term financing for Alliance for Progress through international groups; exposing and repudiating Pentagon's guarantee of loans so that underdeveloped nations can buy modern arms.

August
Fulbright introduces "national commitments resolution," and Undersecretary of State Katzenbach, at hearings, calls Tonkin resolution the "functional equivalent" of a declaration of war. Johnson challenges Senate to seek repeal if it wants to repudiate

resolution. Academic and government witnesses criticize the President's accretion of war-making powers, say that Congress should reclaim its constitutional share of powers to make and fulfill national commitments.

September — Fulbright authorizes Foreign Relations Committee staff to begin quiet inquiry into Tonkin incidents; begins by requesting *Maddox* logs and cable traffic from Pentagon.

December — Pentagon officials seek to dissuade Fulbright from pressing investigation, claiming that evidence is solid and that hearings would hurt national interest. Fulbright refuses, and is supported by Senator Russell, chairman of Armed Services Committee. Informants in Pentagon guide Fulbright staff to key evidence.

1968

February 20 — McNamara appears before closed session of committee.

February 24 — Hearing transcript released which reveals (a) nature of *Maddox* mission; (b) preattack fears of Herrick; (c) revised orders given *Maddox* after August 2 incident; and (d) confusion about August 4 episode, both in Gulf of Tonkin and in Washington.

March 7 — Fulbright tells Senate he considers Tonkin resolution, "like any contract based on misrepresentation . . . null and void."

March 31 — Johnson announces partial bombing halt and his decision not to seek reelection.

December 16 — Fulbright formally ends inquiry with release of volume of supplementary documents.

SOURCES

PROLOGUE

1. Interview with Patrick N. Park, Los Angeles, California, December 2, 1968.
2. Senate Foreign Relations and Armed Services committees, *Southeast Asia Resolution,* Joint Hearings, August 6, 1964 (censored transcript of testimony, published November 1966, p. 7.
3. Senate Foreign Relations Committee, *U.S. Commitments to Foreign Powers* (SFRC-Commitments hereafter), Hearings, August and September 1967, p. 82.
4. *Congressional Record,* February 29, 1968 (floor speeches hereafter are from the *Record* on the day of delivery).
5. Speech to New York State Association of Newspaper Editors, January 1968 (Text given to the author by Moyers).
6. Bureau of Intelligence and Research, Department of State, *Geographic Bulletin #3: Sovereignty of the Sea,* April 1965, p. 3.
7. Senate Forcign Relations Committee, *National Commitments,* Report on Senate Resolution 187, November 20, 1967, p. 6.
8. *Ibid.,* p. 14.
9. *Ibid.,* p. 27.

CHAPTER ONE

1. *New York Times,* August 3, 1964.
2. Quotations from Department of Defense press conferences of McNamara and other officials in this chapter are from official transcripts maintained in the Directorate for Defense Information in the Pentagon.
3. Senate Foreign Relations Committee, *Southeast Asia Resolution,* Hearings, August 6, 1964, p. 30.
4. News briefing transcript, August 3, 1964, Office of News, Bureau of Public Affairs, Department of State.
5. Janeway, Michael, "Bill Moyers Talks About LBJ, Power, Poverty, War, and Young," *Atlantic Monthly,* July, 1968.
6. Hilsman, Roger, *To Move a Nation* (New York, Doubleday & Co., 1968), p. 208.

7. Kennedy, Robert F., "Thirteen Days: The Story About How the World Almost Ended," *McCall's,* November 1968.
8. Transcript from *Department of State Bulletin,* August 16, 1964.
9. *Chicago Tribune,* August 21, 1964.
10. Transcript from *Department of State Bulletin,* August 16, 1964.
11. *Chicago Tribune, op. cit.*

CHAPTER TWO

1. Quotations from floor speeches are from the *Congressional Record* for the date.
2. Senate Foreign Relations and Armed Services Committee, *Southeast Asia Resolution,* Hearings, August 6, 1964. Certain of the material deleted by Pentagon censors prior to publication of the hearings in November 1966 was obtained elsewhere, and is identified in the text by brackets.
3. Senate Foreign Relations Committee, *Supplemental Foreign Assistance, Fiscal Year 1966—Vietnam,* Hearings, January and February 1966, p. 567.
4. Senate Foreign Relations Committee, *U.S. Commitments to Foreign Powers,* Hearings, August and September 1967, p. 139.
5. Transcript is in *Department of State Bulletin* for August 19, 1964.
6. McNamara press conference at 5 P.M. August 6, 1964 (Transcript from files of the Directorate for Defense Information, Department of Defense).

CHAPTER THREE

1. Moore, Robin, *The Green Berets* (New York: Crown, 1965), pp. 164–5.
2. Trager, Frank N., "The Far East," in *National Security: Political, Military, and Economic Strategies in the Decade Ahead,* eds. David W. Abshire and Richard V. Allen (New York: Praeger, 1965).
3. Duncan, Donald, "The Whole Damn Thing Was a Lie," *Ramparts Magazine,* February 1966.

CHAPTER FOUR

1. House Committee on Appropriations, *Department of Defense Appropriations for 1969,* Hearings before the Subcommittee on the Department of Defense, Part 4: Operation and Maintenance, 1968, p. 393 *supra.*
2. The incident concerning the attaché was told to me by a State Department official with long experience in the Middle East.
3. National Broadcasting Company's "Meet the Press," February 4, 1968, quoted in *Department of State Bulletin* for February 26, 1968, p. 271.
4. *New York Times,* March 17, 1964.
5. Kahn, David, *The Codebreakers* (New York: Simon & Schuster, 1967).
6. *Department of State Bulletin* for August 3, 1959.
7. House Committee on Appropriations, *op. cit.,* p. 401 *supra.*
8. *Ibid.,* p. 410.
9. Churchill, Sir Winston, *Their Finest Hour* (Boston: Houghton Mifflin Company, 1949), p. 383 *supra.*
10. Carroll, John M., *Secrets of Electronic Espionage* (New York: E. P. Dutton & Company, Inc., 1966), p. 190.

11. U.S. Arms Control and Disarmament Agency, *Seventh Annual Report to Congress,* January 30, 1968, p. 22.
12. Carroll, *op. cit.,* p. 183.
13. Stimson, Henry, and Bundy, McGeorge, *On Active Service in Peace and War* (New York: Harper & Row, 1948), pp. 368–9. Coincidentally, Bundy was White House national security adviser at the time of the Gulf of Tonkin incidents.
14. Statement read by State Department press officer Carl Bartch at news briefing August 31, 1967, printed in *Department of State Bulletin* for September 18, 1967, at p. 362.
15. Office of the Oceanographer of the Navy, *The Oceanographic Operations Program of the U.S. Navy, Accomplishments and Prospects* (Government Printing Office, 1967).
16. Senate Judiciary Committee, *The Communist Threat to the United States Through the Caribbean (USSR and Cuban Fishermen),* Hearings before the Internal Security Subcommittee, Part 18, 1967.
17. *Ibid.*

CHAPTER FIVE

1. Senate Foreign Relations Committee, *The Gulf of Tonkin, The 1964 Incidents* (SFRC-Tonkin hereafter), Hearings, February 20, 1968, p. 26.
2. Interview with Patrick Park of Los Angeles, California (Park interview hereafter), December 2, 1968.
3. Interview with Captain John J. Herrick, St. Julien's Creek Naval Ammunition Depot, Portsmouth, Virginia (Herrick interview hereafter), July 19, 1968.
4. Interview with James Stankevitz of Stevens Point, Wisconsin (Stankevitz interview hereafter), November 25, 1968.
5. Wise, David, "Remember the Maddox!" *Esquire,* April 1968.
6. Senate Foreign Relations Committee, executive hearing on Asian affairs, September 20, 1966. A one-and-one-quarter page excerpt from Bundy's testimony was issued on December 20, 1967, in the form of a press release.
7. SFRC-Tonkin, p. 15.
8. Wise, *op. cit.*
9. Horton, J. Warren, *Fundamentals of Sonar* (Annapolis: U.S. Naval Institute, 1957), p. 303.
10. Frosch, Robert A., "Underwater Sound," in *Modern Science and Technology,* ed. Robert Colborn (Princeton: D. Van Nostrand Co., Inc., 1965), p. 631.
11. Wise, *op. cit.*
12. Defense Appropriations Subcommittee, House Appropriations Committee, *Defense Appropriations for Fiscal 1969: Operations and Maintenance, Part 4,* Hearings, 1968.
13. SFRC-Tonkin, p. 10.
14. SFRC-Tonkin, p. 58.
15. SFRC-Tonkin, p. 107.
16. Park interview.
17. *Life,* August 14, 1964, p. 21.
18. *Time,* August 14, 1964, p. 14.
19. Stankevitz interview.

CHAPTER SIX

1. Schlesinger, Arthur M., Jr., *A Thousand Days, John F. Kennedy in the White House* (Boston: Houghton Mifflin Company, 1965), pp. 139–40.
2. Alsop, Stewart, "The Anti-Johnson Underground," *Saturday Evening Post,* August 14, 1965, p. 18.
3. Evans, Rowland, and Novak, Robert, *Lyndon B. Johnson: The Exercise of Power* (New York: New American Library, 1966), p. 529.
4. Wicker, Tom, "Lyndon Johnson vs. the Ghost of Jack Kennedy," *Esquire,* November 1965, p. 152.
5. Roberts, Charles, *LBJ's Inner Circle* (New York: Dell, 1965), p. 20.
6. Israel, Fred L., *Nevada's Key Pittman* (Lincoln: University of Nebraska Press, 1963).
7. Byrnes, James F., *Speaking Frankly* (New York: Harper & Row, 1947), p. 7.
8. *Ibid.,* pp. 235–6.
9. Truman, Harry S, *Years of Trial and Hope* (New York: Doubleday & Company, 1956), p. 119.
10. Paige, Glenn D., *The Korean Decision* (New York: The Free Press, 1968), p. 191.
11. Senate Foreign Relations Committee, *Supplemental Foreign Assistance Fiscal Year 1966—Vietnam.*
12. *Ibid.,* p. 714.
13. Preparedness Investigating Subcommittee of the Senate Armed Services Committee, *Worldwide Military Commitments, Part 1,* Hearings, August 1966, p. 2.
14. *Ibid.,* p. 68.
15. National Committee for an Effective Congress, in its *Congressional Report,* August 31, 1967.
16. *Ibid.*

CHAPTER SEVEN

1. Schlesinger, Arthur M., Jr., *A Thousand Days: John F. Kennedy in the White House* (Boston: Houghton Mifflin Company, 1965), p. 252.
2. Salinger, Pierre, *With Kennedy* (New York: Doubleday & Company, 1966), p. 264.
3. Senate Foreign Relations Committee, *U.S. Commitments to Foreign Powers,* Hearings on Senate Resolution 151, August and September 1967, pp. 19–20. Professor Bartlett's statements in the remainder of this chapter come from the hearings.
4. *Ibid.,* page 76. Likewise for Katzenbach's testimony.
5. Wormuth, Francis D., *The Vietnam War: The President Versus the Constitution* (Santa Barbara: Center for the Study of Democratic Institutions, 1968), p. 6. Professor Wormuth's statements in the remainder of this chapter come from this paper.

CHAPTER EIGHT

1. Senate Foreign Relations Committee, *The Gulf of Tonkin, The 1964 Incidents,* Hearings, February 20, 1968 (hearing quotations from the transcript hereafter).

2. Interview with Captain John J. Herrick, St. Julien's Creek Naval Ammunition Depot, Portsmouth, Virginia, July 19, 1968.
3. Biography #01–430, dated August 20, 1965.
4. Transcript of daily news briefing, Office of News, Bureau of Public Affairs, Department of State, September 13, 1968.
5. Strang, David Phillip, *The Walls Beneath the Sea*. U.S. Naval Institute Proceedings, Annapolis, March 1968, pp. 35–36.
6. Carlisle, Captain Geoffrey E., *Three Mile Limit: Obsolete Concepts?*, U.S. Naval Institute Proceedings, Annapolis, February 1967, p. 30.
7. Map supplied to the author by Book and Magazine Division, Directorate for Defense Information, Department of Defense, on September 30, 1968.
8. Ministry of Foreign Affairs, Democratic Republic of Vietnam, *Memorandum Regarding the U.S. War Acts Against the DRV in the First Days of August 1964* (the DRV "White Paper"), Hanoi, 1964, p. 32. The CIA's monitoring service carried the same broadcast in its daily report several days after delivery.
9. Map supplied by Book and Magazine Division, Department of Defense, on September 30, 1968.
10. DRV White Paper.
11. Transcript in files of Directorate for Defense Information.
12. Shalowitz, Aaron L., *Shore and Sea Boundaries* (Washington: Coast and Geodetic Survey of the U.S. Department of Commerce, 1963), pp. 73 and 258.
13. Transcript in the *Department of State Bulletin* for August 16, 1964.
14. *Ibid.*

EPILOGUE

1. Senate Foreign Relations Committee, *The Gulf of Tonkin, The 1964 Incidents: Part II,* Supplementary Documents to February 20, 1968 hearing with Secretary of Defense Robert S. McNamara.
2. Stone, I. F., "The Supineness of the Senate," *The New York Review,* February 13, 1969.
3. Shoup, General David M., "The New American Militarism," *Atlantic Monthly,* April 1969.
4. Flora Lewis of *Newsday* first revealed the Burchinal story, which was later confirmed by State Department officials. *Washington Post,* February 25, 1969.
5. Senate Foreign Relations Committee, *U.S. Commitments to Foreign Powers,* Hearings, August and September 1967, p. 20.

INDEX

Da Nang
  air base for Operation Haylift, 84
  coastal patrols work from, 93
Dale, Edwin A., 36
Dalmo Victor Electronic Warfare
    Systems, 109
De Gaulle, President Charles, 32, 33
Dean, Ambassador Arthur H., 226
Defense, Department of. *See also*
    Pentagon
  announces second Tonkin Gulf
      incident, 34–35
  sets up Armed Forces Security
      Agency, 105–106
  National Security Agency an
      "element" of, 106–107
  Special Security Communications
      System of, 148
  studies of August 4 incident, 157
  map showing *Maddox* and *Turner
      Joy* tracks, 229
Defense Intelligence Agency (DIA)
  functions of, 109–110
  responsibility of, for DeSoto
      patrols, 123
Democratic Republic of Vietnam.
    See North Vietnam
Demokreten (Denmark), 78
DeSoto patrols
  along Sino–Soviet coasts, 123,
      124, 125
  plan of, changed, 137
  Herrick and Sharp disagree over
      continuance of, 140
  by destroyers *Morton* and *Edwards,*
      159–160
  actions to separate, from 34–A
      Operations, 218
DIA. *See* Defense Intelligence Agency
Diem, President Ngo Dinh, 20, 83
Dirksen, Senator Everett, 24–25, 26, 31
Dodd, Senator Thomas J., 168
Dominican Republic
  controversy over sending U.S.
      Marines to, 15
  Administration explanation of
      dispatch of troops to, 165–166
  intervention in, 182
  troops sent to, by Theodore
      Roosevelt, 186
Dorticos, President Osvaldo, 119
Drake, Sir Francis, 225

DRV White Paper on *Maddox* incident,
    79–81; map from, 228
Dulles, Secretary of State John
    Foster, 49, 50, 171, 175 (footnote)
Duncan, Special Forces Sergeant
    Donald, 91–92

Earth Resources Observation Satellite
    (EROS), 113–114
East Wind, 117–118
ECM. *See* Electronic countermeasure
    devices
Edisto, 117–118
Edmondson, Commander G.H., 151–152
Edwards, USS, 159–160
Egypt. *See* United Arab Republic
Eisenhower, President Dwight D.,
    49–50, 104, 164, 166, 171, 194
Electronic countermeasure devices
    (ECM), use of, in espionage,
    110–112
Electronic intelligence ships (ELINT)
  problems caused by, 15–16
  dangers in use of, 104–105, 247
  probing for location of enemy
      warning systems, 110
ELINT. *See* Electronic intelligence ships
Ellender, Senator Allen, 70
EROS. *See* Earth Resources Observation
    Satellite
Ervin, Senator Sam, 20, 64–65, 199
Espionage
  electronic, dangers of, 100–121
  aerial, of U.S., 113–115

First Composite Radio Company, 126
Foreman, Representative Ed, 45
Formosa and Pescadores resolution,
    171, 189
Forrestal, Secretary of Defense
    James V., 210
Fort Meade, headquarters of National
    Security Agency at, 106–107
France
  nuclear tests of, 112–114
  geographic intelligence of, given
      to CIA, 123 (footnote)

Helioaircraft, 83

Helms, Richard, 35, 105

Herrick, Captain John J., as commander
   of Tonkin Gulf Patrol, 123–134,
   135, 137–147, 151–157, 206, 210,
   219, 232–233, 234

Hickenlooper, Senator Bourke B.,
   57, 197–199

Ho Chi Minh, 74, 85

Ho Chi Minh Trail
   attacks on, 86
   reconnaissance on, 91
   North Vietnamese men and supplies
      harassed by Meo along, 96
   Viet Cong continue to use, 99

Hobart, 143

Holleyfield, Captain E. E., 159–160

Holt, Pat, 67, 166, 182 (footnote)

Hon Gio, 129

Hon Mat
   Hanoi claims fishing boats
      chased near, 80
   Maddox comes near, 129
   lighthouse goes dark on, 130

Hon Me
   Morse accuses *Maddox* of shielding
      South Vietnamese raids on, 58
   Hanoi claims South Vietnamese
      shelled, 80
   part of Sullivan plan, 90
   target for attack by South Vietnam,
      90, 96
   South Vietnamese attack on, 127–128
   Maddox turns toward, 130
   North Vietnamese patrol boats
      emerge from, 131
   feints at, by *Maddox* and *Turner Joy,*
      139
   U.S. Navy determined to show
      flag in area of, 141
   messages from, audible to *Maddox*
      monitors, 153

Hon Ngu
   Hanoi claims shelled by U.S.
      and South Vietnam, July 30,
      1964, 80
   South Vietnamese attack on, 96, 128

Horton, J. Warren, 145

Hot pursuit, in relation to Tonkin
   Gulf incidents, 231–232

House of Representatives. *See* United
   States House of Representatives

Huerta, General Victoriano, 187

Hughes, Thomas L., 14–15

Humphrey, Senator Hubert H., 24,
   50, 74

Hussein, King, 101–102

Ignatius, Secretary of Navy Paul,
   204–205, 207

Information, government control of,
   17–19, 33–34

Institute for Defense Analysis, 159,
   234, 244–245

Interior, Department of, puts up Earth
   Resources Observation Satellite,
   113–114

International Control Commission,
   94–95

Israel
   war with United Arab Republic,
      101–102
   shelling of *Liberty,* 101–104

Israel, Fred L., 169, 170

Japan, intercepted fleet messages of, 105

Javits, Senator Jacob, 71

Jefferson, President Thomas, 183,
   185, 189

Johnson Administration
   mishandles reports concerning Tonkin
      incidents, 18–20
   advances possible reasons for
      Maddox attack, 29

Johnson, President Lyndon B.
   preelection promises of, 13, 164
   meets officials after attack on
      Maddox, 23–24
   announces decisions made after
      attack on *Maddox,* 27–28
   effect of Tonkin incidents on
      presidential campaign of, 30–33
   and Premier Khanh, 31–33
   considers retaliation for Tonkin
      incidents, 35
   makes televised announcement
      of second Tonkin Gulf incident,
      37–38

rushes television announcement
of railroad settlement, 46
Morse and, 49
vs. Goldwater in public opinion
polls, 77
appoints Vietnam Working Group to
plan strategy, 87
approves expansion of operations
against North Vietnam, 91
orders reconnaissance of Plaine des
Jarres, 97
orders air strikes on Pathet Lao, 97–98
sends orders to naval vessels
in Mediterranean, 102
calls Kosygin on hot line, 103
claims advantages for electronic
espionage, 105
quote on Cuba overflights, 114
first decision of, after August 2
Tonkin Gulf incident, 135
receives first report of August 4
incident, 148
considers response to August 4
attack, 149–150
calls meeting of key Congressmen, 154
private comment of, on Tonkin Gulf
incidents, 160
sends message to Congress for
military appropriation, 164
and intervention in Dominican
Republic, 165–166, 167–168
opens peace offensive, 171–172
meets with Nguyen Cao Ky, 177
confrontation of, with Fulbright over
senatorial powers, 180
answers reporter's question on Tonkin
Gulf Resolution, 193–195
effect of Tonkin inquiry on political
fate of, 242–244
Johnson, Vice Admiral Roy L.
confers with Maxwell D. Taylor
regarding Navy's share in war,
95
transfers order for Tonkin Gulf
patrol, 123
reply of, to Herrick's cable, 130
supplies information to Sharp, 153
demands verification of attack,
153, 157
conclusion reached after review of
data, 158
questions regarding conduct of, 245

Joint Chiefs of Staff
meeting regarding second Tonkin
Gulf incident, 35
Directorate for Communications-
Electronics (J-6) coordinates
National Security Agency
activities, 106–107
establish Tonkin Gulf patrol,
123, 124–125
military moves decided on by, after
August 2 Tonkin Gulf incident,
136–137
contingency plans of, presented to
McNamara and Rusk, 149, 150
meet with McNamara to determine
actuality of attack, 153
demand confirmation of attacks from
Herrick, 206
and report of Institute for Defense
Analysis, 234–235
Joy, Admiral Charles Turner, 27
(footnote)

Katzenbach, Undersecretary of State
Nicholas deB., 13, 183, 188–192,
195–199
Kearsarge, USS, 136
Keelung
first stop of *Maddox,* 125
Maddox leaves, 127
Kellogg, Secretary of State Frank B.,
178 (footnote)
Kennedy, President John F., 85, 149,
163, 164, 166, 182 (footnote)
Kennedy, Senator Robert F., 34, 243
Khan, President Ayub, 108
Khanh, Premier Nguyen, 29, 31–33,
58, 66
Khrushchev, Premier Nikita, 29, 87,
116, 135
Klocko, Lieutenant General Richard
P., 102
Klusman, Lieutenant Charles, 97
Komer, Robert, 84
Komsomolets Ukrainy, 120–121
Korea, Truman sends troops to, 170
Kosyakov, Soviet Captain, 121
Kosygin, Premier Aleksei, 103, 181

territorial waters of, 226–227
map showing version of, of *Maddox*
    actions, 228
Novaya Zemlya, 113, 117–118

O'Brien, Lawrence, 30–31
Ogier, Commander Herbert L.,
    as commander of *Maddox*,
    127, 128, 131, 132, 138,
    143, 144, 145, 155–156
Operation Farm Hand, 31
Operation Haylift, 84, 85, 86
Operation Market Time, 77, 220
    (footnote)

Paige, Glenn D., 170
Pakistan, National Security Agency
    base at Peshawar in, 107–108
Paramilitary operations before Tonkin,
    83–99
Park, Patrick N., as *Maddox* sonarman,
    11–12, 14, 125–128, 130–132, 141–
    143, 145–147, 155–157, 212, 249–
    250
Pathet Lao
    U.S. admits bombing, 78
    mounts attacks on Laos government,
      96
    positions of flights over and bombing
      of, 97–99
Patil, S. K., 148
Pearl Harbor, 18
Pell, Senator Claiborne, 230
Pentagon. *See also* Department of
    Defense
    makes first announcement of Tonkin
      Gulf incident, 23
    transcript of undated interview with
      Moore, from Directorate for
      Defense Information of, 46–47
    mishandling of order to *Liberty*,
      102–104
    Advanced Research Project Agency
      of, 112
    develops MIRV, 112
Peru, crisis with, over territorial waters,
    247

Peshawar, Pakistan, National Security
    Agency base at, 107–108
Phouma, Premier Souvanna, 96–98
Pickering, USS, 124
Pike, Representative Otis, 103
Pittman, Senator Key, 169
Plaine des Jarres, 97
Ponturo, John, 234, 244
Powers, Francis Gary, 105, 108
Presidential use of armed forces
    without congressional action,
    184–186, 189. *See also* Johnson,
    President Lyndon B.
Press reaction to Administration conduct,
    77–79
Project Delta, 91
Public opinion, before and after Tonkin
    Gulf incidents, 77–79
Public reaction to crisis, government
    manipulation of, 18–19
Pueblo, USS, 15–16, 109, 116–117,
    224–225, 247

Quang Binh Province, frogmen tried in,
    94
Quang Khe, 42, 43, 157

Radford, Admiral Arthur W., 49, 50
Raymond, Jack, 230–231
Reedy, George, 27, 36, 156
Republican platform, quoted, 30
Retaliation
    attempts to verify incidents before,
      232–235
    chronology of decisions on, 259–261
Roberts, Charles, 169
Rogers, Secretary of State William P.,
    248
Roosevelt, President Franklin D., 15,
    117, 170, 187
Roosevelt, President Theodore, 186
Rosenthal, Harry F., 201
Rostow, Walt Whitman, 87
Rowan, Carl, 149
Rowe, James, 30–31
Rusk, Secretary of State Dean
    meets with Johnson after August 2
      attack on *Maddox,* 23–24, 135

comments to reporters on August 2
  incident, 24
attends private meeting of Senate
  Armed Services and Foreign
  Relations committees, 26–27
at National Security Council meeting
  and private meeting with
  Johnson, after August 4 Tonkin
  incident, 35, 149–150
background statement of, to State
  Department correspondents, 42
with McNamara and Wheeler, brings
  Tonkin Resolution to August
  1964 hearings before Senate
  Foreign Relations and Armed
  Services committees, 53–57,
  58–59, 60, 65, 66, 67
interviews with Elie Abel, 76, 233
private remark of, about reading
  mail, 121 (footnote)
directs preparation of Tonkin
  Resolution, 136
with McNamara, seeks information
  regarding attacks from National
  Military Command Center,
  148–149
meets with Johnson after August 4
  Tonkin Gulf incident, 149–150
before Foreign Relations Committee,
  on 1965 Dominican Republic
  crisis, 165–166
before Foreign Relations
  Committee in 1966, 172–175
before Preparedness Investigating
  Subcommittee in 1966, 178
refuses to appear before Foreign
  Relations Committee after 1966
  hearings, 188 (footnote)
on mechanisms for "organization of
  a peace," 189
and military buildup in South
  Vietnam, 235
Russell, Senator Richard
  quote on *Maddox* attack, 25
  suggests addition to Tonkin
    Resolution, 51, 195
  at hearing on Tonkin
    Resolution, 56
  Nelson confers with, on Tonkin
    Resolution, 74
  on result of failure to provide for
    troops, 176

objects to dispatch of troops
  to Congo, 180
speaks for national commitments
  resolution, 181
at private meeting of Nitze and
  Fulbright, 207–208
advises Johnson regarding sending
  more troops, 244

Saltonstall, Senator Leverett, 58
Samos. *See* Satellite and Missile
  Observation System
San Augustin, José R., 151
Satellite and Missile Observation System
  (Samos), 112–113
Satellite reconnaissance
  by Soviets, 112–113
  by U.S., 112–113
Sather, Lieutenant (jg) Richard, 42
Schlesinger, Arthur M., Jr., 163
Scorpion, SS, 120
SEATO. *See* Southeast Asia Treaty
  Organization
Security organization, national
  shortcomings of, 14–15
Senate. *See* United States Senate
Sentel, Seaman Edwin R., 144
Sentry, USS, transferred to South
  Vietnam, 93. *See also Kua Hoa*
Serene, USS. See also Nhut Tao
  transferred to South Vietnam, 92–93
  reinforced by Swift boats, 95
Severnaya Zemlya, 117–118
Seward, Senator William H., 186
Shalowitz, Aaron L., 231–232
Sharp, Admiral Ulysses Grant, Jr.
  makes first announcement of Tonkin
    Gulf incident, 23
  quote on August 2 *Maddox* attack, 24
  transfers order for Tonkin Gulf patrol,
    123
  deploys ships, 136
  orders DeSoto patrol continued, 140
  receives permission to prepare for
    retaliatory strikes, 147
  McNamara asks further information
    from, 152
  demands verification of attack,
    153–155
  phones McNamara, confirming attack
    report, 154

Territorial waters, 224–232, 247
Thailand, fighter bombers ordered into, 136
Thant, Secretary-General U, 33, 154
34-Alpha Operations
    name for naval forays north of North Vietnamese border, 96
    increased activity of, 125
    attack on Hon Me and Hon Ngu, 127–128
    Maddox and *Turner Joy* decoys for, 140
    Maddox mission and, 214–223
Thurmond, Senator Strom, 65–66
Ticonderoga, USS
    provides air cover for *Maddox,* 27, 28
    air strikes by, against North Vietnam bases, 34, 38, 39, 43
    McNamara describes course of, 57
    as stationary target off Da Nang, 122
    gives air support to *Maddox,* 133, 134
    planes from, to remain constantly airborne, 138
    Herrick asks for air support from, 146
    reports from pilots of, concerning August 4 incident, 151–152
    planes leave from, for retaliatory strikes, 156, 157
    chronology of participation in Tonkin Gulf incidents, 261
Tiger Island. *See* Hon Gio
Time, 35, 36, 41 (footnote), 42 (footnote), 157, 158
Time zones, Tonkin Gulf and Washington, 34 (footnote)
Tonkin, Gulf of
    summary of incidents, 13
    mishandling of reports concerning, 18–20
    crisis of, useful to Johnson, 20
    relevance of incidents to today, 20
    August 2 attack in, 23
    Johnson Administration reports incidents of, to Congress and public, 23–47
    August 4 attack in, 34
    retaliation planned against, 35
    press and television accounts, after second incident of, 35–43
    North Vietnamese version of attacks in, 79–81

real story of, 83–99
patrol mission planned for, 122–125
facts vs. claims about, 201–237, 239–242
map showing course followed by *Maddox* in, North Vietnamese version, 228
map showing course followed by *Maddox* and *Turner Joy* in, Defense Department version, 229
and military buildup in South Vietnam, 235–237
report of hearings on, released, 243
supplemental report on, 245
questions raised by inquiry on, 246–247
chronology of events in, 253–261
Tonkin Resolution
    passed by Congress, 13
    history of, 48–79
    quoted, 50–51
    congressional hearings on, 50–75
    amendment offered on, 74–75
    congressional vote on, 75
    length of Senate deliberation on, 75–76
    Rusk directs State Department to prepare, 136
    Johnson orders preparation of, 150–151
    Rusk's testimony on use of, 173–175
    and bombing of Laos, 192
    hearings on, published, 202
Trager, Frank N., 86–87
True, Rear Admiral Arnold E., 176
Truman, President Harry S, 106, 170–171, 189, 194
Tshombe, Moise, 78
Turkish pilots, for Vietnam Air Transport, 84
Turner Joy, USS C.
    nearly fired on by *Maddox,* 11–12
    joins *Maddox* after August 2 attack, 27, 138
    patrol activities of, announced by McNamara, 39–42
    claimed not connected with coastal raids by South Vietnam, 76
    reported fired on by North Vietnamese, 143
    fires at North Vietnamese patrol, 146

information on Tonkin incidents
supplied by crew of, 151
inconsistencies in reports of,
concerning August 4 action, 156
logbooks of, requested by Fulbright,
203
physical evidence of attacks
on, as presented by
Administration, 212–214
Defense Department map showing
tracks of, in Tonkin Gulf, 229
chronology of events on, in
Tonkin Gulf, 255–261

Printed in the U.S.A.